Echoes of The Past

A Family Story

Echoes of The Past

A Family Story

Michael J. Herrick

All rights reserved. No part of this book may be reproduced or transmitted in any form or by any means, electronic or mechanical, including photocopying, recording, or any information storage and retrieval system, without permission in writing from the Author.
This is a work of non-fiction.

Cover design Copyright © by Jane Herrick

Echoes of the Past: A Family Story
Copyright © 2019 by Michael J. Herrick

ISBN: 978-1-7335733-1-3 (Trade Paper)
ISBN: 978-1-7335733-0-6 (Hard Cover)

Second Printing

Printed in the United States of America

To My Children—
Brad and Mandy and their children
Iris, October, Cora, Rio and Perennial

Table of Contents

Preface 1

Part I: 3
Henry's Legacy

Chapter 1. 5
Leicester 1598

Chapter 2. 15
Religion, Churches, Family

Chapter 3. 29
The Big Decision

Chapter 4. 35
Ericke of East Anglia

Chapter 5. 45
Erick the Forester

Chapter 6. 51
Great Stretton: The Eyryks

Chapter 7. 55
Robert and William Eyryk

Chapter 8. 59
The Hericke Trades

Chapter 9.. 63
Sir William and Beau Manor

Chapter 10... 75
Robert and the Grey Friars

Chapter 11... 83
King Richard III, Bosworth

Chapter 12... 89
Robert Herrick the Poet

Part II:.. 97
Henry's Dream: An American Legacy

Chapter 13... 99
Salem 1629: Starting Over

Chapter 14.. 123
Plymouth

Chapter 15.. 141
Joseph Sr.

Chapter 16.. 157
Joseph Herrick Jr., Benjamin Herrick

Chapter 17.. 175
Nathaniel Herrick

Chapter 18............................... 207
Move West: Zadock and John

Chapter 19............................... 215
Beau Manor

Part III:................................ 227
The Modern Family

Chapter 20............................... 229
Civil War and Mahlon Herrick Sr.

Chapter 21............................... 261
Ireland and Sweden

Chapter 22............................... 273
Move to Harbor Springs

Chapter 23............................... 285
Mahlon Jr.

Epilogue................................. 313

Bibliography............................. 317

Index.................................... 339

Acknowledgments

First and foremost, I want to thank my children and grandchildren for being the reason and inspiration for this book. The purpose of this book has always been to provide them a family legacy as I understand it. I can only hope that my life has been as inspirational to them as their lives have been to me.

A special thanks go to the Herrick Family Association, in particular to Richard Leon Herrick, for his tireless work on the third edition of the Herrick Genealogical Register. Those volumes have been my go to source for much of what I included in this book. A special thanks also goes to Alice (AB) Reynolds who did a fantastic job of editing an early and final draft for content accuracy, and to Nancy Johnson who also did a fantastic job of editing for style and form. AB is one of the founders of the Herrick Family Association and her knowledge of Herrick genealogy is unsurpassed. Nancy's work on formatting and advise on publishing were extremely helpful. I wish to also acknowledge fine work of John Brandsen of Chequamegon Art and Photo who designed the book cover and formatted the family tree charts. I also wish to thank Deborah Nelson, Sandy Herrick, and Dale Yoe for editing early manuscripts and giving me suggestions for redirection, which early on were most necessary. I also wish to thank John Irwin who was extremely helpful in helping me to understand more about the Herrick role in founding Granby, VT and for his helpful maps to pin point Herrick property in Granby. On the English side of the pond, I wish to thank Irene Turlington, from Leicester, for directing me to valuable documents and resources about the English Herricks. I also wish to acknowledge Peter Liddle and Roderick Dale, University of Leicester and University of Nottingham respectively, for their expertise on English Vikings. Last but not least, I wish to thank my wife, Jane, for her constant encouragement to complete this work and her encouragements about my research and writing skills even when undeserved. Plus, I wish to thank Jane for allowing me to use one of her art pieces as the cover for this book and suggesting to me how it could relate to the flow of generations. I took the title of her art piece as the title for this book.

The website to the University of Leicester Archeology Services Department found in this book, providing in-depth details about the history, archaeology and science behind the search and discovery of King Richard III, was kindly provided by the University of Leicester. Maps of medieval Leicester on pages 6 and 7 were provided with kind permission of the University of Leicester Archeological Services with artwork by Mike Codd. Other copyrights include:

Quote from The Midland Peasant on page 36 granted by MacMillian UK. The image of Viking bones at Repton on page 38 granted with permission from Oxford University Press. Map of English place names on page 41 granted with permission from Oxford University Press. Website referenced in footnote 41 on page 85 provided with kind permission of the University of Leicester Archeological Services. Photo of Herrick Pewter Porringer on page 109 provided with permission from the Peabody Museum, Essex Institute. Quote by William IV on page 217 granted with permission from the Leicestershire Education Committee. Portrait of William Perry Herrick on page 219 granted with kind permission from Anthony Wessell. Lyrics of "Enlistment Jumpers" on page 231 granted with kind permission from Bruce Burnside. Every effort has been made to contact copyright holders. The author will be pleased to rectify any omissions, if necessary, in future editions.

Preface

This is a true story of one ancestral line of the Herrick family, spanning over 26 generations and over 10 centuries. It is a story of success, failure, joy and sorrow. It is a story of individuals experiencing life's ups and downs within their vastly different environments. It is a story of English and American history through the lens of one single family and ancestral line.

My interest in writing this book started with a trip to Leicester, England with the Herrick Family Association in 2014. It became clear to me then that this one family touched much of the essential events of English and American history by simply living out their lives as best they could. But on a personal level, my interest in writing this book begins with my father, Mahlon Herrick. His interest in Herrick family history goes back to the mid-1970s when he found a copy of the original 1846 Herrick Genealogical Record (HGR I) in the attic of his boyhood home. He started to connect the dots from Henry Herrick of Salem to 1846 when HGR1 was published. Then he traced is immediate family in Michigan back to HGR1. After much research, he found that the link in his Herrick line was John P. Herrick who was one of the last Herricks documented in HGR I. John P. Herrick was finally found at the Carmel Township cemetery in Eaton County, Michigan. From then on, he was hooked on Herrick genealogy and so was I.

As I reviewed all the documents, stories and pictures that I had accumulated from genealogical research and knowledge gained from my visit to Leicester, England, it became clear that I might be the only one in my immediate and extended family who knew this information, and I felt that it needed to be consolidated in one place. So, I started to write it down. The more I wrote, the more I read, the more I researched, the more I wrote. This book is the culmination of that cycle of research, writing and reading.

It was not all serious work, however. Sometimes I felt like the spirits of Herricks past were present as I pursued my research. One day as I was studying the life of Joseph Herrick Jr., I learned that he had donated a portion of his farm to be turned into a community burial ground. During a Herrick Family Association meeting in Salem, MA in 2005, I went to Topsfield to find the South Side Cemetery, where we expected to find the grave of Joseph Jr. We were confident that we had the correct cemetery, so we looked at every single headstone. No Joseph Herrick Jr. Then deep in the woods bordering the cemetery, I noticed a pile of stones and what looked like broken headstones. I proceeded to dig into this pile to see if Joseph's headstone might be amongst the rubble. Found nothing. At least I thought. Disappointed, I began walking out of the cemetery. On the way out, my arm started to itch. Soon red bumps formed and developed into a full-blown case of poison ivy. I thought, "Perhaps I did find Joseph Jr. He was just telling me to tread carefully."

Part I:
Henry's Legacy

Cast of Characters:

Ericke, King of East Anglia - A Danish chief who invaded Britain during the reign of Alfred the Great. He lost and was forced to live in East Anglia. He was known as "Ericke, King of those Danes who hold the country of East Anglia". He tried again to unite the Danes against the English, led by Edward son of King Alfred, around 900 but was defeated again. He was subsequently killed by his own subjects for alleged severities in his government.

Erik the Forester - Fought against William the Conqueror at the Battle of Hastings in 1066. Alleged to be a brother of Erik the Red, whose son, Leif Erikson, founded Iceland and possibly what is now Newfoundland.

Sir William Eyrick - Knighted by King Edward III for service to the Black Prince, Prince of Wales and King Edward III's son, for service at the Battle of Gascony. His brother Robert was Chaplin to Black Prince and built a chapel at St. Giles church at Great Stretton in the mid-14th century.

Thomas Eyricke - First Herrick to appear in the book of the Leicester Corporation 1511 and first Herrick to live in Leicester.

Nicholas Eyricke - First in the Herrick line to leave the iron trades and enter the cloth trades in the mid-16th century.

Robert Eyricke - Built house over Grey Friars and grave of Richard III. Robert was benefactor to Free Grammar School in 1573.

Sir William Eyricke - Purchased Beau Manor in 1595. Granted Coat of Arms with brother Robert in 1598 by Queen Elizabeth. Knighted by King James I in 1605.

Henry Heyricke - Came to New England in 1629 with son Thomas. Was a puritan and was excommunicated by Church of England. Follower of Francis Higginson, a Vicar at St. Nicholas in Leicester, who was also a "non-conformist". Was a freeman weaver from Belgrave, England.

Chapter 1

Leicester 1598

Surrounded by four walls – to the north, south, east and west – medieval Leicester, England, about 100 miles north of London, looked like a fortress. Ancient Leicester was built for protection against foreign invaders throughout its early history. Medieval towns like Leicester were built like fortresses by lords who received the land as gifts from the Kings or Queens who built them for their protection against raiders and armies. But first came the Romans as early as 43AD, then the Anglo-Saxons, then the Vikings, then the Normans. The Normans, like the Vikings, were of Scandinavian decent. They invaded and defeated France and were given the land at Normandy as a spoil of war.

But in 1598, the year Henry Herrick was born, Leicester was a medieval village with each wall complete with a large gate for entry and exit. These large gates were used for village commerce, since they were the only means of entry or exit for tradesmen. The gates were useful mostly for collecting tolls from traders coming into town. This commerce fulfilled the needs of the entire community. Herdsmen, butchers, bakers, tanners, forgers, ironmongers, and textile weavers were common trades in 1598 Leicester. There were churches[1], schools, a hospital, markets for trading, buying and selling, meeting places for civic affairs, a jail (or gaol as it was known), rows of cottage like houses with thatched roofs, and even a castle for occasional royal visits. Built in 1070, the Leicester Castle hosted King Edward I in 1300 and King Edward II in 1310. Just outside the east wall of the village, the river Soar supplied Leicester with fresh water for cooking, cleaning, and crop irrigation. The villagers carried their water in containers on their shoulders.

---

1 The most famous church is St. Mary de Castro built in 1017 and was the site of the wedding of Geoffrey Chaucer and Philippa de Roet in 1366. The church still stands.

But with all this commerce came a down side. Sanitation in Leicester and all medieval towns. The village was dirty, smelly and crowded. There were no sewers and no drains. Rubbish such as rotting vegetables and dirty water were thrown in the streets. Consequently, rats and other vermin were common. Given these conditions, it is not surprising that outbreaks of the plague were common. And the plague did strike multiple times. Towns like Leicester were particularly vulnerable since the disease was so contagious. The plagues that threatened all of England and all of Europe for centuries were only one reason for the average lifespan to be about 35 years. Childhood deaths were especially high. Between one third and one half of children died before the age of 16.

Medieval Leicester surrounded by stone walls

Chapter 1 — Leicester 1598

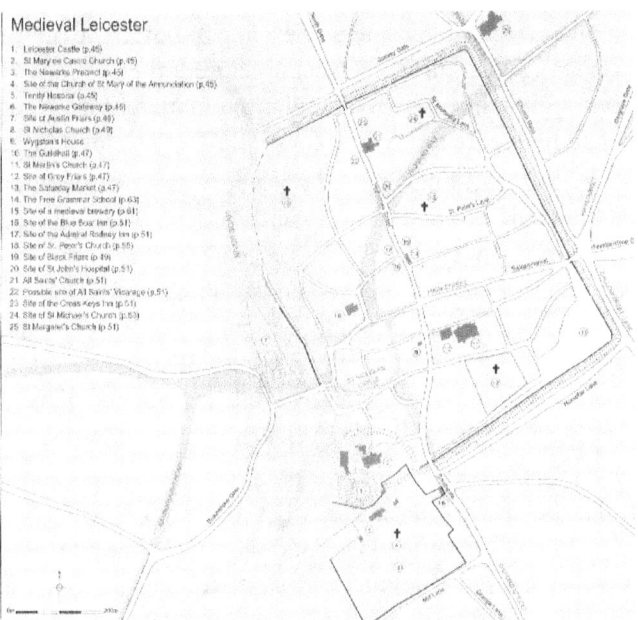

Medieval Leicester. High Street and Highcross Streets are marked in present day locations.

Leicester and the surrounding county of Leicestershire was similar to other medieval English villages with one exception, particularly relevant to Herricks. Leicestershire was home to the family of Eyryk, which by the 16th century had branched out to multiple families and spread around the county. The family name also had multiple spellings, from Eyryk to Eyricke to Hyrick to Hericke and ultimately to Herrick. For the Herricks in America, the year 1598 in Leicester is of major significance because that was the year that Henry Eyricke or Heyricke or Herrick was born, and our branch of the Herricks began.

Henry was the son of Thomas and Elizabeth Eyricke. He grew up with two brothers, Godfrey and George and a sister Ann. Henry was in the 5th generation of Eyrickes who worked in the cloth or textile trades, or "drapers" as they were called. Henry's father, Thomas, however, was a draper and was the apprentice of his father, John Eyricke. Thomas was admitted to the Merchant's Guild in 1598 to become a Freemen. Being a Freeman meant that you were no longer worked as an apprentice, but could practice your trade, create your own business, and make your own money without indenture.

The cloth or textile business was a popular trade in England in Medieval times. Most 'drapers' manufactured their goods outside of town and brought them to town to sell at the markets. In Leicester, those markets would be the Saturday Market or the Wednesday Market.

The cloth and textile business, however, was a different line of work from other branches of the Eyricke family. Many in the Eyricke family were in the "ironmonger" trades in Leicester, which involved various iron works, crafting metal objects and making jewelry. The jewelry business of the Eyrickes used precious metals such as gold and silver to create fine jewelry, typically for the wealthy. The jewelers of the time, because of their wealth, were typically bankers, lenders, and financers as well as metal workers, as were the Eyrickes.

The Eyrickes prospered in the popular cloth trade and prospered very well in the metals or ironmonger trade. But Medieval English society was highly structured around social economic groups. The nobility who owned huge amounts of land were at the top. Below them were the gentry and rich merchants. Gentlemen in the gentry typically owned large amounts of land and were commonly educated and may even have a family coat of arms. Below the gentry were the yeomen who could be as wealthy as the gentry but they worked alongside their employees, whereas the gentry did not. The Eryicke family in both the cloth and metals trades were probably considered either gentry or yeomen. Below yeomen were the tenement farmers who leased their land from the rich landowners. They were wage laborers who were mostly illiterate and very poor.

These social classes were designed to be visible. In the 16th century, Sumptuary laws were passed that defined what clothes a person could or could not wear. These laws said that only people of a certain wealth could wear clothes made with expensive materials such as velvet or silk. They didn't care, since they couldn't afford expensive clothes anyway. But the laws were supposed to keep the classes separate. There were defined punishments for violation of the sumptuary laws, and they were largely ignored.

Given the cloth trades in Henry's line of Herricks, their prosperity could have been accentuated by catering to the wealthy for their rich taste in clothing, even with their relatives. Hose made for the rich were made from pieces of cloth or linen and knit by hand. The Herrick Letters reveal that in 1578, Mary Erycke writes to her son William (later Sir William) "I have sent you a pair of knit hose, and a pair of knit Jersey

CHAPTER 1 —LEICESTER 1598

gloves. I would have you send word of how they serve you ; for if the gloves be too little for you, you should give them to one of your brother Hawes's children, and I would send your another pair". Then is a letter from Robert to his brother William, he writes, "I have sent up by Henry White this bringer 40 pair of good worsted hose, tied together in four bunches, which I pray you will sell for me for 12li. or else lay them up in your press. I cannot aford them for less". Then in 1582, William receives this letter from his friend, Richard Hudson, from Leicester "The cause of my writig ujto you at this time is to let you understand that I have sent you the pair of knit stockens which you sent for by Richard Penne, and I have received a crown of him for them ; They did cost five shillings at Doncaster and if you do not like them of the price, I pray you to get them coloured of the same colour as the stockons are which you had on your legs when I was with you. I take it they were a murrey, and I will pay you for them, and will send you your five shilling again. Moreover, friend William Erycke, I have a pair of worsted stockens, the legs of them I pray you to get me a purse, a large one, made of them, with a lock ring, and I will pay you for it. I would have the fringe that shall go about it to be of silk".

Medieval England was not considerate of its poor. In villages like Leicester, jobs were not easy to find and those out wandering looking for jobs, called vagabonds, were considered a threat to law and order. The only concession to the poor was that the old and disabled poor were given licenses to beg. However, anyone roaming around without a job was tied to a cart and whipped until they were bloody. Then they were banished from town and sent to the parish where they had been born or lived for the last 3 years. What's more, in 1547 a law was passed that said that vagabonds could be made slaves for 2 years.

Since Henry's branch of the family had been in the cloth business for five generations, Henry too entered the cloth or textile trades and became apprenticed to Edward Peabodie, a local tailor. In 1621 at the age of 23, Henry was admitted to the Merchant's Guild and was made a Freemen in the textile trades, meaning that he could establish his own textile business free of the oversight and tutelage of Mr. Peabodie. Henry and his father worked as Freemen in the textile business in Belgrave, a small village just outside the Leicester walls, for three years until Thomas died in 1624.

As a youth Henry would most likely accompany his father to the Saturday Market, located in the southeast corner of the village wall and adjacent to the East Gate. The Saturday Market was a hub of activity and trading, and was established centuries before in 1298. It was clearly a landmark in the village and in young Henry's time, a place to frequent, given the high level of commercial activity. The market offered a wide variety of products for sale, not only foodstuffs such as grain, beans, meat and fish, but also wool, clothing and drapery. Because of cloth commodities the Saturday Market was sometimes referred to as the 'Housewives Market'. Because Henry's family business was cloth such as drapery, clothing, gloves, linens, and other assorted textiles; his father Thomas would sell his woven goods at the market. It was here, or perhaps at the Wednesday market, that Henry had his first lessons in the business side of his father's trade.

The Wednesday Market was just as popular or perhaps more important to young Henry. The market was right in the center of the village on High Street[2], which was the main street in Leicester connecting the East and West gates. Not only was there lots of activity due to all the trading going on, including the nearby Sheep market, but there were interesting landmarks in the area, some of which related to Henry's family. Right at the market at the intersection of High Street and the Swinesgate[3] was the famous High Cross of Leicester. The High Cross marked the center of town. Only a short block away was the famous Blue Boar Inn where King Richard III spent his last night before the Battle of Bosworth on August 22, 1485. Since the Battle of Bosworth, only 14 miles from Leicester and a famous battle in English history, stories were often told about how the inn changed its name from the White Boar Inn, the colors of Yorkist King Richard III, to the Blue Boar Inn after Richard was killed in the Battle.

Despite the importance of the Battle of Bosworth to English monarchy and history and the fact that it occurred only 100 years before Henry's time, Henry as young boy was probably more interested and proud in his namesake on a list of donors to the Free Grammar School. Built in 1573 and located on High Street (now Highcross Street) across the street from the Blue Boar Inn and only a block from the Wednesday market, the Free Grammar School was a significant addition to village life in Leicester. The school was originally housed in St. Peter's Church, but the church became in a poor state of repairs and was demolished. The

---

2 Now High Cross Street
3 Now High Street

CHAPTER 1 —LEICESTER 1598

school, a free all boys school, was still needed. So, the school was re-founded when Queen Elizabeth I made an annual grant of 10 pounds to the school. Others in Leicester followed the Queen's lead and contributed funds for the school's construction and maintenance. They included Robert Herrick and his son, Tobias Herrick. It is very possible that young Henry Herrick attended the Free Grammar School. It is not known how much schooling Henry had, but he needed enough to conduct business in his chosen trade.

Young Henry had to be proud of the many accomplishments of his extended family, particularly his cousin Robert Herrick[4]. Robert Herrick and his son Tobias were publicly listed on a plaque of benefactors to the Free Grammar School. This plaque still remains on the outside the grammar school. Also, on this list of benefactors was none other than Queen Elizabeth I herself! One can only imagine how Henry might have felt as a young boy seeing evidence around the village of his family's importance when on the same public list as the Queen of England.

What certainly had to be known at the time was that the stones used to build the Free Grammar School were the same stones used after the demolition of St. Peter's church not far away. St. Peter's was built in the 10th century, so it went back to Saxon times about 600 years before Henry. Not only was the Free Grammar School cherished by the village as place for free education for its youth, it also held strong historical value. But most of all to young Henry, it was his school. Even if you were of modest means and particularly if you were a boy, you almost certainly attended the Free Grammar School at least for a few years.[5]

It is likely that little if any of this history mattered to Henry at the time he entered school for the first time. It is also likely that Henry entered the Free Grammar School since he would have known High Street well, not far from the High Cross at the center of town and the Wednesday market. Further, it is highly likely that Henry's father and mother encouraged, if not insisted, that he go to school so he could learn to read, write and be able to trade and barter in the market. That with his skill as tailor or draper would surely ensure him a good and prosperous life in Leicester like so many in his family before him.

---

4 Robert and his brother Sir William were Henry's first cousin, 3 times removed. Both were wealthy and prominent ironmongers.
5 The school with its old Saxon stones still stands today as a popular restaurant. The name, of course, is 1573, the year it was built.

What can only be imagined, however, is what Henry may have thought about his famous and benevolent relatives who were in the metal trades when Henry and his wing of the family were in the textile trades. However, both the metal and cloth sides of the family were successful and prominent citizens of Leicester. It can be assured that Henry, because of his immediate and extended family, was proud to be a Herrick.

But there was also a mysterious danger lurking in this area of High Street. The borough gaol[6] was located not far from the grammar school. It is easy to imagine that Henry and his friends heard many stories and legends about the criminals incarcerated in the gaol, since it was particularly known for being unduly harsh and repressive on the prisoners. Added to this was the sense of ancient mystery to the building itself. The first known prisoner was sent there centuries before - as early as 1297.

Much of Leicester during Henry's time in the mid to late 16th century still had remnants of Roman times. The medieval High Street (now Highcross Street), for example, used stones from the old Roman forum walls, suggesting that the walls were still visible by medieval times. Also, many of the medieval buildings were constructed with re-used Roman walls. In fact, the Roman baths of Leicester were located adjacent to St. Nicholas Church and stones from the ruins of the baths were used in the construction of the church. These ruins and the ancient stones in the church are still visible today. The Roman town walls were maintained throughout most of the medieval times, but by the time Henry was growing up in Leicester, the walls were starting to crumble and the stones came down and were carted away. By this time, defenses against invaders were not considered as necessary. In fact, "suburbs" had started to be developed outside each of the stone walls near the gates into the town. Surrounding the town were three great open fields, which provided produce for the inhabitants and grazing for livestock.

Leicester Castle was the center of power in Henry's time and had been since the Norman times. The castle was built near the southwest corner of town in 1068, two years after the Norman invasion, and still stands today. The castle was used as the resident for English kings, earls and dukes and other dignitaries while visiting Leicester. Next to the castle was St. Mary de Castro, a catholic church built around the same

---

6 Similar to a county jail today.

time as the castle. The first Earl of Leicester, Robert de Beaumont, established a college of cannon (community of priests) at the church in 1107. Then in 1330, Trinity Hospital, a hospital for the elderly and infirm, was built in this same southwest corner of town. Trinity Hospital was one of the favorite philanthropic interests of Robert Herrick's[7] benevolences. All these ancient landmarks were vibrant and active during Henry's life in Leicester.

Other landmarks located near the southeast quarter of Leicester were the Greyfriars, St. Martin's Church (now Leicester Cathedral), and Guildhall. Greyfriars was a Franciscan monastery built in 12th century and St. Martin's, built in the 13th century, was Leicester's wealthiest parish. The Guildhall, built in 1390, was the meeting place of all the guilds or associations of craftsmen and merchants. Starting in 1494, the Guildhall became the meeting place for town business, including meetings of the town council and mayor. Greyfriars has become most noteworthy as the burial place of King Richard III and the site of Robert Herrick's manor house. All that remains today of the Greyfriars is a fragment of one of its stone walls. St. Martin's was the church attended by Robert Herrick, and today as the Leicester Cathedral, includes a side chapel known as Herrick Chapel where the remains of both Robert and Sir William Herrick are interred. As mayor and alderman (councilman), Robert Herrick, as well as other Herricks, conducted the business affairs of Leicester. St. Martin's church and the Guildhall were important Leicester landmarks in Henry's day, and, because of their historic family connections, are Herrick landmarks today.

One would only have to take a short walk from the cathedral and the Guildhall in the center of town to the west side of town to St. Nicholas church. Undoubtedly, Henry would make this walk many times as a young man, since his church, St. Nicholas, is located in this side of town. The old Roman baths would still be present next to the church with its imposing stone arches (now known as Jewry Wall) built for men and women entries into the baths. St. Nicholas is the oldest church in Leicester, built by the Anglo-Saxons in 880 AD. Much of the church building used bricks and stones in its construction from Roman baths, which were located just a few steps from the church. The baths were

---

7 The same Robert Herrick who was benefactor of Free Grammar School

built in 159 AD, and much of the baths still remain, although in ruins since the stones were used in the church construction[8].

Near the church was a butchers' "shambles" where animals were butchered and the meat sold. Butchers shambles was on a street called "Holy Bones", since the bones were discarded nearby. One or more tanneries were also located near here as well. Cattle hides were processed into leather here and sheep skin was de-haired before being sold. Undoubtedly, the skins and leather goods were sold at the Wednesday Market nearby in the center of town at what is now the junction of High and Highcross Streets. Henry would have been to the Wednesday market many times to buy meat, hides and other goods and would certainly have stood near the stone Highcross which was located at this corner.

A short walk up High Street (now Highcross Street) from the Wednesday Market was the northeast quarter, leading to the North Gate. Before Henry's time this area of town was thriving, but probably due to successive years of poor harvest, starvation became epidemic. This plus the Black Plague, which struck this area of Leicester hard in 1348, caused the population to decrease dramatically by the time Henry lived in Leicester. The current Highcross Street leads through this area to the North Gate; pass the Blue Boar Inn, where Richard III spent his last night, Saint Peter's Church, whose materials were used to build the new Free Grammar School in 1573, and All Saints Church. All Saints was built in 1066 by the Vikings, or Normans, in the same year of the Norman conquest at the Battle of Hastings, thus beginning Viking rule of England and closing Anglo-Saxon rule. The tower of the church was built in 900 AD[9], thus dating it back to Saxon times. A short walk up Highcross Street (now High Street) from the Wednesday Market leads to the East Gate, also known as Belgrave Gate[10]. Outside this gate was the small village of Belgrave[11].

---

8 The Roman baths were excavated in the 1930's and the foundation is visible and on display. The entrance to the baths consists of two stone arches and are still standing and called Jewry Wall
9 The church and the Saxon tower still stand today on High Cross Street.
10 The Haymarket Memorial Clock Tower now stands where the old East Gate was located.
11 Today Belgrave is a Leicester suburb.

Chapter 2
Religion, Churches, Family

Henry VIII became King of England in 1509. Despite his well-known conflicts with Rome over the validity of his six marriages and his ultimate break with Rome, he was a very religious man. Henry was raised to be Archbishop of Canterbury and would have been if his older brother Arthur had not died before he became king. As a result of this grooming, Henry grew up a very pious Catholic and in fact expressed unshakable loyalty to the Pope against the attacks of Martin Luther during the reformation. Henry VIII's "divorce" from Rome came when he was unable to produce a male heir to the throne beginning with his first wife Catherine of Aragon, his brother Arthur's widow. Somehow Henry began to feel that this inability to produce an heir was a result of God's anger with him for marrying his brother's former wife. After studying scripture, Henry figured that God willed that his marriage was illegitimate and therefore should be annulled. Because the Pope refused to annul the marriage, Henry began his separation from Rome. Then in 1533, Parliament passed the Act in Restraint of Appeals, which cleared the way for the annulment of Henry and Catherine's marriage without the Pope's approval. At the same time, a decree proclaimed his marriage to Anne Boleyn to be valid. This infuriated Pope Clement, so Henry VIII was excommunicated by the Pope in that same year. Thus, began the Church of England.

The new church, called the Anglican Church in England, was very similar to the Catholic Church except that the Pope had no authority over the church or over the king. However, the Church of England was a protestant church, separating itself from Rome like other protestant churches arising during the time of the Protestant Reformation. In 1537 the new national Church of England authorized a new Bible in the English language. This new Bible was a combination of William

Tyndale's interpretation of Martin Luther and Miles Coverdale, an ex-friar.

Before the creation of the Church of England under the authority of the English monarch, there were 502 monasteries in England. These monasteries were very rich. Collectively, the total income of all the monasteries was over 160,000 pounds a year – a tidy sum in the mid-16th century. In the spring of 1536, in an attempt to rid England of the Pope's control, Parliament passed an Act for the dissolution of all religious houses with a net income of less than 200 pounds per year. Then the next year, 1537, the government dissolved all monasteries in England, and in 1538 all monks and nuns were stripped of their religious commitments, meaning that their religious vows were no longer valid. The monks and nuns were relocated to other houses and given a small grant to begin ministries as secular clergymen or to seek lay occupations. Those who resisted were executed. All the monastic wealth was diverted to the Crown, which aimed to make money out of the dissolution. Henry VIII was in need of cash and Parliament was not anxious to raise taxes, so this monastic dissolution worked well for Henry and Parliament. The lands owned by the monasteries were sold at market prices, which meant that the big winners in the dissolution were those who purchased the former monastic lands. Sales began in 1539 at very reasonable prices.

So, why is this important to the Herricks? Robert Herrick, the brother of Sir William and future benefactor to the Free Grammar School, was one of those purchasers. The Greyfriars monastery was torn down and Robert bought a track of Greyfriar land from the Crown in 1558. The long-term effect of the dissolution was a general sense of religious freedom. As the Church of England became established with theological influences of Lutheranism, there were rebel groups wanting to return to strict Catholicism. Plus, "immigrante" theologies of Zwinglianism and Calvinism started to have influence. Then in 1549, the Act of Uniformity was passed by Parliament. This act, through the force of civil law, required uniformity in religious worship. As a result, the Book of Common Prayer[12] was published and used in all churches in England. As one can imagine, there were pockets of reluctance to worship from the Book of Common Prayer since it disallowed even the slightest variation of worship by a clergyman, a worshiper, or from the

---

12 The Evensong, a collection of prayers for an evening service, is part of the Prayer Book common in Anglican churches today.

Chapter 2 — Religion, Churches, Family

congregation. This Act of Parliament resulted in even more significance for the Herricks, as we shall see.

When Henry VIII died in 1547, his son from Jane Seymour, Edward VI, became King. He was an ardent protestant. At Edward's death in 1553, Mary, daughter of Henry VIII and Catherine, took the throne. She, however, was a committed Catholic. At Mary's death 1n 1558, Elizabeth I, daughter of Henry VIII and Anne Boleyn took the throne. Queen Elizabeth was a protestant and ardent supporter of the Church of England. All during this time religious life in England was in turmoil.

Out of this turmoil arose a radical form of Protestantism called Puritanism. Puritans wanted to "purify" the church. It wasn't so much the wealth and corruption of the church's bishops, which had reached epic levels, but the rituals and ceremonies of the Prayer Book that had become meaningless and irrelevant to parishioners that caused such a strident and "purifying" movement. Puritans were not even concerned about issues of theology or doctrine. However, many evangelically minded clergy who had been profoundly influenced by Calvinism in Geneva were inspired to remodel the entire governance of the church. Basically, the Puritans wanted to purge the church worship of any remnants of Catholic rituals and to base its services entirely upon preaching and prayer. Queen Elizabeth consistently opposed the Puritan principles from the very beginning of her reign and she never changed her opinions. When a Bill was introduced in Parliament in 1571 to revise the Prayer Book and adopt the Geneva Prayer Book, she not only opposed the Bill but ordered her bishops to repress any attempt to change the church. Because of this repression, Anti-Puritan sentiment continued in the succeeding monarchies of King James I and King Charles I. Puritan congregations had started to leave England as the 17th century began – first to Holland, then to New England.

The reason Queen Elizabeth, and King James after her, rejected Puritanism so fiercely is because Puritanism was a threat to the monarchy. Despite the fact that Puritans were protestant as was Elizabeth and James, Puritans were militant in their belief that the Word of God as expressed literally in the Bible held far greater authority than the monarchy. Further, they not only believed that the Bible was the sole source of religious authority, but Puritans believed in the sanctity of individual interpretations over church or government interpretations. Puritans were dogmatic. They were highly assertive in their beliefs that theirs were the only "true" beliefs and any deviation from those beliefs were wrong. Such views, particularly when mixed with a militant and elitist voice, were intolerable to English monarchs.

Puritans in Leicester at this time were called "hoters", which was an even more radical form of Protestantism than that of Queen Elizabeth. Because Leicestershire was 100 miles from London, the county was less affected by the political and religious swings of the capital city, so Leicestershire felt a bit insolated, and less inhibited to express their beliefs. Because it felt isolated from the stranglehold of London, Leicestershire had long been considered a center of religious non-conformity and dissent. The Eyricks of Leicester were generally considered non-conformists even by Leicestershire standards. In fact, Henry's uncle, John Eyricke, was found to be in possession of a Geneva Bible, the bible of the Puritans, when he died in the early 1600s. Also, Henry's uncle John was accused throughout the period of 1623-28 of entertaining Puritan preachers in Leicester. Such offences to the official church were considered serious dissents to the church and to the King.

The Queen introduced a new English Prayer Book for the Anglican Church of England, but the Puritans, including many in the Eyricke family, took exception. Due to this religious dissent in and around Leicestershire, a pattern of persecutions began around 1620. These persecutions began in the reign of King James I, who became King at the death of Elizabeth in 1603, despite the fact that he was initially more liked by Puritans because he was Scottish and the Scottish adopted protestant Calvinism. However, conformity to the King James version of the Bible, written during the reign of King James, was strictly enforced.

Then Francis Higginson entered Henry's life. Francis Higginson was a close friend of Henry Eyricke (or Heyrick by this time), probably encountering each other while Francis was preaching in various Leicester churches. Francis was a free-thinker and became a Puritan early in his career. He started his education at Cambridge and received his BA degree at Jesus College at Oxford University in 1610. Jesus College was the first Protestant college founded by Queen Elizabeth in 1571. Higginson grew up in a very religious family. His father, John Higginson, was a priest and appointed by the Queen as one of the eight founding fellows of Jesus College.

In 1619, Francis Higginson became minister at Claybrooke, one of the parishes of Leicestershire. He soon became disenchanted with the Church of England and began to associate himself with Puritan congregations and became Vicar of St. Nicholas Church in Leicester.

Chapter 2 — Religion, Churches, Family

Higginson gained great influence as a preacher in Leicestershire, and through his association with Arthur Hildersham and Thomas Hooker, two other religious dissenters, his disenchantment with the Church of England intensified.

Below is an account by historian, Sidney Perly, about Higginson's gradual movement from the Church of England to Puritanism, which drove him to venture in the new world to New England.

Tobey Mathew, archbishop of York, his title being curate of Scredingham,' and priest at Bishopthorpe by the same archbishop Dec. 8, 1614. He was collated or instituted April 20, 1615, by the same archbishop to the rectory of Barton-in-fobis, in Nottinghamshire, which he resigned April 4, 1616, having never served under that appointment. From about 1617 to 1629, he was the minister in the churches connected with the parish of St. Nicholas, in Leicester, where he styled himself "lecturer" as well as "minister." He was a worthy man² and an attractive speaker, having a pleasing voice, and was greatly successful in his service.

He practised the full ritual of the Church of England for many years; but, having made the acquaintance of Mr. Arthur Hildersham and Mr. Thomas Hooker, he became interested in the controversy that had begun to agitate the church as to whether it was right to recognize certain ceremonies. He began to investigate the matter, and became convinced that many of the rites had neither the support of scriptural authority nor ancient practice. He therefore became a conscientious non-conformist; and consequently was deprived of his position in the church in which he had so long and favorably officiated. Nevertheless, his ministry was so desirable that his people procured for him the liberty of preaching a constant lecture³ on one part of each Sunday; and brought into it for safety. Eleven hundred people were slain in the streets, and the houses and public buildings plundered.

At the close of the delivery of the sermon he thanked the magistrates and Puritans of the place for the liberty, countenance and encouragement they had given to his ministry, and told them of his intended removal to New England, the principal end of the plantation there, he then declared, being the propagation of religion; and of the hope he had that New England might be designed by Heaven as a refuge and shelter for the non-conformists against the storms that were coming upon the nation, and a region where they might practise the church-reformation unto which they had been bearing witness. He concluded with a most affectionate prayer for the king, the church and state, and particularly for Leicester.

With his family, he then took his journey to London. As they left the town, the people generally came into the street and bade them farewell, with benedictions upon them and loud prayers for a safe voyage and prosperity.

At London he found that three ships were nearly ready to sail for New England, and that two other vessels were to follow about three weeks later. There were servants of the Company and passengers sufficient to fill the three ships and among them were the two clergymen already mentioned, Messrs. Bright and Skelton.

As Higginson gained great influence as a preacher in Leicestershire, he was increasingly persecuted by the Church of England for his dissenting views. These persecutions were for such offences as refusing to wear a surplice, which was a white linen vestment; or to conform to the worship prescribed in the Book of Common Prayer. Then in 1619 Higginson was accused by the church of not using the sign of the cross when baptizing children, and again he was criticized for celebrating marriages without rings. All of these seemly petty offices were in strict violation of the Book of Common Prayer. In 1613, several of Higginson's parishioners were excommunicated by the Church of England for refusing to kneel for communion. Higginson continued to preach but refused well-paying jobs within the church due to his beliefs. He was able to support himself by preparing young men for the university. Bishop Williams of Lincolnshire protected Higginson and others in Leicester for years, but he died in 1628, but the new Bishop, Bishop Laud, was much more traditional and began to persecute nonconformists. Perhaps the strong Viking origin in and around

CHAPTER 2 — RELIGION, CHURCHES, FAMILY

Leicestershire affected their independent thinking and beliefs about religion.

As the Eyrickes in Leicester were becoming increasing non-conformists, young Henry Eyricke became increasing radicalized by the Puritans, and Higginson in particular. To a great extent, the Herricks in America today owe their family heritage to the influence and friendship that Henry formed with Francis Higginson. Although it is not clear exactly how Henry and Francis met and became friends, but it is clear that our Henry Herrick was very much influenced by the preaching of Rev. Higginson.

Although knighted by King James I, Sir William Herrick, brother of Robert who purchased monastery land, was a known non-conformist. Very influential in the Woodhouse church near his home at Beau Manor, Sir William appointed a pupil of Francis Higginson, John Bryan, as curate (assistant to the priest) at the Woodhouse church – the Herrick's church. Later this curate was charged by the Church of England of giving communion to people sitting rather than standing, again a violation of church rules. If that wasn't bad enough, John Eyricke, Sir William's brother, was accused of entertaining Puritan ministers, even providing them overnight stays. Despite his many benevolences to the community, Robert Herrick was also under suspicion. When a friend of Robert's, who ministered to a Puritan, died, Robert became the guardians of his two children. These events certainly did not go unnoticed by the church.

Even Sir William's wife, Lady Joan Heyrick, was long embroiled in disputes with the church for activities at the Woodhouse church, particularly Sir William's appointment of John Bryan. The Woodhouse dispute started around 1627 when one of the church wardens (councilmembers), Robert Thurbarne, charged the Herricks and others of "illegal practices" at the church involving contact with Puritans. Lady Joan Heyrick became so infuriated that she broke a church window. The dispute between Lady Heyrick and Robert Thurbarne continued for years, even into the courts. However, court proceedings did not go well with Lady Heyrick because, "as a married woman she was unable to commence a cause." Sir William then stepped to defend his wife and his own decision regarding the Puritan Bryan, thereby "beginning a fresh cause on the same grounds". At this time Sir William and Lady Heyrick began attacking Thurbarne as failing in his duties as churchwarden. The disputes back and forth became revengeful and personal. This dispute finally culminated in two court cases, "Heyrick vs. Thurbarne" and

"Thurbarne vs. Bryan". Records are incomplete, but Lady Heyrick either took her case to a higher court or she abandon all her suits. Nonetheless, in December, 1637, Lady Heyrick received an order from the church, "The Ladie Heyrick's seate (in the Woodhouse chapel) to be abated and mad lower, on both sides and at the entrance a foot or thereabouts, or turned banisters to be sett instead of the upper pane thereof." Then on July 6, 1639, after over a decade of disputes, Lady Joan Heyrick was accused of not standing up for the gospel reading. The church was relentless, as such transgressions were recorded and publicly noted.

As Puritans or Puritan sympathizers, many of the Herricks in Leicester believed that people should worship in a manner that they felt was right. In strong contrast, the king insisted that people believe and worship in only one way, no matter who you were, and were punished for not doing so.

As his friendship with Francis Higginson deepened, Henry's thinking became more radical in the eyes of the church. It may have been of some concern to John Mobbes, Mayor of Leicester in 1609, that his daughter Alice would marry such a radical Puritan as Henry Eyricke (or Hericke). Or perhaps John Mobbes became more liberal and radicalized himself by the time his daughter married. But Alice and Henry did marry at All Saints Church, an old Norman (Viking) church on High street on September 22, 1622. The wedding ceremony was conducted by Henry's good friend and fellow Puritan, Francis Higginson.

Since All Saints was not the Eyricke family church, it is more likely that it was the Mobbes family church. Not only did Henry, Alice, and Francis think along the same lines, but All Saints was considered a radical congregation during this time. Since Higginson also served All Saints at the same time that he served St. Nicholas, both churches were suspect by the Church of England. A few years before Alice and Henry were married, All Saints parishioners were accused of "separating yourselves from other people of God" and being "in conformable and refactoring", meaning it was changing the official practices of the church. Clearly the official Church of England was a strong political force in England at the time as well as a strong influence on the personal lives of the citizenry. However, Henry and Alice were so strongly influenced by Francis that they developed the courage to think for themselves and courage to act according to their beliefs even when it was considered illegal by the Church of England.

CHAPTER 2 —RELIGION, CHURCHES, FAMILY

Alice and Henry started a family. Samuel was born in 1623, one year after Henry and Alice were married. Samuel was baptized by Rev. Higginson at St. Nicholas Church, the Eyricke family church. Three years after the birth of Samuel, Alice and Henry moved to Belgrave, a small residential village just outside the East Gate of the Leicester wall. Here a second son was born. Thomas was born in 1626 and baptized by Higginson at St. Peter's church in Belgrave. Only one year later in 1627, Francis Higginson was fired by the Church of England, or as the church proclaimed it, "deprived of curacy". Despite his release, Higginson continued to preach at various churches in Leicester and Belgrave, and Henry continued his friendship with him. Then life caved in on Henry Herrick[13].

Interior of All Saints Church

---

13 By this time the surname Eyricke, Heyricke or Hericke were used intermittently.

Back view of All Saints Church with Saxon bell tower

St. Nicholas Church

CHAPTER 2 — RELIGION, CHURCHES, FAMILY

Interior view of St. Nicholas Church

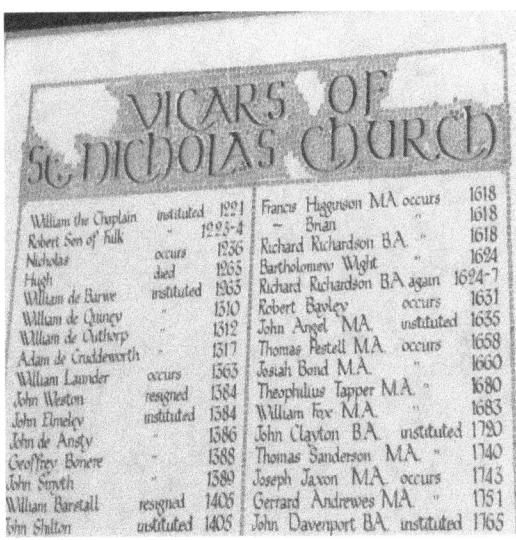

Vicars of St. Nicholas Church, Francis Higginson, 1618

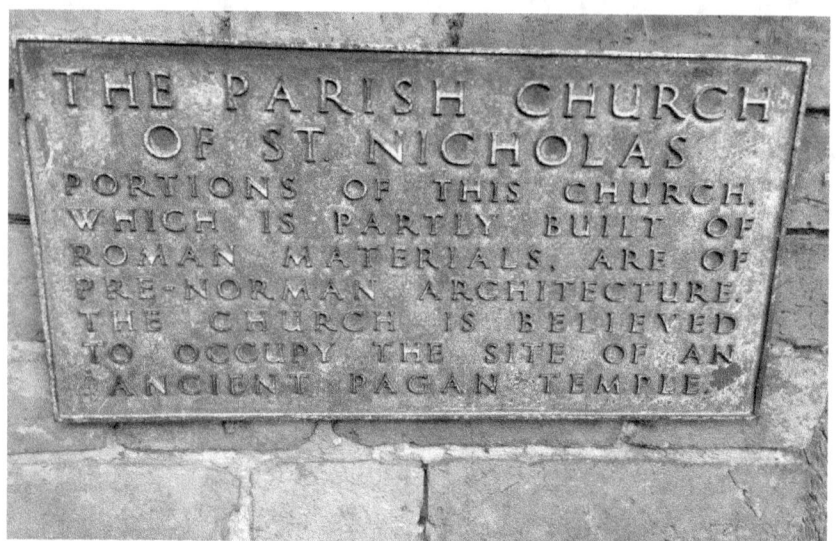

Plaque on St. Nicholas Church explaining that the stone used in construction came from the Roman ruins next to the church

Jewry Wall, remaining structure of the Roman Baths. Stone from the bath were used to build St. Nicholas Church in background.

CHAPTER 2 —RELIGION, CHURCHES, FAMILY

Henry developed a reputation of dissent and non-conformity, not to mention guilt by association with the "outlaw" Francis Higginson. The records are not clear on exactly when or why, but it appears that both Alice and their son, Samuel, died around 1627 or 1628.[14] Then in March 1628, almost within a year of the death of his wife and son, Henry Herrick was excommunicated by the church.

---

14 The death of Alice and Samuel in 1627 is a theory that is yet unsubstantiated. There is also evidence that Thomas may not have traveled to Salem with Henry. More research is needed.

Chapter 3

The Big Decision

    Sometimes when the seas are calm, the air is fresh, the sun warms the heart and mind, and all seems perfect in the world, but that is when the storm may erupt and change life forever. Such was the case for Henry Herrick. Life was good in Belgrave. Henry was happily married with two young boys, and had become a freeman in a prosperous trade. Not long after Thomas was born and baptized, Alice became ill. Then Samuel. It is not clear what illness it was, but it is entirely possible that one of many outbreaks of the plague ran through Leicester at the time. Whatever the disease, it took them very quickly. Henry had to be beyond despair. In the wink of an eye, he went from highest joy to the lowest grief. He now had to move on with life as sole parent to Thomas, his remaining son.

    But there was also the church. He had not only lost his wife and son, but also lost the church. And for what? At the bottom of personal despair, the church excommunicated him for "not kneeling for communion received and taken for last visitation on Easter day last and next Sunday". But the church was not finished. Henry was summoned to appear in the church court to explain and repent is "sins". But by this time Henry had different ideas and refused to appear. Perhaps it was the weight of despair, the anger of the church's claim on his life, or fear of the future. But he could not and did not appear. Consequently, as the church records show, he was fined 7 schillings for not appearing. To make matter more insulting and grievous, Henry was given the additional charge of "inhibition", which meant that he couldn't conduct trade with other church members and church members could not trade with him. The storm arrived. His business was gone, along with his wife and child.

    However, his friend Francis Higginson was never far away. In the same month that the church left Henry, Higginson embraced him. Rev. Higginson himself was bitterly involved at this time in proceedings against him in the church's Court of High Commission. Perhaps it was an act of true friendship. Perhaps it was providence. Regardless, during the very same month of March, 1628, Francis Higginson offered Henry and 350 other Puritans the opportunity to join him in a new life with the Massachusetts Bay Colony. A new life in America, where they could start life over, free to worship as they wished and as they believed to be true and honest.

One year later, Henry Herrick set sail for America with his son Thomas[15]. There was a small fleet of six ships with Henry and Thomas on the Lyon's Whelp. Francis Higginson, his wife Ann, and their 8 children sailed on the Talbot. The other ships in this fleet bound for Massachusetts Bay were the George Bonaventure, Four Sisters, and the Mayflower (not the Pilgrim's Mayflower), and the Pilgrim, which carried only supplies. The Bonaventure carried Rev. Samuel Skelton and his family. Once in Salem, Skelton and Higginson were selected as Pastor and Teaching Minister respectively at the First Church of Salem[16]. All total, this fleet of six ships carried "300 men, 60 women and maids, 26 children, and 140 head of cattle."

The small fleet of ships left Yarmouth or Southampton, in the Isle of Wright. The Talbot, carrying the family of Francis Higginson and the Lyon's Whelp, carrying Henry Herrick and Thomas, left Gravesend on April 25, 1629, but due to slight winds, it only went 12 miles. A few days later they sailed to Gorin Road, where they anchored for the night. The next day, they proceeded a little further, anchored at Margaret Town and waited for a stronger wind to carry them out to sea. They sailed to Lizzard Head and again anchored for the night. Then on May 13th, they passed Land's End and saw England for the last time. Their destination, as stated by John Winthrop who joined the colony in 1630 as its third governor[17], was described as "the city on the hill", which is a quotation taken from the Book of Matthew. The intention to characterize New England with such a biblical quotation was to proclaim to the world that

---

15 Evidence has been gathered by the Herrick Family Association that Thomas came to New England with his father on the Lyon's Whelp. However, contrary evidence has been produced by some English Herricks that Thomas (or another Thomas) stayed in Leicester married Isobel Hoyes in 1646/7, became a Freeman as a tailor or ironmonger in 1647, and died in 1675. Research on this discrepancy is continuing.
16 Now the Unitarian/Universalist Church of Salem
17 Roger Conant was first governor and John Endicott was second governor.

Chapter 3 — The Big Decision

such a settlement was a venture of the godly, particularly in light of the fact that England's Protestant Church was in such disarray.

But the church was not finished. On June 2nd, 1629 the church proclaimed that it would absolve Henry of all his wrong doings if he would repent. Little did the church know that Henry had already made a life change, beyond the reach or imagination of church doctrine. Henry Herrick was in the middle of the Atlantic Ocean on his way towards a new life in Salem.

Francis Higginson upon leaving England on the Talbot made perhaps the poignant comment about this new venture of Puritans in comparison to that of the Pilgrims who arrived in Plymouth nine years earlier. As he and his family stood on the stern of the Talbert watching England fade into the distance, Higginson wrote into his diary, "We will not say, as the separatists (Pilgrims) were wont to say at their leaving of England, 'Farewell, Babylon!' 'Farewell, Rome!' but we will say, 'Farewell, dear England! Farewell, the church of God in England, and all the Christian friends there!' We do not go to New England as separatists from the church of England; though we cannot but separate from the corruptions in it; but we go to practice the positive part of church reformation and propagate the gospel in America."

The Lyon's Whelp was one of a private fleet of 10 three masted Lyon's Whelps built by the Duke of Buckingham in 1628. All the Lyon's Whelps were armed merchant ships. The Lyon's Whelp, which carried Henry to Salem, weighted 120 tons and was equipped with eight cannons. The Lyon's Whelp master was John Gibbs and carried 6 fishermen and 40 planters including Henry.

The Lyon's Whelp. Built 1628 and carried
Henry Herrick to Salem in 1629

The boards on the ship's haul creaked to a steady melodious tune as they slowly parted the continuous oncoming waves across the water. The sails high above the deck took the wind from the gentle breeze pushing the Lyon's Whelp slowly and assuredly forward. The ship he was on had made up its mind. It was going forward with confidence and courage. But was he? Did he know what he was doing? Had he made the right decision? Henry talked to himself. No, there was no turning back! There was no more doubt. No more hesitation. What will be his fate in the unknown land ahead? What of his old life was he taking to his new life? Only memories, he thought. Some bitter, some prideful and sustaining. Henry looked back as the land slipped into the horizon. Too far out to sea to see England again. He held Thomas's hand as his anxieties shifted slightly to hope. As he looked out from the ship from what seemed like

Chapter 3 — The Big Decision

small buoy bobbing in the sea, his senses started to swell. In sight was only endless sea, he felt wind against his face, he smelled the salty air, and the only sound was the creaking ship pushing against the waves. His mind was empty. Memories filled the void.

He recalled the stories his father, uncles, and cousins told to him about his past, his famous ancestral name. He recalled Beau Manor, the home built by his famous cousin, and the civic and benevolent roles of his relatives. He recalled the stories of how his family long before had shifted from the metal trades to the cloth trades. He contemplated the stories repeatedly told by his relatives of his ancestral heritage going back centuries in Leicestershire. The stories, the places, the family were gone now. Gone, except for those sacred memories.

Chapter 4
Ericke of East Anglia

It is often said that truth is stranger than fiction. While pondering his voyage to the new world, Henry stretched his memory as far back as he could and contemplated what his relatives claimed as truth about the earliest English Herricks. Growing up Henry heard many stories about the "true" beginnings of his ancestors. These stories and family traditions always claimed the Herricks descended from Ericke, a Danish Chief during the reign of King Alfred the Great.[18] Family tradition holds that it is entirely possible, in fact probable, that Ericke either participated in the Viking Great Invasion of 865 AD, or what the English called the Great Heathen Invasion, or was part of an invasion shortly later. The 865 invasion was called a heathen invasion because the invading Vikings were pagans.[19] This single invasion, involving 3000 men and hundreds of fleets, was the beginning of series of Nordic invasions involving a combined force from Sweden, Norway and Denmark lasting 14 years, all during the English reign of King Alfred the Great. The Danes were the prominent Vikings in England, while Norwegians and Swedes were the prominent Viking invaders in Ireland and Scotland. The Great Invasion of 865 was the first Viking invasion that resulted in Viking settlements in England. These Scandinavian Vikings were in England to stay. Previous

---

18 This linage is well documented in each edition of the Herrick Family Register. However, Dr. Roderick Dale, a noted Viking expert from the University of Nottingham commented to the author in private correspondence that Eric or Eryke, etc. are very popular Viking names and it would be very difficult/almost impossible to determine the exact linage back to Ericke of East Anglia, and that the citation in the HGR are probably from the early historian Holished or a similar later historian.

19 A genetic heritage study was commissioned in 2000 to determine through DNA precisely where the Nordic invaders came from. The results indicate that the Danish Vikings originated from areas concentrated on the Jutland peninsula of Denmark.

Viking invasions, the first recorded in the Anglo-Saxon Chronicle was in 793 at Lindisfarne, were essentially raids in which the Vikings took what they wanted and returned home. There were raids after the Great Invasion but they were often orchestrated by Vikings who had already settled in England. It was also the case were Viking invasions were conducted in England in order to sue for peace. The Danes soon realized that the English were often willing to pay large sums of money for the sake of peace, however temporary. So, raiding parties became profitable for the Vikings.

> It seems likely that the Herricks could trace their ancestry back to one Erik, one of the original Danish settlers, perhaps, of the past quarter of the ninth century in the same village (i.e. Wigston and Stretton); and that they may well have occupied the same piece of land since that distant date knowing what we do of the immense continuity of village ownership in medieval times. They above all emerge into recorded village history from the mists of pre-Conquest days, from the Danish army of the ninth century and the sokemen of the eleventh, and we find them flourshing vigorously in the village when Henry VIII came to the throne.
> —The Midland Peasant, W.G. Hoskins, 1957, p.42

Viking invasions were never under a unified command but were led by many different kings and earls with mostly a Danish command. The invasions occurred up and down the English eastern coast, mostly in Northumbria and East Anglia. They were largely successful. The Vikings subsequently invaded and settled what was then called Mercia in central England.[20] Alfred's base during this time was Wessex, which before London was the capital of England. The boundary between Danish

---

20 Recent excavations in Repton, Derbyshire, about 30 miles north of Leicester, have discovered the remains of Viking settlers believed to be part of the Great Heathen Invasion. There were settlers not warriors, since woman remains were found. Artifacts found at the grave sites are exactly like those found in Denmark about the time of the invasion. It is estimated that about 5000 Vikings made their winter camp at Repton. The remains of Ivar the Boneless, one of the primary leaders of the Great Heathen Invasion are believed to be among them.

CHAPTER 4 — ERICKE OF EAST ANGLIA

dominated England and Anglo-Saxon England lay directly through Mercia in a line running north-west to south-east from Chester along Watling Street to London. This line runs directly through what is now Leicestershire. Danish England was known as Danelaw, since Danish law and governance dominated the Anglo-Saxon population.

Because these Nordic invaders were pagans, as descripted in the Anglo-Saxon Chronicles[21], the English Anglo-Saxons were even more resentful of their brutal and violent hit and run tactics. Beginning with the Great Viking Invasion of 865, the subsequent invasions were not the typical Viking hit and run raids of the past. The purpose of these invasions, subsequent to 865, was to conquer and settle. Ericke of East Anglia could very likely have been a participant in the Great Heathen Invasion, a Danish chief or warlord in East Anglia and later traveled inland with other Vikings to Mercia.

The Vikings under the command of Guthrum, later King Guthrum, took full control of East Anglia in 869 when they killed Edmund, the English king of the East Angles. The Vikings were able to move inland from East Anglia and Northumbria because their long boats floated high in the water, permitting them to travel along rivers to victimize small villages and create new settlements. They most likely traveled up the river Trent, deeper into the richer lands of Mercia. In 874, the Great Heathen Army invaded and conquered Mercia and seized Repton, a royal center, and began their winter settlement there.[22]

Below is an account from the Anglo-Saxon Chronicle describing the first Viking invasion and raid at the Lindisfarne Monastery in 893:

> DCCC.XCIII. In this year dire forewarnings came over the land of the Northumbrians, and miserably terrified the people: these were excessive whirlwinds and lightnings, and fiery dragons were seen flying in the air. A great famine soon followed these tokens; and a little after that, in the same year, on the the Ides

---

21 The Anglo-Saxon Chronicles were accounts of Anglo-Saxon history and maintained in monasteries from the 9th century. They were written from a Christian perspective, thus referring to the Vikings as pagans or heathens.
22 Little was known about this Viking winter encampment until excavations began in the 1970s and 80s. These fortifications are significant because they are the only archaeologically excavated Viking built fortifications in Britain.

of January (Jan. 8th), the havoc of heathen men miserably destroyed God's church at Lindisfarne, through rapine and slaughter.

In 867, two years after the invasion the Great Army tuned on Mercia and made peaceful terms with the people there. They meant to settle, since the Mercian town of Repton presented the key to the kingdom of Mercia. After they arrived, the Vikings drove the Mercian King, Burgred, into exile. But around 877, the Viking Army at Repton split into two distinct units. The Viking chieftain, Halfdan, headed north to Northumbria and another Viking chieftain named Guthrum, along with other chieftains Oscetel and Anwend, headed south. The purpose of the southern unit that split at Repton was to colonize the five boroughs or shires of Nottinghamshire, Lincolnshire, Derbyshire, Leicestershire and Rutland, thus ultimately creating Danelaw. There were many Viking chieftains in those days with different roles to play, but one of the chieftains that headed south from Reptan could have been Ericke of East Anglia. Ericke, or his immediate descendants, and could have settled in Leicestershire, but until further research is done, this is conjecture.

Remains of 250 Viking men and women
excavated at Repton in 1980-86

Chapter 4 — Ericke of East Anglia

The Anglo-Saxon Chronicles state that in 880 Danish Viking soldiers settled as farmers, dependent on the army bases established in main towns in the area, such as Leicester. The Doomsday Book of 1086[23] recorded Scandinavian names for parishes and the area north and northeast of Watling Street, including Leicestershire, indicates a sharp distinction between English and Danish Mercia. It is estimated that over 500 place names (parish names) are in the five boroughs alone. It is possible that the Herricks originating from Leicestershire resulted from this Viking split shortly after the Viking invasion and settlement in Mercia.

The village of Leicester was an important place for Viking military fortifications since it had been established centuries before by the Romans, who left the area around 410 AD. Shortly after that, the Anglo-Saxons occupied Leicester and later the Vikings built upon the Anglo-Saxon settlement.

The Danes were mostly successful in their conquests and settlements in Northumbria, Mercia, and East Anglia, so they purchased peace from the Danes with horses and other necessary goods. However, in 878 King Alfred's English army defeated the Danish King Guthrum at Edington. Guthrum and his fellow Danes agreed to settle in East Anglia. Given the dates and records pertaining to Ericke, Ericke was likely a part of that battle and subsequent defeat.

---

23 The Doomsday book was like a modern day census started by William the Conqueror to count residences and their incomes for taxation purposes.

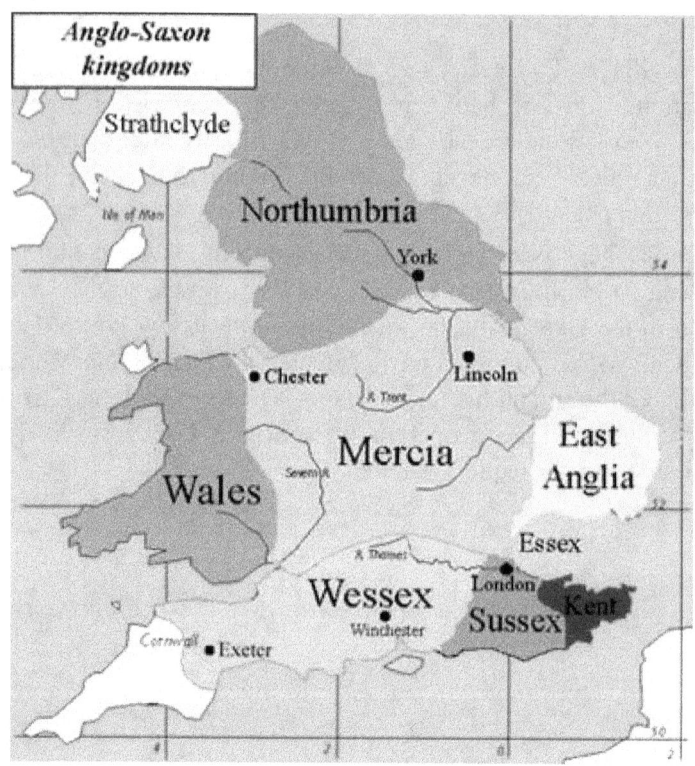

English States Under Danelaw at the time of Alfred the Great

Chapter 4 — Ericke of East Anglia

Scandinavian Place Names as recorded in Doomsday Book 1086

The line dividing English and Danish Mercia at the time of Alfred the Great

The maps above show the English states as they existed during the time of King Alfred and the during the time of Ericke of East Anglia. Leicester was in the center of what was then the Kingdom of Mercia, directly west of East Anglia. It is very possible that Ericke and his next generation migrated from East Anglia to Mercia via the long boats on interior water ways, and on to Leicestershire after the Viking army split.[24]

The dotted line on the last map shows the boundary of English Mercia to the west and Danish Mercia to the east. Danish Mercia and East Anglia was governed by Danelaw. Danelaw originated from Viking expansion in the late ninth century. Danelaw is a region and a government. It was a region in England governed by Danish law by decedents of Viking invaders and settlers. The governed were both Danes and Anglo-Saxon English.

Leicester is located in Danelaw just east of the boundary, which continued from Watling Street in London to Chester, and was established through a treaty between the Danish King Guthrum of East Anglia and the English King Alfred. By the late 10th century, Danelaw had become so prominent in England that the Danish King Sven and his son, Cnut, were considered King of all England. Interestingly, after becoming King of England, Cnut's chief concern was protecting his kingdom from fresh Viking raids from former members of his own army.

> The traditions of this very ancient family (Herrick), claim their descent from Ericke, a Danish Chief who invaded Britain during the reign of Alfred, and having been vanquished by that Prince, was compelled, with his followers, to repeople the wasted districts of East Anglia; the government of which he held as a fief of the English crown. He is recognized in history as 'Ericke, King of those Danes who hold the Countrie of East Angle.
> —Herrick Genealogical Record, Jedediah Herrick, 1846, p.5.

---

24 Further evidence that the Herrick roots go back to Viking times is that the excavations at Repton reveled a medieval axe of an identical type found in Fyrkat, Denmark and 5 silver coins, that were struck around 872.

CHAPTER 4 — ERICKE OF EAST ANGLIA

It is very likely that this citation in the Herrick Genealogical Record refers to the Danish defeat at Edington. Guthrum and Ericke and perhaps other Danish "kings" and their followers did settle in the region of East Anglia and their "kingdom" was held as a fief of the English crown. But in 903, Aethelwald, the King of Essex, which was within the kingdom of East Anglia, incited all the East Anglian leaders to break the peace with the English and initiated a battle with England. So, in an attempt to "unite the Danish power against the Englishmen," Gunthrum and Ericke again rose up in battle against England. Again, the Danes were defeated by the English, this time by King Edward 'The Elder', the son and successor of Alfred.

It is here citations about who Ericke is gets somewhat confusing. The Anglo-Saxon Chronicles state that both Aethelwald and the Danish King Eohric (Eirikr in Danish), son and successor of Gunthrum, were killed in the battle of 903. However, the chronicles continue to cite English and Danish wars after 903. In 911, the English again defeated the Danes at Tettenhall. With Gunthrum and Eohric now dead, Ericke was now King of the Danes. Polydore Vergil's Anglica Historia, states that in 911:

> Ericke, the King of those Danes which held the country of East Angle, was about the procure new war, and to allure other Danes to join with him against the Englishmen, that with common agreement they might set upon the English nation and utterly subdue them. King Edward having intelligence hereof, proposed to prevent him, and thereupon entering with an army into his country, cruelly wasted and spoiled the same. King Ericke having already his people in armor, through displeasure conceived hereof, and desire to be revenged, hasted forth to encounter his enemies, and so they met in the field, and fiercely assailed each other. But as the battle was rashly begun on King Ericke's side, so was the end very harmful to him, for with small ado, after great lose on both sides, he was vanquished and put to flight. After his coming home, because of his great overthrow and fowl discomfiture, he began to govern his people with more rigor and sharper dealing than beforetime he had used. Whereby he provoked the malice of the East Angles so highly against him, that they fell upon him and murdered

him; yet did they not gain so much hereby as they looked to have, for shortly after, they being bought low, and not able to defend their country, were compelled to submit themselves to King Edward.
—Herrick Genealogical Record, Appendix B2, 1846, p.64.

So, it appears that the chronicles cite two East Anglican kings with similar spellings, King Eohric, killed in battle in 903 and King Ericke, killed by his own people after 'severities' in his government shortly after his defeat at Tettenhall in 911. Since Polydore's account is based on the chronicle record of Ericke and not Eohric, Herricks are likely descendants from the Danish King Ericke. Quoting Dr. Dale from the University of Nottingham, "If the Herricks originated from Leicestershire they almost certainly had them (Danish Viking roots)."

Chapter 5

Erick the Forester

Ericke, the ancient Danish King of East Angelia started a long line of Danes in England. Before long, that line led to Erick the Forester, who lived in Leicestershire in the 11th century. He was certainly a man of great character. During this time, the Danish King, Cnut or Canute, was also the King of England. As the Danes settled Danelaw in Mercia, they set up encampments of armies as well. The towns in Danelaw at this time, including Leicester, became military bases for the invading forces against the English Anglo-Saxons. As time passed, the Viking warriors in these military bases, such as the ones in Leicestershire became colonists and landowners. Erick the Forester evolved from that transition in Leicestershire. Viking historians have long claimed that Erick the Forester lived in Leicestershire and possessed extensive domains going all the way west to the border of Wales.

As a young man, Henry could have easily wondered about stories of ancient times and the role that his ancestors played. Perhaps he had those thoughts has he watched England fade from sight on the deck of the Lyon's Whelp to a new life in Massachusetts. "What would my ancestors do if they were in my shoes today and experienced my life", he may have thought. Perhaps he thought of the stories of Ericke, King of East Anglia and of Erick the Forester of Leicestershire and the tough decisions that had to make. Since Polydore wrote Anglica Historia in 1555, Henry may have heard stories about King Ericke from his family and relatives in Leicester based of these accounts. If stories of the ancient Herrick family were part of family conversation, surely Erick the Forester would have also been a topic of discussion.

Erick the Forester was born in 1040 and raised in Leicestershire, in the middle of what was then the Kingdom of Mercia and ruled under

Danelaw. He was most likely the great-great-great grandson of King Ericke of East Anglia.[25]

Erick the Forester was part of a notable Viking heritage. Not only was he a descendent of a Danish warrior and king but also is alleged to be the brother of Eric the Red[26], who settled in Iceland and Greenland. Erik the Forester also had a unique relationship with a very famous English king – William the Conqueror.

In 1066, William, Duke of Normandy, later to be known as William the Conqueror, was planning an invasion of England from his home in Normandy, a Viking settlement in northern France.[27] The popular King of England at the time was Edward the Confessor. He died in January 1066 and the Norwegian, Harold Godwinson, became the next King of England. Given this event, William felt that he was in a good position to press his claim to the English throne and so he began his plans for an invasion. King Harold, however, had inherited a staggering task with multiple enemies scheming to overcome England. The initial invasion came in May, 1066 by his own brother, Tostig. By September, Harold had fought off three invasions including the bloody battle of Stamford Bridge, killing his brother Tostig. His army was exhausted, but by this time William had assembled his army on the coast of Normandy and was ready to cross the channel for his invasion. After the Battle of Stamford Bridge, Harold marched his army 240 miles from York to Hastings to engage William. On October 14, the Battle of Hastings was fought all day long. For the English, it was the third major battle in less than four weeks. King Harold was killed in the battle and William claimed victory.

Once Erick the Forester learned of the impending invasion, he raised a large army at Copt Oak, Charnword, an area around Leicestershire. His goal was to repel the invaders, dispossess the Normans of other recent conquests, and to drive them out of England for good. It is entirely possible that Erick the Forester and his army was part of the military force that defended England with King Harold. His efforts

---

25 Evidence of this linage is found in all editions of the Herrick Family Register.
26 This account appears unlikely since Eric the Red was from Norway not Denmark and was born in 950, 90 years before Erick the Forester.
27 William was partly French and his people were called Normans and their settlement called Normandy because they were Norse or Northmen. Vikings invaded France in the mid 8th century and settled in the northern part of France named Normandy.

CHAPTER 5 — ERICK THE FORESTER

failed, as William won the Battle of Hastings, and henceforth was known as William the Conqueror, King of England. The Normans were in England to stay and the Anglo-Saxon period in all of England came to an abrupt end. Without power, finances, or estates, Erick and his followers were no longer a threat to the Normans. William the Conqueror stripped Erick and his followers of their estates and all sources of their former power. Although a one-time enemy, William noticed and favored Erick due to his bravery in battle and, therefore, and quite ironically, entrusted him with important offices, made him one of his army generals, and permitted Erick to retire back to his home in Leicestershire.

It is important to note, however, that the Norman conquest of England did not end with the Battle of Hastings. There were a series of English revolts for years following, particularly in the north, and William was brutal to those who resisted, but forgiving to those who submitted. In the summer of 1068, two years after the Battle of Hastings, William commenced his "second campaign" into Oxford, then into Warwick, and after that into Leicester. Edwin, the Earl of Leicester, was killed when he attempted to escape to Scotland.

> The town (Leicester) was taken and almost utterly destroyed. The castle and the church dedicated to St. Mary, standing near thereto, shared the same fate. The obstinacy of the resistance made by the townspeople may be inferred from the injury done to their houses and defenses. From Leicester, the Conqueror marched upon Derby, Nottingham, Lincoln, and York, where similar scenes of havoc and slaughter were enacted.
> —The History of Leicester, James Thompson, 1849, pp 21-22.

There is no account if Erick the Forester had submitted to William the Conqueror prior to the attack on Leicester or as a result of the attack. It is just clear that he did submit and was granted his home and property and allowed to remain in Leicestershire.

By all accounts, William the Conqueror ruthlessly put down rebellions that sprung up after the Norman Invasion, but he could be fair and compassionate to those who did submit. When the English who fought against William surrendered and they "came before the Conqueror", they gave hostages and swore oaths to him. William promised them that he would be a "gracious lord". Historians agree that

William promised "many wise, just and merciful provisions", including allowing London's leading men and their laws would be maintained as they were in the "time of King Edward". William is often considered the "first chivalrous king of England" when compared to earlier English kings. Erick's submission to the new king, allowed his return to Leicestershire and his appointments to official positions with King William. However, the lands and property of William's former enemies were confiscated and could only be repossessed through purchase or a grant from the new king. It is not clear whether or not the return of Erick's property in Leicestershire was purchased or granted as a favor due to his respect for Erick.

Despite William's commitment to rule fairly, he nevertheless imposed heavy taxes on the citizenry. In order to establish a basis for that taxation, William ordered the creation of the Doomsday Book in 1086, which was an exhaustive census of all England's people and property. It was called Domesday, because like the day of judgment, its decisions were unalterable.

William the Conqueror was a man a great stature and by the age of 24 was the mightiest feudal lord in France. After the Battle of Hastings, he seized the English crown but was never popular with the English Saxon population. However, William's iron rule brought social order and stability to England.

Below are various accounts of the Battle of Hastings taken directly from the Anglo-Saxon Chronicles.

> A.D. 1066. Then, during this, came Harold, king of the Angles, with all his forces, on the Sunday, to Tadcaster, and there drew up his force, and went then on Monday throughout York; and Harold, King of Norway, and Tosty the earl, and their forces, were gone from their ships beyond York to Stamford Bridge, because it had been promised them for a certainty, that there, from all the shire, hostages should be brought to meet them.
> A.D. 1066. This year came King Harold from York to Westminster, on the Easter succeeding the midwinter when the king (Edward the Confessor) died. Meantime Earl William came up from Normandy into Pevensey on the eve of St. Michael's mass; and soon after his landing was affected, they constructed a castle at the port of Hastings. This was then told to King Harold; and he gathered a large force and came to meet

Chapter 5 — Erick the Forester

him at the estuary of Appledore. William, however, came against him unawares, ere his army was collected; but the king, nevertheless, very hardly encountered him with the men that would support him: and there was a great slaughter made on either side. There was slain King Harold, and Leofwin his brother, and Earl Girth his brother, with many good men: and the Frenchmen gained the field of battle, as God granted them for the sins of the nation. This battle was fought on the day of Pope Calixtus: and Earl William returned to Hastings, and waited there to know whether the people would submit to him. But when he found that they would not come to him, he went up with all his force that was left and that came since to him from over sea, and ravaged all the country that he overran, until he came to Berkhampstead; where Archbishop Aldred came to meet him, with child Edgar, and Earls Edwin and Morkar, and all the best men from London; who submitted then for need, when the most harm was done. It was very ill-advised that they did not so before, seeing that God would not better things for our sins. And they gave him hostages and took oaths: and he promised them that he would be a faithful lord to them; though in the midst of this they plundered wherever they went. Then on midwinter's day Archbishop Aldred hallowed him to king at Westminster, and gave him possession with the books of Christ, and also swore him, ere that he would set the crown on his head, that he would so well govern this nation as any before him best did, if they would be faithful to him.

A.D. 1066. And the while, William the earl landed at Hastings, on St. Michael's-day: and Harold came from the north, and fought against him before all his army had come up: and there he fell, and his two brothers, Girth and Leofwin; and William subdued this land. And he came to Westminster, and Archbishop Aldred consecrated him king, and men paid him tribute, delivered him hostages, and afterwards bought their land.

A.D. 1068. This year King William gave Earl Robert the earldom over Northumberland; but the landsmen attacked him in the town of Durham, and slew him, and nine hundred men with him. Soon afterwards Edgar Etheling came with all the

Northumbrians to York; and the townsmen made a treaty with him: but King William came from the South unawares on them with a large army, and put them to flight, and slew on the spot those who could not escape; which were many hundred men; and plundered the town.

The Norman invasion was a dramatic turning point in English history as it was for the descendants of Erick the Forester. Before the invasion, the English Anglo-Saxon population was ruled by Scandinavian kings, but post invasion England was ruled by Norman authority. Erick and his ancestors were of Danish (Scandinavian) origin, but Danelaw ended with William the Conqueror. It is believed, and highly likely, that Erick the Forester settled in Great Stretton in the middle of Leicestershire, since his son and grandsons, were landowners at Great Stretton, known then as Stretton Magna. The great grandson of Erick the Forester was named Henry but was always referred to as Eyryk of Stretton, from whom the Herrick linage continued to descend.

Given the many English derivations of the surname[28], it isn't surprising that the name could have evolved from Erick, which was and is a Viking name. The earliest Scandinavian spelling would have been Eirikr. Turi King[29], a geneticist at the University of Leicester, studied the Herrick surname extensively and points out that no one prior to the Norman Invasion in 1066 had a surname. People were given a personal name and sometimes a nickname, such as Edward the Confessor, or William the Conqueror, or Erik the Red, or in our family Erick the Forester. Surnames evolved from those personal names. Turi King's family DNA research concludes that the Herrick surname name is "single source", meaning that all Herrick surnames come from a common source. Her research also led to the finding that the Herrick surname in the 13th century was most commonly found in Leicestershire, an area of intense Danish settlement in the 9th and 10th century. Subsequent DNA research shows Herricks to be the same haplogroup as the Vikings in the area, confirming that Herricks have Viking roots.

---

28 Henry of Great Stretton spelled his name Eyryk, Robert of Houghton spelled his name Eyricke, his son Thomas spelled it Eyrick, and his son John spelled it Eyrek. Nicholas, father of Robert the poet, spelled his name Heryk. By the middle of the seventeenth century the name was spelled Heyrick or Herrick.
29 Turi King was the lead geneticist who conducted the DNA testing on the skeletal remains found in Leicester in 2012 and conclusively identified those remains as King Richard III.

Chapter 6

Great Stretton: The Eyryks

When a boy or young man hears stories about his family going back over 300 years across 13 generations, facts and details get blurred and questionable to say the least. And that may have been the case when Henry heard about his Great Stretton connection. Almost legendary were the commentaries about the first Eyryks to settle at Great Stretton, only a short distance from Leicester. It was commonly thought that Eyryk of Stretton, thought to be one of earliest Eyryks at Great Stretton, was born in 1216 and died at Great Stretton in 1272. There is some evidence that his name was actually Henry and his father and grandfather's names were also Henry, all of them living at Great Stretton. If true, the grandfather of the legendary Eyryk of Stretton was Henry born in 1125.

In Old English, Stretton means 'street' and in medieval times it was referred to as the "settlement on a Roman Road". Great Stretton, or Stretton Magna, as it was called then, was indeed on a well-traveled road, a road built by the Romans, which originated from London and traversed Leicestershire. The road was built around 500 AD and wove its way through forest and meadows north from London to Leicester and beyond. As with most Roman roads, the Great Stretton Road was a long stretch of road made of stones from the surrounding area connecting English villages, primarily for military purposes. The settlement at Great Stretton, about 10 miles from the village of Leicester and only a few miles up the Roman Road to Houghton on the Hill, was occupied by eight generations of Eyryks.

In 1086, the year of the first Doomsday recordings, Stretton was listed as one estate, but later was split into two townships - Great Stretton and Little Stretton. The Eyryks or Heyricks, as it was sometimes spelled at this time, were probably the most important family in Great Stretton. They were substantial free tenants and first mentioned by name at Great Stretton in 1274 when Richard Heirek (again a spelling variation) was described as a local clerk. In 1327 and again in 1332, Richard Heiek and Robert Heysrick (Robert de Stretton) paid between them about one third of the whole estate in the parish. The Herricks (Eyryks) were the oldest of all families residing at Stretton Magna or Wigston Magna, a nearby village. The name of Henry Eyrig (a spelling variation) was listed as a subsidy grant witness sometime between 1247 and 1260.

Great Stretton is now abandoned, but in medieval times it was a village devoted primarily to agriculture. The villagers were peasants, providing goods for themselves, the Eyryks who owned the land, and often times to the community at large. In addition to the village and St Giles church, built between 1150-1075, Great Stretton included a moat and two fish ponds. The moat was built by Robert Eyryk to surround his manor house. The fish ponds were used to harvest fish and for fresh water. Great Stretton is listed in the Domesday book for tax purposes. In 1381, the Doomsday book recorded 21 taxed persons residing at Great Stretton. In 1563, there were 15 households and in 1670 only 5 households resided at Great Stretton.

It was during this time the Eyryks of Leicestershire became prosperous and noteworthy as they were well known residents of Great Stretton. But Eyryks settled over a wide area of Leicestershire. Many Eyryk families lived only a short distance from Great Stretton in a similar village called Wigston Magna. The Eyryks were integral families at both Stretton and Wigston, as their names appear many times as witnesses on land charters and grants. Henry Eyrek's signature was perhaps most common during the 13th century. But the Eyryk family in Wigston wasn't all upright and righteous. Ancient records show that Adam Eyryk murdered a man named Simon, the clerk of Wigston, a crime for which he was pardoned in 1299. There were a string of murders during this time and the motives were and still are unclear.

It was recorded in the thirteenth century at Wigston Magna that Richard Eyryk occupied a messuage (farm house without buildings) and paid rent to the local hospital, which owned the property. Records show that Henry Eyryk, Richard's direct ancestor, was living at the farm in 1463. This Eyryk line continued to live on this farm until 1540.

During this time a sort of renaissance in the Midlands took place. People were becoming more mobile, commerce was becoming more active, giving people more freedom and wealth. Education was starting to be considered the path to the future, and people were exercising more freedom of thought. The common belief was that one could move from

CHAPTER 6 — GREAT STRETTON: THE EYRYKS

being a villain (peasant) to middle class through education. During the 14th century a new form of freedom started to be expressed in Leicestershire and throughout the Midlands. This was a belief in religious freedom. A group called the Lollards, formed by John Wycliffe an Oxford professor, was a resistant group against the Catholic church due to the papacy's corruption and politicization. The movement was of course forbidden by the Pope and was ultimately put down and the rebels hanged or burned. But it was the beginning of free and independent religious thought in England. Today the Lollard rebellion is considered a precursor to the reformation. It is also a precursor to the Puritan rebellion against the Church of England in the 16th century.

But at the same time three events took its toll on Leicestershire and all of England. The Black Death began during this time and over the next few centuries killed two thirds of city populations in England and all across Europe. Secondly, the 100 Years War with France and the War of the Roses between the House of Lancaster and the House of York broke out and continued for decades. The War of the Roses ended at Bosworth Field just 14 miles outside of Leicester. Thirdly, the peasants started to protest against their landowners and the Peasant Revolt began. Even though the peasants lost militarily in their uprising, they ultimately were given concessions.

These three events, although highly disruptive, established a sort of cultural background for the progressive movements brought forth through increased skilled trades, commerce, and education. For the most part, the people of Leicestershire in the 12th and 13th century were ordinary people just trying to get by, doing their best to survive, and doing what they thought was right. The more well to do, including the Eyryks of Great Stretton, generally considered their good fortune to be middle class land owners. They were considered responsible citizens. The facts that probably stuck with Henry about his Great Stretton ancestors and which Henry probably had most confidence were the famous stories of Robert and Sir William of Great Stretton and their service to the Black Prince and his father, King Edward III. The brothers, Robert and William Eyryk (or Heyrick) and their families held land in Great Stretton until the 15th century, then moved to Houghton on the Hill and ultimately to Leicester.

Chapter 7
Robert and William Eyryk

The fame and wealth of brothers Robert, born 1540, and Sir William Heyrick, born 1557, of Leicester and Beau Manor respectively was carved deeply into family history, and the fame of Robert Herrick the poet is well known. But there was another Herrick story often overlooked. One story that could easily been told during the days of young Henry was of two family members who lived over 200 years before Henry. This is the story of two other brothers also named Robert and William Eyryk. This Robert and William, both born around 1300 at Great Stretton, were very much like their family namesakes of the 16th century. Robert drew his notoriety as the Chaplain to the Black Prince, known at the time as the Prince of Woodstock. The Black Prince was the eldest son and heir to King Edward III. William, the older of the two, drew his notoriety by being knighted by King Edward III.

William served King Edward III by attending to his son, the Black Prince, at various military conflicts, including the Battle of Gascony in 1355, the Battle of Crecy, and the Battle of Poitiers, all part of the 100 Years War between England and France. For this service to the King, William was knighted by King Edward III, and since then William was known as Sir William. But questions always remained. What valued service did William perform for the Black Prince that qualified for knighthood? When did William return to Great Stretton and why ? And why was William knighted by the king when his brother Robert, who fell into great favor with the prince and the king, was not?

After taking his Holy Orders, Robert Eyryk became chaplain to Edward, the Black Prince, whose favor he enjoyed for the rest of his life. Robert was consecrated Bishop of Litchfield and Coventry on the Prince's recommendation in 1360 and was sometimes referred to as the Bishop of Chester. However, since Robert lacked sufficient education, the Archbishop of Canterbury refused to consecrate him. Robert apparently was so illiterate that a complaint was made to Pope Innocent VI concerning his unfitness as Bishop. But the king, favoring Robert, was persistent over many years of attempts and finally managed to have him consecrated in 1360. The Pope, however, did not perform the consecration, but rather had two of his suffragans (assistants to an Archbishop) perform the consecration, which they did reluctantly. That same year, he was asked to be one of the auditors of the Rota at the Vatican in Rome. Robert presided over the diocese of Coventry and Lichfield for a period of 25 years.[30]

Back at Great Stretton, Robert founded and endowed a Chantry in the chapel at St. Giles church at Great Stretton on September 4th, 1378. He supplemented his endowment with "4 messuages and 8 virgates containing 198 acres of land". Given that both Robert and William served the king by attending to the Black Prince, it is likely that both joined the prince as he entered battle with the French during the 100 Years War, which lasted from 1337 to 1453. How they divided their time in service to the king and operating their properties in Great Stretton is a mystery. It is also unknown how they survived and prospered during the Black Death, which broke out in 1348. Most of the victims of the disease resided in the cities where sanitation was very poor and populations were more dense. But they did survive and others who did, both landowners and peasants, prospered because there were fewer people to work more land. Despite relative prosperity, a Peasant Revolt broke out in 1381 due primarily to landowner attempts to keep wages low. It is not known how Robert or William or their sons responded to this revolt, if it affected them at all.

Robert, due to his devotion and service as Chaplain to the Black Prince was made Bishop of Lichfield and Bishop of Chester, but to the people around Leicestershire he was affectionately known as Robert de Stretton. According to available records, Robert and William were the 5th generation to live at Great Stretton. Great Stretton was occupied not just by the landowners, the Eyryks, but by 15 peasant families who worked the land. In addition to the peasant homes, clustered closely together in a tight community, Great Stretton subsumed 10 acres of meadow, a home where the Eyryks lived, and St. Giles church. The Great Stretton peasant villagers or serfs worked the land to sustain themselves

---

30 Robert Eyrke's acts as Bishop are preserved in two volumes of his registers which are extant at Lichfield. Much of his work was done by suffragans.

CHAPTER 7 — ROBERT AND WILLIAM EYRYK

and to pay the Eyryks their rent. That payment was made either in money or produce such as grain, honey, eggs or other produce. The work of the peasants was hard, owning nothing but the obligation to work for their master or land owner, who received their property through inheritance.

St. Giles was built in the 12th century, well before Robert and William were born. This was the church that the Eyryks attended along with the village peasants. Robert built his own private chapel adjacent to the church for family worship. Although his family had resided at Great Stretton for over a century, Robert built a large manor house on the property. The manor house was a short distance of about 200 yards from the church. It was a sharp contrast to the poor and simple peasant homes just on the opposite side at St. Giles. Not only was the manor house elaborate for its time, Robert built a deep moat surrounding the house. Between the manor house and the church was a large pond, which supplied water for the moat. On the other side of the moat was a smaller pond to drain the water when necessary. The moat was not needed for protection but was used primarily as a water supply.

By Henry's time, 200 years later, Robert's manor house was dilapidated, vacant, and nearly falling down. By this time, all the Eyryks had left Great Stretton, for Houghton-on-the-Hill and then to Leicester. The church was still there during Henry's youth and still very active. Many of the peasants still worked the land. The last Eyryk to live at Great Stretton was Robert Eyricke, the great grandson of Sir William of Great Stretton. Robert left Great Stretton and moved a few miles up the Roman Road (Gartree Road) to Houghton-on-the-Hill in about 1475. Robert's son Thomas became an ironmonger and perhaps the first ironmonger in the Eyrick family. Thomas was the first in the Eyrick family to be listed in the book of the Leicester Corporation[31] in 1511 and the first to live in Leicester. He served as Borough Chamberlain in 1511 and his two sons, Nicholas and John, both became Mayors of Leicester – Nicholas in 1552 and John in 1557. After Thomas died 1540, his wife Agnes was recorded in Wigston Magna as receiving a Lay Subsidy in 1545 as a widow. By this time, she took her name as Agnes Heyryke.

---

31 The Leicester Corporation evolved from Merchant Gilds or Freemans, which go back to before the Norman Conquest in 1066. The corporation is the forerunner of the city council with Major and Alderman, which exists today. The members of the Corporation chose the burgesses to send to the House of Commons.

St. Giles Church, Great Stretton

Serf's fields of Great Stretton and St. Giles

Chapter 8

The Hericke Trades

Standing on the deck of the Lyon's Whelp, Henry snapped out of his thoughts. He couldn't believe he could recall the stories of his ancient family in such detail. "Maybe because I'm alone at sea, separated from family and everything I've ever known", he thought to himself. Thomas asked him what he was thinking. Henry didn't answer, still amazed at his heritage or at least the heritage stories that he was always told. Then reality set in again.

With grief and anguish still fresh and with emotions beginning to flash rapidly through his mind, his thoughts went beyond Alice and Samuel and were now with his father. Thomas Heyricke died only 5 years earlier at the age of 48, so Henry had little time to properly grieve his loss. Henry had learned this weaving trade at the feet of his father as a young boy. His father was instrumental in procuring Edward Peabody to serve as his apprentice. Henry started reflecting on the family business and the stories of how it began so long before him. He particularly pondered how and why his family line decided on the cloth trades when other branches of the family were active in the metal trades.

There were many facets to the wool trades, including raising and sheering sheep, preparing and weaving the wool, selling the wool, making garments from the wool, selling woolen garments, etc. Henry and his father, Thomas, were known as weavers from Belgrave so it seems likely that they were most involved in the weaving side of the trade and most likely selling those products locally in Leicester or across England or even abroad. Like most trades at this time, the wool or cloth trades were starting to specialize, but it is not clear if or how Henry's family specialized in the trade. Since Sir William and his side of the metals family were doing business in London, across the continent and beyond, it is not unreasonable that Henry and his side of the family were doing the same.

Will Of Thomas Hericke, Of Belgrave, Weaver, 1624.
Dated 16 Oct. 1624. My dau. Anne, wife of Henrie Corpson.
My sons Henrie, Godfrey, & George. My wife Elizabeth. My
two grandchildren. My son Godfrey to be executor.
Witness: Rob: Hericke, &c.

Abstract of Thomas Hericke's Will

Like other families of the same class, the Herricks moved into commerce and various trades. Many in Leicester became ironmongers (blacksmiths, iron craftsmen, and jewelers). During this time, ironmongers meant that they supplied consumer goods made of metal, such as iron, brass, steel, and other metals. The Herricks, particularly Sir William, moved into precious metals and became jewelers. His business became so successful that he moved into lending money and operated much like a bank. The Herrick ironmongers practiced their trade from about 1534 to 1633.

Henry surely heard stories about his ironmonger family but perhaps even more about his great grandfather Nicholas. Nicholas Heyricke was the first in his family to start the cloth trade as a draper, which turned out to be very successful for generations. Nicholas's brother, John, was an ironmonger and may have started the metals trade in that branch of the family or at least continued with the family business. Why one branch of the family, starting with Nicholas, started the cloth trades while another branch of the family stayed with the metals trades is not clear. What was common, however, is that when a young man was apprenticed by his father or his father was instrumental in procuring an apprentice for his son, the young man stayed with the family business. If that did not happen, a young man may have branched out to another trade. That may have happened when Nicholas and John chose separate trades. John may have apprenticed with his father Thomas as an ironmonger while Nicholas branched out on his own.

The cloth trades, however, were not new to England at the time. In fact, the cloth trades go back to Anglo-Saxon times. England has long been known for its highly regarded sheep and wool business.

Chapter 8 — The Hericke Trades

Consequently, trades such as drapers, clothiers and glovers were very prosperous in Leicestershire and throughout England. So, it is not surprising that a member of a family, even a prosperous family, would split off into the cloth trades.

Henry pondered this split in the trades of the Heyricke family back nearly 100 years before he was born. The Heyrickes were successful in both lines of work. The ironmongers or metal tradesmen in the family began to transition primarily into silver and gold, thus becoming jewelers. Silversmiths and goldsmiths were the first bankers in those days. In the case of the Heyrickes, that line of work resulted in great wealth. The cloth traders were also core to the economy and Henry's side of the family was successfully in that trade. Because of his work in the cloth trades, Henry had money when coming to New England. He and his father were in the merchant class and did well. Henry became a weaver because his father, Thomas, arranged his apprenticeship with a weaver. Thomas was apprenticed by his father John, a tailor, and John was apprenticed by his father Nicholas, a draper. Apprenticeships keep many young men in the family business and it did just that for the Heyricke cloth business.

Chapter 9
Sir William and Beau Manor

The cloth business was good to the family for four generations. But as Henry pondered the business activities of the broader family, he reflected with pride and perhaps a bit of jealously about that wing of the family that stayed with the metals trade, continuing as ironmongers. It is very likely that whenever he thought of wealthy and noteworthy family members, it would be easy to think of his grandfather's first cousins, William and Robert Heyricke.

How many Englishman can claim that one of their family members was knighted by the King of England? Yet his grandfather's cousin, William, was now Sir William. Henry was 7 years old when King James I knighted William Heyricke in 1605. Henry must have remembered the fanfare of that day and may even have been present. As a 7 year old boy, he probably wondered why everyone was so excited, but to be recognized by the King was surely something. But for what? For doing what he and the family had always done? Making metal objects and jewelry and then selling them? But William was particularly successful in his trade, apprenticing as a goldsmith with his other brother, Nicholas, in London and then taking over his brother's goldsmith business in London's Cheapside after Nicolas's tragic death. The goldsmith business was lucrative in itself, but it also gave one a definitive edge on a whole other lucrative business. The goldsmith business gave one the exclusive power of coining money, which gave them the power to act as both banker and pawnbroker. He made money, loaned money, and became noteworthy as a banker as well as continuing as a goldsmith in the capital city. William Heyricke became one of the most eminent goldsmith in London. Queen Elizabeth herself was one of William's best customers and the relationship continued when James I took the throne after the queen's death. There can be no doubt that William took good care of his customers. As a money lender, he also had prominent customers who were well known throughout England.

The metals side of the family were actually bankers before there was a designation of banker. Sir William and his brothers Robert, the ironmonger from Leicester, and Nickolas, the goldsmith in London, were essentially bankers, or money lenders, which was primitive by modern standards, yet generated great wealth for them. In 1613, Robert writes to William, "I have spoke and sent to all that be likely in the market this day, and cannot find one to return until the 17th of this present". Then in 1616, Robert again writes to William, "I have such ado to return any money up, but they will have all before hand or else no bargain ; and I cannot tell certainly their soundness, which makes me quake when I do pay them, and yet I am desirous to return it with what speed I may".

There is no evidence that a reception was held in Sir William's honor at being knighted, but if there was it probably occurred at Beau Manor. None-the-less, there is a record of what William's brother Robert said about the occasion. Imagine the possibility of Henry overhearing laughter among a small group of adult relatives, who Henry remotely knew, discussing William's merit for such an honor, at which time Robert commented, "The truth of the matter is that William found a way to drill a hole through the King's Diamond". However, the King loved that diamond and wore it often, as William did his job well. William Heyricke's fine jewelry work is what turned cousin William into Sir William. When the king commissioned William to be his official court jeweler, William was on his way to knighthood.

CHAPTER 9 — SIR WILLIAM AND BEAU MANOR

Sir William Heyricke of Beau Manor,
King's jeweler, Exchequer and MP

Sir William's wealth and fame preceded knighthood, however. In 1595, three years before Henry was born, William purchased Beau Manor. During the times that Henry visited Beau Manor, they probably were care-free days playing around the vast wooded grounds upon which Beau Manor was situated. He may not have always been sure who he was playing with, since there were so many cousins, even distant cousins, about his same age. These rare family gatherings would have been festive, fun, and exuded a richness that he would not have known at home. Imagine Henry pondering the wealth and fame of Sir William and his childhood play at Beau Manor, then coming out of his day dream and noticing that he was standing on the deck of a ship looking out at a vast passionless sea. Again, the wind blew into the sails and the wood beams gently carved through the water. The ship sailed onward, further from home.

Henry would have thought about what his son Thomas may recall. Thomas, although born in England would probably never have memories of Leicester, memories of his extended family, or memories of Beau

Manor. Henry may have thought on this voyage that someday when Thomas is older, stories about Beau Manor should be told. Henry tried to recall the history of Beau Manor as told to him by his father, grandfather and other relatives.

When William Heyricke purchased Beau Manor in 1595, the house was run down and dilapidated. So, William immediately started repairing and altering the estate. The Beau Manor that William purchased was the original medieval home built in the 13th century. Beau Manor in Henry's time had a moat surrounding it with a drawbridge giving access to the house.

The interior of Beau Manor, after its renovation, was impressive. In the main parlor was a huge painting of William. But the painting was unusual and highly distinctive in that William was wearing an odd looking costume characteristic of the Ottoman Empire. The painting was painted on William's return from an "errand", as it was described, to Turkey requested by Queen Elizabeth. The errand was actually an important embassy visit in 1575 to the Ottoman Port, the Sultan of Turkey, which was commissioned by Queen Elizabeth. Before becoming Sir William, he was ambassador to Turkey. His success in negotiating with the Turks won him great favor with the Queen and was thus given an appointment in the Exchequer, which he held throughout the Queen's reign and into the reign of King James. As Exchequer, William was in charge of a government department responsible for the collection and management of taxes and revenues, and for making payments and auditing accounts on behalf of the monarch. In addition to this official role, William loaned money to the monarchs, took orders from them for gems and other luxurious jewelry. King James I continued the Court's respect for William and conferred upon him the title of Principal Jeweler to the Crown. Truly Sir William Heyricke was well connected in business and in politics throughout the reign of both Queen Elizabeth and King James. His wealth and fame also won him elections as a Member of Parliament from Leicester in 1600, 1605, and 1620.

Yet this house, with such elegance, owned by a family member with such notoriety, surely had a prominent history that Henry must have thought should not be lost. The earliest record of William's home at Beau Manor, or at least the land upon which it sits, goes back to the tax records recorded in the Doomsday Book of 1086. Beau Manor was, and still is, located in the Charnwood Forest not far from Leicester. According to Highways and Byways of Leicestershire, "It is quite the

Chapter 9 — Sir William and Beau Manor

most romantic district in Leicestershire and to the geologist, Charnwood presents features unsurpassed in the British Isles."

The Doomsday Book records that Hugh Lupas, Earl of Chester, owned the forested land at the time Doomsday was first written. Then in the early 13th century, the Despenser family acquired the land and held it for many generations. The Despensers used the property as a hunting estate with a lodge and deer park. Hugh Despenser was a close friend of Simon de Montfort, Earl of Leicester, who led a revolt against King Henry III. Both de Montfort and Hugh Despenser were killed in the Battle of Evesham in 1265. Hugh Despenser's son, also named Hugh, supported the King and so his land, which included the Beau Manor grounds, were restored to him. Hugh Despenser, and his son Hugh III, ultimately became a favorite of King Edward II and held great power in parliament. However, when King Edward II was murdered in 1327, both Despensers were hanged.

Then in 1327, Lord Henry Beaumont was granted the property by the new king, King Edward III. Henry Beaumont built the original Beau Manor in 1330, thus the new manor house was named Beau Manor after Lord Beaumont. Henry Beaumont's son John became the second Lord Beaumont, his son Henry became the third Lord Beaumont, and his son John became the fourth Lord Beaumont – all residing at Beau Manor. Due to military successes, John and his wife on two occasions were honored to receive King Richard II and his Queen at Beau Manor.

The next Beaumont at Beau Manor was Henry Beaumont, the fifth Lord Beaumont and his son John was the sixth Lord Beaumont. John Beaumont was living at Beau Manor during the War of the Roses, a war between the Lancastrian and Yorkist families. He held many senior level government positions and was named the first Viscount of England by King Henry VI, but in 1460 John Beaumont fought for King Henry and died at the Battle of Northampton. The seventh and last Lord Beaumont was William Beaumont. He was a loyal Lancastrian, so he fought the Yorkist's, and soon to be King Edward IV, at the Battle of Towton in 1461. Edward was successful in the battle, and consequently all Lord Beaumont's land including Beau Manor were forfeited to the new King.

Beau Manor became vacant for a short time. William Hastings of Leicestershire was a loyal Yorkist and supporter of King Edward IV, so in 1462 he became the next owner of Beau Manor. William Hastings was man of great wealth and also very involved with the King's foreign affairs. However, he became unwittingly involved with Thomas Grey in a plot to overthrow the King, and in 1483 was beheaded. Beau Manor then fell to Thomas Grey's son Leonard in 1524 and he owned it until 1540, when Beau Manor again was forfeited. His older brother, Henry Grey, then inherited Beau Manor. Henry Grey and his wife Francis, a niece of Henry VIII, had three daughters, the oldest being Jane. Lady Jane Grey grew up at Beau Manor and became an innocent and tragic figure.

Jane was manipulated by her family and skillfully married off to the son of John Dudley, Duke of Northampton. A plot was hatched to put Lady Jane Grey on the throne, but the plot failed and Lady Jane Grey, her husband, father and uncle all were beheaded in 1554. Lady Jane Grey was only 18 years old, and accounts indicate that she was an innocent, well-meaning and refined young woman. Her mother, Francis, retired to Beau Manor in grief. Later Francis remarried Adrian Stokes, and upon his death Beau Manor became the possession of his brother. Soon after that, the Earl of Essex owned Beau Manor for three years. The Earl was a favorite of Queen Elizabeth and became the Privy Councilor and Foreign Secretary to the Queen. However, he later incurred the Queen's displeasure, by plotting to take her throne, which was enough to lose his head on the block in 1601. Before his demise, the Earl of Essex sold Beau Manor in 1595 to Sir William Herrick for an annual rent of 70 pounds. Beau Manor remained in the Herrick family for 7 generations[32].

---

[32] There were three Beau Manors occupied by the Herricks. The first was purchased by Sir William in 1595, the second was built on the same site by William Herrick V in 1726, and the current Beau Manor was built on the same site by William Perry Herrick in 1846.

CHAPTER 9 —SIR WILLIAM AND BEAU MANOR

Top: Beau Manor purchased by Sir William Heyricke in 1595
Bottom: Beau Manor built by William Herrick V in 1726

Beau Manor built by William Perry Herrick
in 1846 and still stands today

After acquiring Beau Manor, William continued to rise in status in Leicestershire and in London, where he continued as a goldsmith. Shortly after he purchased Beau Manor, he and his brother Robert applied to the crown for a family Coat of Arms. Prior to this time the Heyricke family had always used the Bond coat of arms. Mary Bond was Robert and William's mother. Robert and William decided that the Heyricke family should have their own coat of arms, and so they went about the task of designing their own family crest. Then on May 8th, 1598, the year Henry was born, the family crest was confirmed by William Dethick, Garter, and William Camden, Clarenceux, and thus granted by Queen Elizabeth I.

In medieval England the family crest and coat of arms reflects family heraldry. English heraldry is the family insignia, represented in a family crest or coat of arms. Coats of arms in England were and still are regulated and granted to individuals by the English Kings of Arms of the

College of Arms. It was popular within the upper classes to have a distinctive family mark for competitions and tournaments. It found particular use with knights, for practice and in the thick of battle, where heraldry was worn on embroidered fabric covering their armor. Their houses or family signs became known as coats-of-arms. They were also worn on shields, where they were known as shields-of-arms. Most known symbols on a coat of arms were white or red roses used by the houses of York and Lancaster during the War of the Roses. Other common symbols for a family crest were eagles or lions. It is certainly curious, why Robert and William Heyricke chose a horned bull to symbolize the Herrick family. The bull is associated with strength and perhaps that is what Robert and William were trying to convey in the coat of arms. It is doubtful that they have thought of themselves as "bull headed"!

The original grant of the Heyricke coat of arms is shown below as it is displayed at Beau Manor. At the top of the grant are three shields charged with the following "coats":

1. Argent, a fess vair or gules. INSIGNAI PATRIS
2. Argent, on a chevron sable between three hurts as many estoils or, on a chief gules three cinquefoils or. INSIGNAI PATRIS
3. Gules, a fess between eight billets or; impaling, Argent, on a chevron sable three bulls' heads caboshed argent. PATER ET MATER MATRIS.

At the left of the grant is the family shield with a prominent horned bull's head at the top. Also, the confirmation proclamation as printed on the grant is shown.[33]

Original Grant of Arms Awarded to
Robert and William Heyricke by Queen Elizabeth in 1598
as it is currently displayed at Beau Manor

---

33 The grantees of this crest and coat of arms were Robert and William Heyricke (later Sir William Heyricke, Knight of Beau Manor). They are assigned to specific grantees and, therefore, can only be used by direct descendants of Robert and Sir William Heyricke. Changes and modifications to the original can only be made by descendants.

Chapter 9 — Sir William and Beau Manor

To all Nobles and Gentles' to whome theis presentes shall come Will'm Detheck al's Garter, Principall King of Armes and Will'm Camden al's Clarenceux King of Armes of the Southe, East and West p'tes of this Realme of England from the Ryuer of Trent southwarde, send theire due comendacons, & greeting. Knowe yee That whereas Richard Lea, late Clarenceux in his life tyme did by l'res Pattent vnder his hand & Seale of Office giue & graunt vnto Robert & Will'm Herick, the sonnes of John Herick, the sonne of Herick al's Erick of Haughton in the County of Lecester gent., A certeyn Creast, or Badge, viz.: on a wreath of their colours a Bull head argent, yssuing forth of a lawrell Garland, the Mussell, eares, and hornes tipped sable: to be annexed, and borne with their auncient Coat of Armes, which is Siluer, a ffeese verrey or and gules. The which Patten, for that vpon the dissolving of the saide Clarenceux Lea's Office where it did remayne to be recorded, amongst dyuers other things is nowe lost, and by no meanes, search or inquiry to be founde; So that vpon the instant sute & request to vs made by the saide Rob't and Will'm Herick who haue produced theire Signett and stamps before vs, as also vpon the credible report, and testimony of Will'm Segar al's Norry King of Armes of the North, whoe being then Somersett Herauld, both wrytt the saide Pattent and passed the same for them with the saide Clarenceux. Wee the saide Garter, & Clarenceux Kinges of Armes, doe by theis present confirme and allowe vnto the saide Rob't and Will'm Herick, and their posteritye for euer, the aforesaide Creast, or Cognisans, in like manner, and forme, as yet was formerly gyuen by the daise Clarenceux Lea and as it is here on the margent sett forth, and with their Armes depicted. And the Same to vse, beare, and shewe for the in Signett Shielde, Coat Armor or otherwise, at their free liberte, and pleasure, w'out the lett or molestacon of any person or persons whatsoeuer. In witness whereof wee the saide William Detheck al's Garter, and Will'm Camden al's Clarenceux Kinge of Armes hauw herevnto put or handes and seales of Office, Geven in the Office of Armes the viijth day of Maij. In the fortith yeare of the raigne of or Soveraigne Ladye Elizabeth by the grace of God Queen of England, ffrance and Ireland defendor of the faith &c 1598.

WILL'M DETHICK, GARTER	GUILIELMUS CAMDEN,
Principall King of Arms.	CLARENCEUX, REX ARMOR'.

Herrick Coat of Arms showing the complete proclamation

Chapter 10

Robert and the Grey Friars

Sir William, although wealthy, civic minded, and connected to royalty, had a brother Robert who Henry admired as much as William. In addition to being an Alderman along with his brother, Robert was elected Mayor of Leicester three times - 1584, 1593 and 1605. He was also elected as a Member of Parliament from Leicester in 1589, during the reign of Queen Elizabeth I. Robert also was involved the family business of metals, but because of his wealth he too was involved in banking, specifically lending and trading. Robert's trade business involved shipping all across the Mediterranean Sea and into Indonesia to purchase gems and other valuable materials for his business.

As Henry contemplated Robert's and William's local civic contributions, he would have thought of the Guildhall as the center of government in Leicester and the focus of Herrick civic contributions. The Guildhall was where all the city business was transacted, so as Alderman and Mayor, Robert spent much of his time at the hall. Henry's grandfather, John, and his great grandfather, Nicholas, were also city officials in the past and attended many meetings there. In addition, his grandfather and his father-in-law also served as mayor for a short period of time. Nicholas was mayor from 1552-1553. The Guildhall was old, built in the 13th century, and probably had particular memories for Henry, since it was only a block from the city center where he likely joined his father at the Wednesday market when he was very young. Undoubtedly, Henry would have recalled that his father, or other family member, would take him inside the Guildhall to see the Mayor's Parlor, where the Heyrickes met to transact city business. The Mayor was chosen by the Aldermen, who in turn were chosen by the Council. The Council was elected by only the wealthy men in the town or borough. Given such a structure, only a small number of wealthy families controlled local government.

Probably the most memorable thing about the Guildhall would be the Mayor's Chair, a huge dark leather chair designated only for the mayor. It was here that Robert and other Heyrickes presided over city business for many years[34]. Off from the Mayor's Parlor was the Great Hall, which was a large meeting room used for community gatherings. Entertainment was often held in the Great Hall, mostly musical and theatrical productions. It was a well-known fact that a famous playwright from London had traveled north to Leicester to put on a play in the Great Hall. His name was William Shakespeare.

Guildhall Leicester, built in 13th century

---

34 The mayor's chair used by Robert Heyricke and other Leicester majors of the time still exists in the Mayor's Parlor at the Guildhall

CHAPTER 10 — ROBERT AND THE GREY FRIARS

Mayor's Chair, Guildhall

Great Hall, Guildhall

The time Henry spent thinking about William and Robert were surely pleasant thoughts. Thoughts of Sir William probably were mostly directed to pleasant boyhood memories of Beau Manor and William's honor of knighthood. Thoughts of Robert would more likely be focused on his civic duties, business success, and his philanthropy.

Regarding Robert, the first thing that likely came to mind would be the Free Grammar School where Henry likely went to school. When the Free Grammar School was built in 1573, Robert donated 13 shillings and 4 pence for its construction. In addition to the Free Grammar School, his Will states, "I give more forth of the Grey Fryers yearly forever to be paid unto the School Master that teaches the 'petties', 13 shillings and 4 pence." Robert Heyricke's extensive Will, written a year before he died in 1618, documented many of his benevolences and charities. His Will indicated that he provided funds for the purchase and repair of Trinity Hospital in Leicester and for the repair of St. Martin's Church.[35]

The Names of the Several Benefactors to the School	
Queen Elizabeth	10-0-0
Henry Earl of Huntingdon	20-0-0
Sir William Wigston	10-0-0
Sir Ralph Rawlett	3-6-8
Mr. William Norrice	3-6-8
Mr. James Ellis Snr.	1-6-8
Mr. James Ellis Jnr.	3-0-0
Mr. John Stanley	3-15-0
Mr. Thomas Gilbert	5-0-0
Mrs. Dorothy Baker	1-0-0
Mr. Robert Heyrick	13-4
Mr. Tobias Heyrick	6-8
Mr. Thomas Clarke	1-0-0
Mrs. Margaret Hobby	10-0

Benefactors to the Free Grammar School, 1573

---

35 St. Martin's Church is now Leicester Cathedral.

CHAPTER 10 — ROBERT AND THE GREY FRIARS

In addition, he provided for "twenty six poor persons in the new hospital (Trinity), 3 shillings and four pence each". He also contributed funds for repairs to the churches of St. Mary's, St. Margaret's, St. Nicholas, and All Saints. His Will also provided funds for the Spital hospital in Leicester with 3 shillings and 4 pence apiece for the 26 inmates.

Robert was particularly generous to poor families and widowed women. His Will stated that he bequeathed "one shilling per year to poor households of Leicester forever." He also stated that 40 shillings will be paid to "poor widows in Leicester each year forever." But the charity that he started before his Will was written, and later documented formally in his Will, was the charity for which he was most known. That is the Herrick Bread Charity. This charity insured the distribution of bread to poor households throughout Leicester each year. Specifically, his Will stated, "To be paid yearly forever, 5 pounds into the Mayor's hands for the purpose of purchasing loaves of bread, 2 penny loaf at least, to be distributed to every householder of 'old body' in all the parishes of the town."[36]

Robert was the proud owner of a manor house, which he built on top of the Grey Friars monastery after the dissolution of the Catholic monasteries in England in 1538. The story of Robert's house, his famous gardens, and the Grey Friars is a story that Henry must have related to his family as it is a story that should be remembered and retold to all Herricks.

When the official state religion changed under King Henry VIII from Catholicism to Protestantism, all the monasteries in England were dissolved. Under King Henry VIII the official, and therefore legal, church was the Church of England, which no longer took its authority from the Pope in Rome. Prior to Henry VIII, the Catholic Church was a paramount influence in English politics and English life, and monasteries of a variety of Catholic orders were common all over England. The small village of Leicester had three monasteries prior to the dissolution. There were the Black Friars, a Dominican Order; the Augustinian Friary; and the Grey Friars, a Franciscan order. The Grey Friary was demolished immediately in 1538 and all the monasteries in England were gone by

---

36 This bequest through the Herrick Bread Charity, administered through the Major and church wardens, continued at least 250 years after Robert's death.

1543. The land upon which the monasteries stood were sold off in various sized parcels.

Robert Heyricke was interested in building a manor house, and he wanted it to be located in the village center, close to the Guildhall and St. Martins Church, unlike his brother William who opted for Beau Manor about 10 miles outside Leicester in Loughborough. Since the Grey Friar monastery had been demolished and it stood nearly adjacent to St. Martins and Guildhall, Robert purchased enough of the land where the Grey Friary once stood to build his manor house and extensive gardens. Robert purchased the land in 1558 not long after the dissolution of the monastery from Sir Robert Catlyn, Chief Justice to Queen Elizabeth I.

Robert and most of the townsfolk knew that King Richard III was buried in the Grey Friar monastery after he was killed in the Battle of Bosworth in 1485. But not long after the monastery was demolished, memories faded, stories spread, and people assumed that the King Richard's body was removed and thrown into the River Soar. However, when Robert built his manor house, he knew the body of Richard III was probably still interred somewhere in the monastery grounds, perhaps even in his garden! These gardens were visited in 1611 by one of Robert's close friends from London, Christopher Wren[37]. Christopher Wren was a well-known architect. Henry remembered as a 13 year old boy about the news around town that his cousin Robert was receiving this London celebrity. Unbeknownst to Henry at the time, Robert had in fact erected a stone pillar in his garden at a spot he felt might be the location of King Richard's body. Robert showed this stone pillar to Mr. Wren who recorded the inscription on the pillar in his journal. It read, "Here lies the body of Richard III, sometime King of England"[38]

---

37 This refers to Christopher Wren Sr. He was the father of Christopher Wren the famous architect who designed the new St. Paul's Cathedral after the original was destroyed in the great London fire in 1666.
38 Robert's manor house stayed in the Herrick family for three generations.

CHAPTER 10 — ROBERT AND THE GREY FRIARS

Robert Heyricke, Alderman and Mayor of Leicester and MP

Robert Heyricke's manor house, center left.
Built over the demolished Grey Friars Monastery.
The house was demolished in 1887.

When Robert Heyricke died in 1618, his body was interred at St. Martins Church. His body and that of his father John and his brother Sir William were interred in St. Katherine's Chapel[39] at St. Martin's church. A slate tablet in the chapel commemorates Robert Heyricke's life. It states, "Here lies the body of Robert Herricke, ironmonger and alderman of Leicester, who had been thrice Mayor thereof. At his death he gave away 16 pounds 10 shillings a year to good use".

As the Lyon's Whelp continued to sail steadily and confidently east to New England, the events Henry enjoyed and learned to take for granted surely became more important and fascinating to him. The personal memories of Beau Manor, the visits to Guildhall, and the mystery of an English King buried beneath his cousin's house somehow took on new meaning. He needed a better life for himself and for his remaining son, Thomas. He thought that the only way to gain that was to separate himself forever from the life he knew in Leicester.

Robert had died 15 years before Henry left for America, but the memories and stories surrounding his manor house, the Grey Friars, and King Richard may have been fresh in Henry's mind. One can only imagine that as the Lyon's Whelp pushed on across the sea in one direction, Henry's memories of his family legacy pushed in the opposite direction.

---

39 St. Katherine's Chapel is now known as Herrick Chapel, given all the benevolences given to the church by the Herrick family. Sir William, Robert and their father John are buried under the floor of the chapel.

Chapter 11
King Richard III, Bosworth

Henry was born 113 years after the Battle of Bosworth, but the battle still held strong implications for England and significant meaning for Leicester. The battle was legendary around Leicester and Henry knew all about it growing up.

The White Boar Inn was just a short block off High Street and Henry inevitably would see it nearly every day as a youth on his way to school or to the Wednesday market. It was nothing special. Just a typical English Inn. Henry and everyone in Leicester would hear conversations that the name of the inn referred to the White Rose, the emblem of the Yorkist branch of the Plantagenets. Old timers in town would speak of the time it was called the Blue Boar Inn. As Henry got older, he learned that the name was changed shortly after the Battle of Bosworth in 1485 because the King of England, Richard III, stayed there the night before the battle. The War of the Roses, was signified by the White Rose of the Yorkist's and the Red Rose of the Lancasters. As a young man, Henry finally realized this old inn was no ordinary tavern. King Richard III actually spent his last night before the battle in this small inn in Leicester.

The War of the Roses was still raging after decades of conflict between the House of York and the House of Lancaster. The King of England, Richard III, was a Yorkist from the Plantagenet family, which had ruled England for centuries. The Battle of Bosworth was a culmination of the war to determine who would rule England, Richard III continuing in the Plantagenet tradition or his rival, Henry Tudor. Tudor claimed rights to the throne, despite the fact that his family hailed from Wales. The armies of Richard III and Henry Tudor met at Bosworth Field about 14 miles from the West Gate of Leicester.

Richard was confident of victory over Henry Tudor, leader of the Lancastrians, because Richard had amassed a large army and had supporters who amassed large armies to defend the monarch. However, Henry Tudor had also amassed a huge army while in exile in France, sailed to Wales picking up more supporters as he went, and invaded England from the west. Richard, on the other hand, was beginning to lose supporters that he had counted on, even up to and during the day of the battle. The day before the battle while in Leicester, Richard received news that one of his loyal supporters, the Welshman Rhys ap Thomas, had defected to Tudor as he marched through Wales. On August 21, Richard led his army out of Leicester to engage Tudor. He left to join his army through Leicester's West Gate and onto his demise. The Battle of Bosworth may have been King Richard's undoing, but it enlarged the history and notoriety of Leicester and Herrick family legacy - not to mention Shakespearian literature.[40]

The morning of August 22, 1485, after a restless night at his camp at Market Bosworth, Richard III donned his battle armor, put his crown on his head, and mounted his horse. Looking out over the field, he saw thousands of loyal soldiers and his confidence grew, despite news of more defections. But he knew that his most loyal supporters with huge armies themselves were to join his armies in battle at Bosworth. Brothers, Sir William and Thomas Stanley (Lord Stanley) would surely greet him. They did not. Not only that, but John Savage, Brian Sandor and Simon Digby would join the Stanleys in joining Henry Tudor against their former friend, Richard III. Once hearing of these defections, Richard quickly ordered the execution of Thomas Stanley's son, George, by beheading.

The battle raged on for hours before it became clear to Richard's forces that the battle was lost. Richard's commanders offered him a fast horse to make his escape, but Richard refused by replying, "God forbid I yield one step. This day I will die as a king or win".

Richard, still ever confident, entered the fray himself and charged his arch rival, but was knocked off his horse by Tudor loyalists. Richard was attacked savagely with swords and knives until killed by a halberd piercing the back of his head. At that moment the King of England, the last King to die in battle, was dead. The War of the Roses finally ended. The Plantagenet dynasty ended and Henry Tudor became King Henry VII. The Tudor dynasty began.

---

40 William Shakespeare first performed his famous play, Richard III, in 1591- only 7 years before Henry was born.

CHAPTER 11 — KING RICHARD III, BOSWORTH

After the battle, Richard III was stripped of his armor and his clothes, his body draped over his horse while enemy combatant's continued inflecting knife wounds into his corpse, and his crown placed on Henry Tudor's head by non-other than Sir William Stanley, Richard III's one time loyalist, with the words, "Sir, here I make you King of England".

Richard III's body was taken back to Leicester, through the same West Gate that he had left. His body was put on public display in the Church of the Annunciation next to Leicester Castle. Henry Tudor and the Lancastrian army wanted the townsfolk of Leicester to see for themselves that the King of England was dead. After three days the body began to decompose, so it was taken down and hurriedly buried in a plain unmarked grave in front on the choir in the Grey Friars monastery. After the dissolution and demolition of the monastery, 53 years later, the whereabouts of King Richard's body began to get lost and confused. Given the rumors and confusion about the location of King Richard's remains, Henry Herrick began to think, "would it really be possible that King Richard III could be buried under my cousin Robert's manor house or his gardens". Indeed, it was possible[41].

---

[41] In 2012, the remains of King Richard III were discovered under a car park over what was once the choir of the Grey Frair's monastery and later the gardens of Robert Herrick. Richard III's head was in a cocked position against the trench indicating a hurried burial. Today a museum to King Richard covers the tomb of King Richard and Robert's garden. King Richard III was reinterred in the Leicester Cathedral in March, 2015, adjacent to the Herrick Chapel. In-depth information about the discovery and scientific investigation into archaeology of the Grey Friars 2012 and 2013 excavations can be found at the University of Leicester website www.le.ac.uk/richardiii

Blue Boar Inn (formally White Boar Inn), High Street, Leicester

Route of King Richard III in Leicester, Battle of Bosworth 1483. White line shows entrance through North Gate and exit from Blue Boar Inn to Bosworth. Black line shows return of his body to Church of the Annunciation for public display and then to Grey Friars.

Chapter 11 — King Richard III, Bosworth

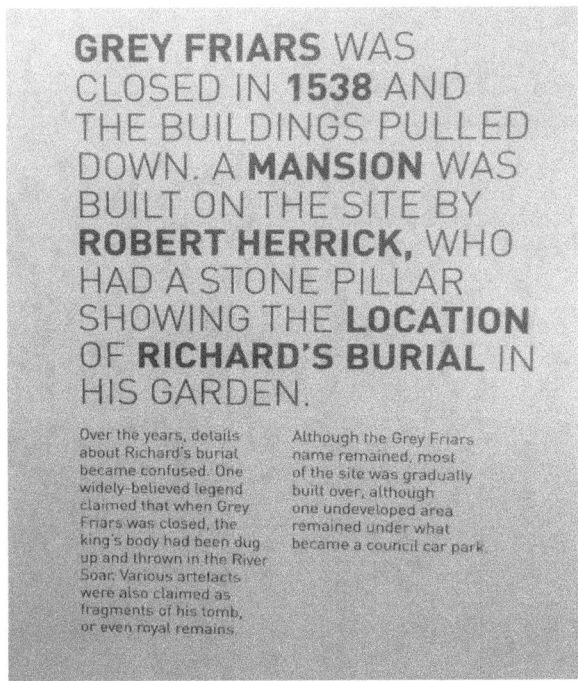

GREY FRIARS WAS CLOSED IN **1538** AND THE BUILDINGS PULLED DOWN. A **MANSION** WAS BUILT ON THE SITE BY **ROBERT HERRICK,** WHO HAD A STONE PILLAR SHOWING THE **LOCATION** OF **RICHARD'S BURIAL** IN HIS GARDEN.

Over the years, details about Richard's burial became confused. One widely-believed legend claimed that when Grey Friars was closed, the king's body had been dug up and thrown in the River Soar. Various artefacts were also claimed as fragments of his tomb, or even royal remains.

Although the Grey Friars name remained, most of the site was gradually built over, although one undeveloped area remained under what became a council car park.

From Richard III Museum, Leicester

Uncovering the tiles from Robert Herricks's garden during the exccavations for the remains of King Richard III. Richard III Museum, Leicester

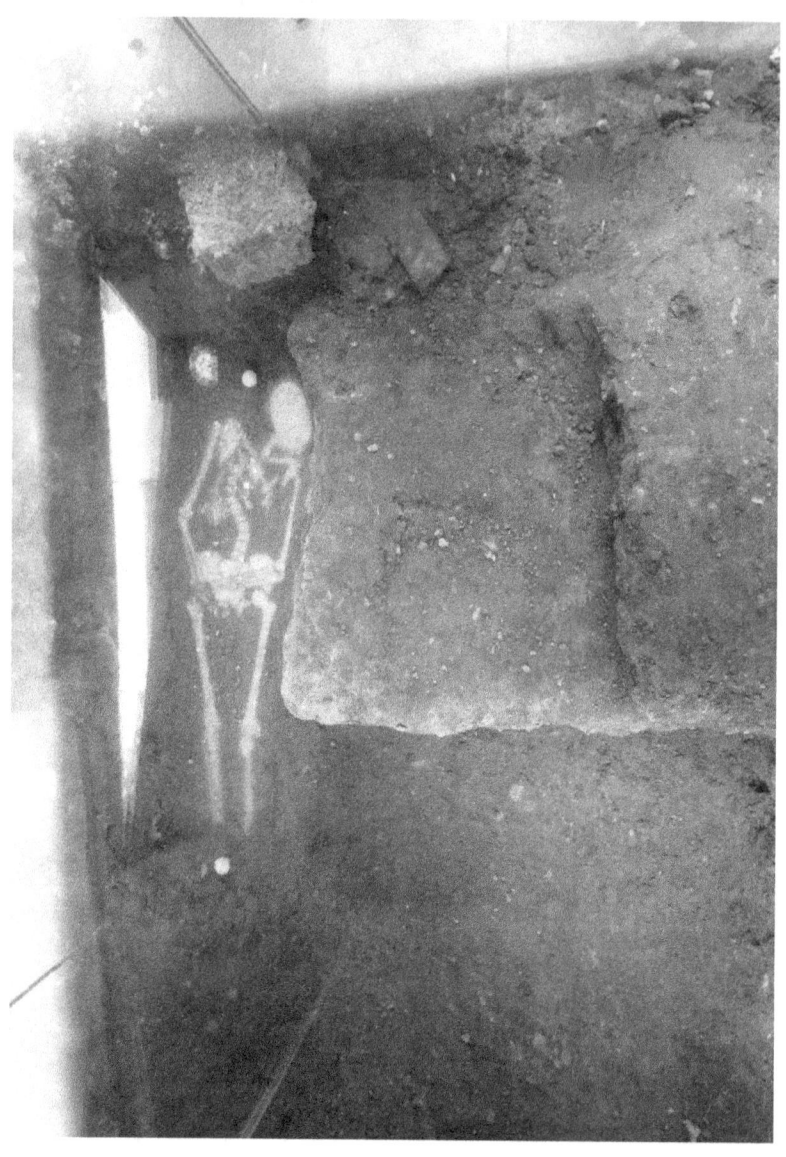

Reconstruction of King Richard III's remains below the gardens of Robert Herrick's manor house. Richard III Museum, Leicester

Chapter 12
Robert Herrick the Poet

It is easy to imagine how Henry growing up must have felt about the success and fame of the Herrick family. Although his side of the family, the cloth traders, were prosperous, it was the metals side of the family that seem to get the most fame and fortune. It was the ironmongers and the jewelers who seem to make the family name. Even though the split in the trades happened nearly 100 years before he was born with his great grandfather Nicholas, the significance of that split was still felt. Not only did Sir William and Robert gain incredible fame, wealth and notoriety, but their brother Nicholas, also an ironmonger who specialized in gold and precious stones, gained notoriety through his son, Robert.

This Robert Herrick was no ironmonger, however. He was a preacher who wrote poetry on the side. Robert Herrick was born in 1591 in London's prestigious Goldsmith's Row. His father, Nicholas was the son of John Eyricke and brother of Robert and Sir William. Nicholas moved from Leicester to London to continue to grow his flourishing goldsmith business. The youngest of seven children, Robert was only one year old when his father died from a freak fall out of their home window. It is entirely possible that Henry got to know Robert since they were about the same age. Robert was 7 years older than Henry. Plus, Robert would return to Leicester for long stays with his uncle Robert at his Grey Friars manor home or with his other uncle Sir William at Beau Manor. At the age of 16, Robert began a ten year apprenticeship with his uncle Sir William in London to learn the goldsmith trade. His intent was to follow in his father's footsteps. But he gradually grew disinterested in the trade, due primarily to his love of literature, which grew as he strolled through the bookstalls around St. Paul's churchyard.

In 1610, Robert wrote is first poem, dedicated to his brother Thomas upon his decision to leave London to farm in Leicestershire. This event plus his own talent for writing caused Robert to leave the apprenticeship with Sir William with 4 years left on his contract in order to go to Cambridge to study law. While at Cambridge, Robert became rowdy, enjoyed good drinks at London taverns, and ran up huge debts. He had to ask for loans from Sir William and those loans were always granted. Soon he realized that he needed a quieter environment, so he transferred to Trinity Hall where he received his Bachelor of Arts and Master of Arts degrees. Three years later in 1623, Robert was ordained a priest. Returning to London, however, he restarted his drinking at various London pubs and, in doing so, became a close friend and admirer of another poet by the name of Ben Jonson[42], to whom he wrote a poem about their friendship.

In 1627 Robert became a young clergyman acting as Army Chaplain to the regiments of the Duke of Buckingham. As Army Chaplain, Robert served on a military expedition to the Isle of Rhe, where two-thirds of the soldiers were killed due to foolish incompetence of the Duke[43]. Henry had not heard much from Robert after this debacle since it happened only two years before he left for Salem. It may have occurred to Henry standing on the deck of the Lyon's Whelp that he and his distant cousin Robert had much in common. Robert tragically lost his father when very young and sought replacements all his life, and witnessed a senseless loss of life as Chaplain during the expedition to the Isle of Rhe. Henry lost his wife and child in an untimely death early in his young marriage, and felt that his business and his beliefs were taken from him by the very institution that should have sustained them. It is likely that Henry wondered what had happened to his distant cousin over the past couple of years and what would become of him. He would never know[44]. As it turned out, Robert retreated to verse. Henry retreated from England.

---

42 Benjamin "Ben" Jonson was a famous English playwright, poet, actor, and literary critic, whose artistry exerted a lasting impact upon English poetry and stage comedy.
43 Interestingly, Robert was on the Lyon's Whelp during the expedition to Isle of Rhe, the same ship that Henry was on two years later in route to Salem, Massachusetts.
44 In 1630, Robert Herrick was installed as vicar of a parish called Dean Prior, which was in far off Devonshire. Robert remained the Vicar at Dean Prior for 17 years until the Cromwellian Government ejected him from Devon for his strong royalist leanings.

CHAPTER 12 — ROBERT HERRICK THE POET

Returning to London, he continued to write and in 1648 his collection of 1,402 poems were published until the title, "Hesperides, or The Works both Humane and Devine". Robert eventually returned to Devon where he died in 1674 and was buried in Dean Prior. Robert never married but was acquainted with many women, the most frequent was Julia to whom he wrote about in many poems. His poetry is often associated with classic romanticism but also dealt heavily with death and time. His most famous poem captures his sense of 'seize the day', for our time on earth is short.

Gather ye rosebuds, while ye may. Old time is still a-flying:
And this same flower that smiles today, Tomorrow will be dying.

Robert Herrick, the Poet

Tree I: Ancient Generations
850-1275 AD

(**Bold** indicate direct line to Henry Herrick of Salem)

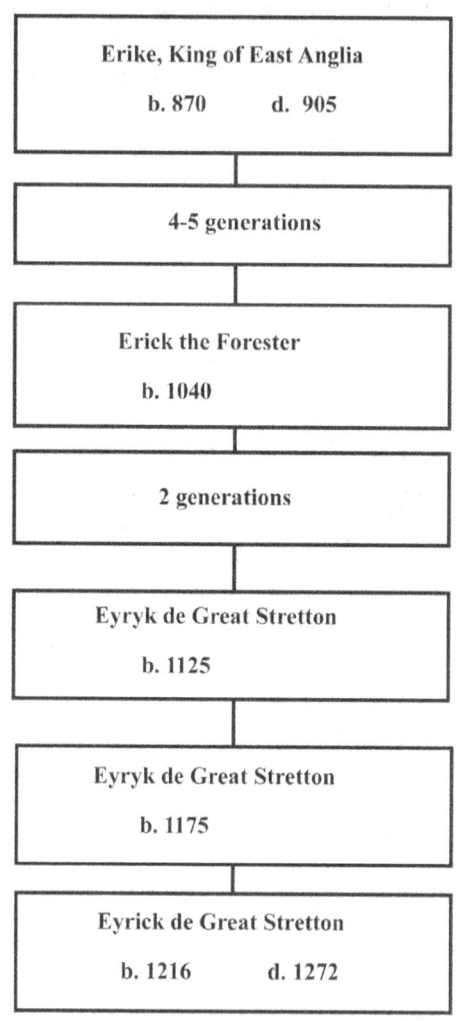

Chapter 12 — Robert Herrick the Poet

Tree II: Stretton and Houghton Generations 1275-1500

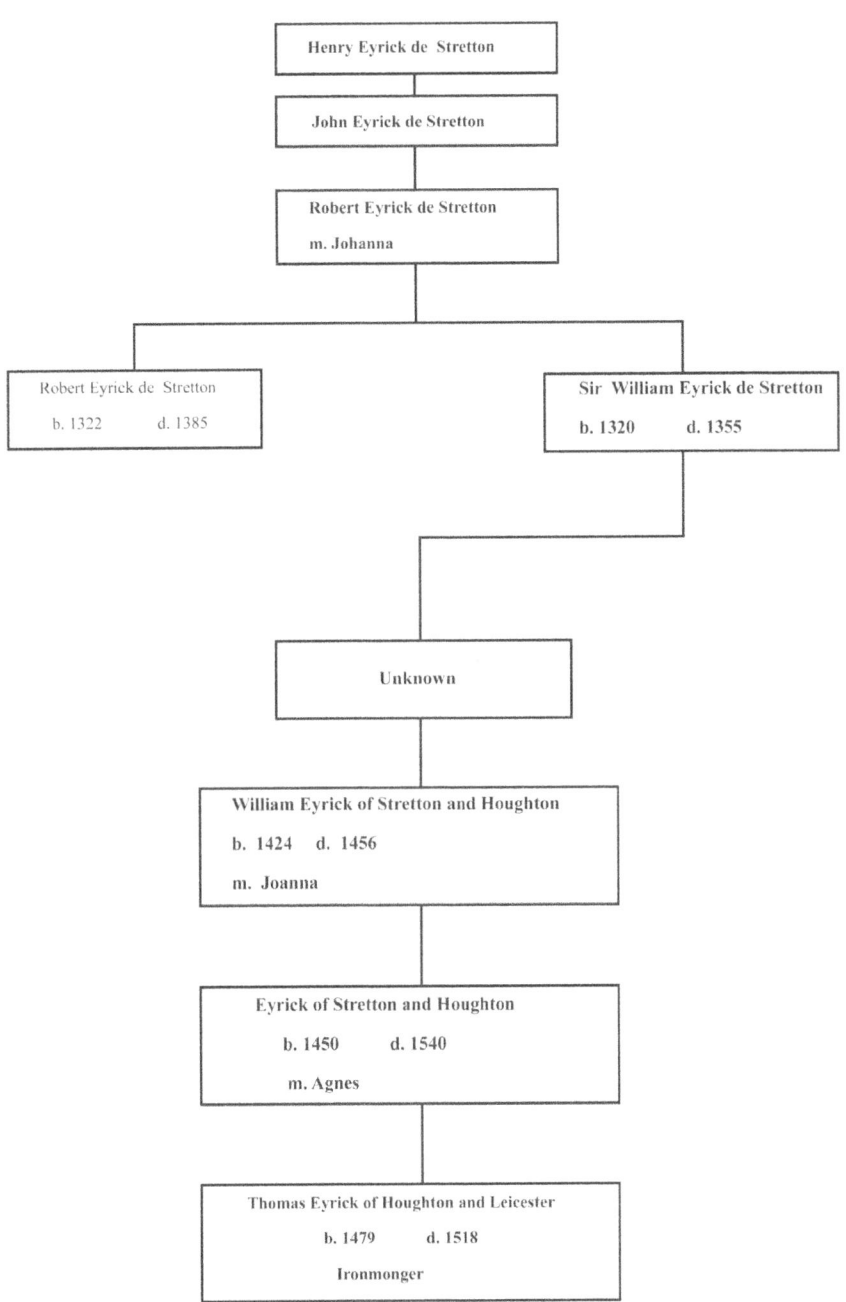

Michael J. Herrick

Tree III: Leicester Cloth and Metals Trades in Leicester 1500-1650

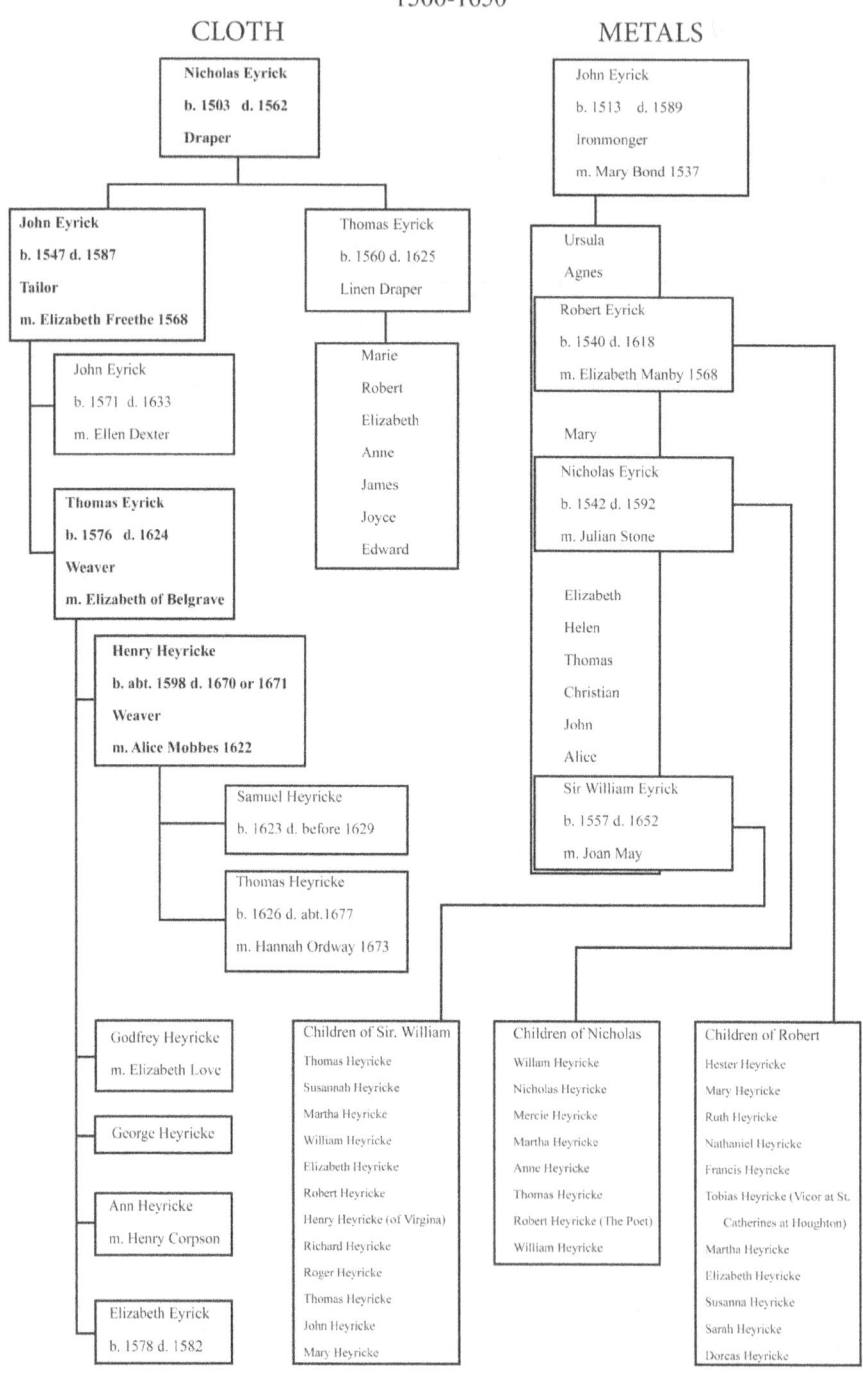

CHAPTER 12 —ROBERT HERRICK THE POET

It was a long voyage, with not much else to do but contemplate. Daydreams, recollections of family stories, perhaps myths. Was he like his ancient ancestor the Danish King Ericke? Invading and settling a new land? Should this be the Herrick legacy?

The crossing took about three months - too much time to simply look out at the expansive sea, inhale the salty air, listen to the creaking ship bounce through the ever present waves. It must have seemed to Henry that most of the other passengers were content to do just that. Was he the only one who was thinking? Feeling at least some remorse for leaving? Thinking about the family he will never see again? One can only imagine that he had these questions, but ultimately he got a hold of himself and convinced himself that he had done the right thing for himself and for Thomas.[45] But what was to become of Thomas, now only three years old? Henry must have asked himself, "How will I raise him by myself"? "Will I find another wife, start another family, continue my trade?" "Am I moving to a complete wilderness?" "What is my future? What is my dream?"

---

45 Recent research from Richard and James Herrick in England have raised questions about Thomas. Their research indicates that Thomas stayed in Leicester, apprenticed as a tailor or ironmonger in 1647, married Isobel Hoyes in 1646, and died in 1675. It is known, however, that Henry had a son Thomas in Salem, but no birth records can be found in the US. More research is continuing to resolve this.

Part II:
Henry's Dream: An American Legacy

Cast of Characters:

Henry Herrick - Came to New England in 1629 with son Thomas as part of the Massachusetts Bay Colony. Was a puritan and was excommunicated by Church of England. Follower of Francis Higginson, a Vicar at St. Nicholas in Leicester, who was also a "non-conformist". Was a freeman weaver in Belgrave, England. Remarried and started a new family in Salem. Founder of the First Church of Salem. Became a prosperous farmer. His farm site in Salem is now the site of Beverly High School located on Herrick Street.

Joseph Herrick - Was governor of one of the West Indies (probably Barbados or Neves). Traveled back to England on business in 1674. Constable of Salem Village during Witchcraft Trials in 1692. Later apologized for his actions and lead the action to end the witch trials. Founder of Second Congregational Church of Beverly. Grave and headstone remains at North Beverly Ancient Cemetery.

Nathaniel Herrick – Militiaman during the Revolutionary War battles of Lexington and Concord and Battle of Bunker Hill. Later was at Valley Forge as part of the Continental Army. After the war, moved his family to Granby, Vermont.

John P. Herrick – Moved west, first with his family from Vermont to Nunda, New York; then as an adult to Carmel Township, Michigan near Vermontville. Homesteaded forested land shortly after the removal of the Indians.

Chapter 13
Salem 1629: Starting Over

The Lyon's Whelp, along with the 5 other ships in the Higginson/Skelton fleet sailing to the Massachusetts's Bay Colony, arrived at Naumkaeg on June 19, 1929. Shortly after their arrival, the name of the settlement was changed from Naumkaeg to Salem in reference to a hoped for peaceful adjustment. Naumkaeg was the Indian name for the area at the time. Less than a month after arriving, Salem was the name given to this new settlement by Henry's friend and confidant, Francis Higginson, who derived the name from the Hebrew word "Shalom", meaning "peace". This was in remembrance of a peace settled at a meeting between themselves and their neighbors, the Pilgrims at Plymouth Colony, after expecting a possible confrontation. Or the "peace" could be the avoidance of a confrontation between Roger Conant and the Old Planters with the Naumkaeg settlers. Conant had been in charge since 1623, then John Endicott arrived in 1628 with a letter saying that he was governor, then John Winthrop arrived in 1630 with a letter saying that he was governor. This certainly could cause conflict.

Upon arriving at Naumkaeg, Francis Higginson wrote this reflection in his diary:

Of the Present Condition of the Plantation, and What It Is.

When we came first to *Nehumkek*, we found about halfe a score Houses, and a faire House newly built for the Gouernor, we found also aboundance of Corne planted by them, very good and well liking. And we brought with vs about two hundred Passengers and Planters more, which by common consent of the old Planters were all combined together into one Body Politicke, vnder the same Gouernor.

There are in all of vs both old and new Planters about three hundred, wherof two hundred of them are setled at *Nehumkek*, now called *Salem*: And the rest haue planted themselues at *Masathulets* Bay, beginning to build a Towne there which wee doe call *Cherton*, or Charles Towne.[2]

We that are setled at *Salem* make what haste we can to build Houses, so that within a short time we shall haue a faire Towne.

We have great Ordnance, wherewith wee doubt not, but wee shall fortifie our selues in a short time to keepe out a potent Aduersary. But that which is our greatest comfort, and meanes of defence aboue all other, is, that we haue here the true Religion and holy Ordinances of Almightie God taught amongst vs: Thankes be to God, wee haue here plenty of Preaching, and diligent Catechizing, with strickt and carefull exercise, and good and commendable order to bring our People into a Christian conuersation with whom wee haue to doe withall. And thus wee doubt not but God will be with vs, and *if God be with us, who can be against us?*

Francis Higginson was a very influential person on this new settlement. Not only was he Henry's friend and confidant, but he was recognized as a primary religious leader in the colony. Clearly, our Herrick legacy in America could not have happened without the influence of Francis Higginson on Henry Herrick back in their days in Leicester.

Upon their arrival in Salem, Francis Higginson was quickly recognized for his ministry and was given the position of Teaching Minister at the First Church of Salem, founded in August, 1629. Four clergymen in England were considered for leadership roles in the new church in Salem: Francis Higginson, Samuel Skelton, Francis Bright, and Ralph Smith. Rev. Bright was eliminated from consideration because he was not in favor of some of the congregational practices. Rev. Smith was eliminated and subsequently left Salem because he felt that the church was not Separatist enough. Both Higginson and Skelton were chosen as

CHAPTER 13 —SALEM 1629: STARTING OVER

ministers for the First Church of Salem. His friend and fellow minister, Samuel Skelton, was chosen as Pastor. The choice of Pastor and Teaching Minister was done by the church Incorporators. Each Incorporator wrote his choice on a slip of paper in the first recorded instance of the use of a written ballot in America. Also, on his date, the first Congregational Society in America was organized. Higginson's first duty as Teaching Minister was to write a confession of faith and a covenant, which formed the basis for the Puritan faith in Salem. As teacher, he was considered the authority of Puritan doctrine.

The confession of faith and covenant as written and presented by Francis Higginson on August 6th, 1629 is below:

6th of 6th Mo^{n}th 1629.
This Covenant was
publickly Signed
and Declared

Gather my Saints together vnto me that haue made a Covenant with me by facrifyce. Psa. 50: 5:

Wee whofe names are here vnder written, members of the prefent Church of Christ in Salem, haveing found by fad experience how dangerous it is to fitt loofe to the Covenant wee make with our God; and how apt wee are to wander into by pathes, even to the loofeing of our first aimes in entring into Church fellowship: Doe therefore folemnly in the prefence of the Eternall God, both for our own comforts, and thofe which shall or maye be joyned vnto vs, renewe that Church Covenant we find this Church bound vnto at theire first begining, vizt: That we Covenant with the Lord and one with an other; and doe bynd our felues in the prefence of God, to walke together in all his waies, according as he is pleafed to reveale himfelf vnto vs in his Bleffed word of truth. And doe more explicitely in the name and feare of God, profeff and proteft to walke as followeth through the power and Grace of our Lord Jefus.

1. first wee avowe the Lord to be our God, and our felues his people in the truth and fimplicitie of our fpirits.

2. Wee giue our felues to the Lord Jefus Chrift, and the word of his grace, fore the teaching, ruleing and fanctifyeing of vs in matters of worship, and Converfation refolveing to cleaue to him alone for life and glorie; and oppofe all contrarie wayes, cannons and constitutions of men in his worship.

3. Wee promife to walke with our brethren and sisters in this Congregation with all watchfullnes & tendernes, avoyding all jeloufies, fufpitions, backbyteings, cenfurings provoakings, secrete riseings of spirite against them; but in all offences to follow the rule of the Lord Jefus, and to beare and forbeare, giue and forgiue as he hath taught vs.

4. In publick or in private, we will willingly doe nothing to the ofence of the Church but will be willing to take advise for our felues and ours as ocafion shalbe prefented.

5. Wee will not in the Congregation be forward eyther to shew oure owne gifts or parts in fpeaking or fcrupuling or there difcover the fayling of oure brethren or fifters butt atend an orderly cale there unto; knowing how much the Lord may be difhonoured, and his Gospell in the profeffion of it, fleighted, by our diftempers, and weaknefses in publyck.

6 Wee bynd our felues to studdy the advancment of the Gospell in alltruth and peace, both in regard of thofe that are within, or without, noe way fleighting our fifter Churches, but vfeing theire Counfell as need shalbe; nor laying a ftumbling block, before any, noe not the Indians, whofe good we defire to promote, and foe to converfe, as wee may avoyd the verrye appearance of evill.

7 Wee hearby promife to carrye our felues in all lawfull obedience, to thofe that are over vs, in Church or Common weale, knowing how well pleafing it wilbe to the Lord,

CHAPTER 13 — SALEM 1629: STARTING OVER

that they should haue incouragment in theire places, by our not greiveing theyre spirites through our Iregularities.

8   Wee refolue to approve our felues to the Lord in our perticuler calings, shunning ydlenes as the bane of any state, nor will wee deale hardly, or oppreffingly with Any, wherein we are the Lords stewards;

9. alfoe promyseing to our beft abilitie to teach our children and fervants, the knowledg of God and his will, that they may ferue him alfo, and all this, not by any strength of our owne, but by the Lord Christ, whofe bloud we defire may sprinckle this our Covenant made in his name.

Rev. Francis Higginson, 1620s

Below is a plaque currently on the wall of the First Church of Salem, showing Francis Higginson's term of ministry from 1629 to until his death in 1630.

FIRST CHURCH IN SALEM

The Succession of Ministers

1629	Francis Higginson	1630
1629	Samuel Skelton	1634
1631	Roger Williams	1635
1636	Hugh Peters	1641
1640	Edward Norris	1658
1660	John Higginson	1708
1663	Nicholas Noyes	1717
1714	George Curwen	1717
1718	Samuel Fiske	1735
1736	John Sparhawk	1755
1755	Thomas Barnard	1776

Succession of Ministers at First Church in Salem

Henry, now in his new adoptive land, severed forever from his friends and family in England and his cloth trade, wasted no time in creating a new life. Immediately after arrival, Henry was among the 30 men who founded the First Church of Salem in August 6, 1629. Also, among those who joined the church with Henry were Hugh Laskin, Henry's future father in-law, John Endecott, Roger Conant, Peter Palfrye, John Balch, John Woodberry, William Trask, and Richard Rayment.

CHAPTER 13 —SALEM 1629: STARTING OVER

However, Francis Higginson was not to survive another year. In fact, he became ill and died August 6th, 1630; exactly one year to the day of his covenant and the founding of the church. Rev. Cotton Mather of Boston wrote that Rev. Higginson had "crossed the sea with a renowned colony, and that having seen an old world in Europe, where a flood of iniquity and calamity carried all before it, he also saw a new world in America; where he appears the first in a catalogue of heroes, and where he with his people were admitted into the covenant of God may therefore be called the Noah or Janus of New England."

Another founding member of the church was Hugh Laskin, who arrived at Naumkaeg a year before Henry in September 1628 on the Abigail, the same ship carrying the colony's leader John Endicott. It is believed that Henry and Thomas stayed with the Hugh Laskin family upon arrival in Salem, since it was common for new immigrants to stay with residents. This was fortuitous for Henry. Again, wasting no time, Henry met Hugh Laskin's daughter Editha while staying with the family, and soon thereafter, in 1632, he married her. Henry was starting a new marriage, a new family, a new home, and a new life. When the first church records were published in 1636, Henry and Editha were listed as church members.

Only one year after arriving in Salem in October 1630, Henry petitioned for the status of Freeman, which granted him rights of citizenship, the right to vote, membership in the General Court, and allowed him to purchase land. He was admitted as a Freeman and took the Oath of Freemen on May 18, 1631. This first grant of Freeman was given to 108 men, Henry Herrick among them, and included 20 of the Dorchester Company, including Roger Conant.

The Oath of Freemen was not taken lightly. The original charter of the Massachusetts Bay Company was written such that the first settlers had no political rights. However, the Court immediately made arrangements for extending the privileges of freemanship to all "suitable persons". Suitable meant that one had to be a mature male, church member, and must have experienced "a transforming spiritual experience by God's grace", as attested by himself and confirmed by church leaders. In addition to church membership and baptism, the transforming spiritual experience by God's grace was a long and arduous spiritual journey toward Grace. This journey had to be publicly narrated before the church congregation and had to be accepted by the congregation.

Even though the original charter provided no political rights for the settlers, it did entitle them to set up a provisional government and make whatever laws they needed so long as those laws were not contrary to the laws of England. The Oath of Freemanship was modified periodically, but the first oath of 1631 made by Henry Herrick is written below:

> I, Henry Herrick, being, by the Almighty's most wise disposition, become a member of this body, consisting of the Governor Deputy Governor, Assistants and a commonalty of the Mattachusets in New England, do freely and sincerely acknowledge that I am justly and lawfully subject to the government of the same, and do accordingly submit my person and estate to be protected, ordered, and governed by the laws and constitutions thereof, and do faithfully promise to be from time to time obedient and conformable thereunto, and the authority of the said Governor and Assistants and their successors, and to all such laws, orders, sentences, and decrees as shall be lawfully made and published by them or their successors; and I will always endeavor (as in duty I am bound) to advance the peace and welfare of this body or commonwealth to my utmost skill and ability; and I will, do my best power and means, seek to divert and prevent whatsoever may tend to the ruin or damage thereof, or of any the said Governor, Deputy Governor, or Assistants, or any of them or their successors, and will give speedy notice to them, or some of the, of any sedition, violence, treachery, or other hurt or evil which I shall know, hear, or vehemently suspect to be plotted or intended against the said commonwealth, or the said government established; and I will not at any time suffer or give consent to any counsel or attempt that shall be done, given, or attempted for the impeachment of the said government, or making any change alteration of the same, contrary to the laws and ordinance thereof, but shall do my utmost endeavor to discover, oppose, and hinder all and every such counsel and attempt. So help me God.

Henry Herrick's signature

Chapter 13 — Salem 1629: Starting Over

On January 25, 1635, Henry was granted a small farm ("a fearme of ground") two or three acres on the "north side of Jeffery Massey's Cove". This lot was "bounded by the Rock on one side and Wollaston's River on the other". On the same day the town granted to William Trask, John Woodbury, Roger Conant, Peter Palfrey and John Balch (five of the old planters) on a thousand acres of land together at the head of the Bass River. Then in the Salem land grant of 1636, Henry received forty acres of land and another forty acres nearby.[46] This 80 acres was on what was then referred to 'Cape Ann-Syde' of the Bass River. The other side of the river was referred to the 'Ryal-Syde'.

About this time, the Pequot War broke out and lasted between 1636 and 1638. The dispute was between the local Pequot tribe and an alliance of English colonists in New England. The Pequots were joined by their allies, the Narragansett and Mohegan tribes, while the colonies combined the Massachusetts Bay Colony (Salem) and the Plymouth colonies. The colonists were trying to break the Pequot control of the fur trade, while the Pequots were trying to maintain their political and economic dominance in the region. This was the first significant clash between the English settlers in New England and the Native Americans.

Henry Herrick was 38 years old and 6 years into his marriage to Editha. But Henry was still active in the local Salem militia, as were most men at the time, as it was required of all able bodied men. It is likely that Henry was called up to volunteer to fight the Pequots in the war. At the outbreak of war, John Endicott, the governor of the Massachusetts Bay Colony, sent a group of Salem settlers to make demands of the Pequots. It was not successful. It is only speculation, but Henry Herrick could have been among those sent to negotiate with the tribe.

The war resulted in the virtual elimination of the Pequot tribe and cleared the way for English expansion. No more conflicts with the Indians were encountered until King Phillips War 30 years later.

Henry and Editha went on to have 7 children of their own who lived to adulthood. Including Thomas, who came with Henry from England, Henry and Editha raised seven boys and one girl. Thomas may have turned out to be a disappointment to his father. He never married until

---

46 These land grants are near the United Shoe Corporation in Beverly and Beverly High School on Herrick Street. Herrick Rock was used as a border marker and overlooks United Shoe today.

Henry's Will explicitly stated that he would not receive a portion of his brother Benjamin's estate if he continued to "live his life as a single man." At the time he wrote this into his Will, Thomas did marry as his father wished. He married Hannah Ordway but was divorced from "his reputed wife" within a year for "impotence". Officially, the marriage was annulled. Hannah Ordway was 20 years old when she married Thomas, who at the time was about 47, over twice her age. One can easily speculate that Thomas was a gay man, but it is clear that marriage was only of interest to him when inheritance was involved. This was very possibly a huge problem for Henry and Editha since marriage was an essential part of the ideal Puritan society. Puritans believed that women were created for men so they might be helpmates. In the home, the husband and father were the "godhead". In Puritan society, the man rules his household as Christ rules the church and as the minister rules his congregation. Whatever the case may be, Thomas was not included in Benjamin's Will, nor of any of his siblings. Not only that, there are no records of Thomas purchasing land or serving as a witness in any Essex County court proceedings. However, Thomas did build a house on this father's land, which, as Henry stated in a land deed, was "that farm I bought of Mr. Alford." Thomas may very well have been the black sheep of the family, Henry's son of a previous marriage, who either had a sexual dysfunction or perhaps, most grievously for Henry and Editha, a gay man.

Zachariah was the first born of Henry and Editha and baptized in December 1636. Following Zachariah in the growing family were Ephraim[47], Henry, Joseph, Elizabeth, John, and Benjamin in that order.

---

[47] Ephraim had two descendants worthy of note. Colonel Samuel Herrick was Ephraim's great-grandson. Colonel Sam was a Revolutionary War hero who was appointed Colonel of the Vermont Rangers, captured Fort Ticonderoga and Crown Point. Under the command of General John Stark, defeated the British at the Battle of Bennington. Myron T. Herrick was Ephraim's 7th grandson. Myron T. Herrick was from Lorain, Ohio and became a successful lawyer, banker, statesman, diplomat, U.S. Ambassador to France and Governor of Ohio. A close friend of President William McKinley, he was offered to be U.S. Treasury Secretary when McKinley became president. Presidents Theodore Roosevelt and William Howard Taft also offered him appointments. His election to governor in 1903 was the largest majority vote in Ohio history. He was a lifelong genealogist of Herrick family history, and donated the altar to St. Catherine's church at Houghton-on-the-Hill near Leicester, England. He died in Paris attending the funeral of Marshall Foch, a WWI French war hero.

All of Henry's sons, made their livelihood solely from farming, with the possible exception of Joseph.

Pewter porringer, owned by the Herrick family (presumably Elizabeth).

Made by John Waite of London and registered with The Worshipful Company of Pewterers of London in 1673-1674. Made during the reign of William and Mary. Their profiles adorn the bowl and lid. Owned by The Essex Peabody Museum, Salem MA

Henry Herrick was now a planter and started to prosper as one. Then in 1653, Henry purchased a hundred acres of farmland from Francis Skerry north of Beverly and west of Wenham Pond, which was called Birch Plain or Cherry Hill. According to Henry's Will, this land was to be divided between Zachariah, Joseph, Ephraim and John. All farmed Birch Plain except Joseph who lived on Cherry Hill.

Below are a series of maps of ancient Beverly showing locations of tracts of land granted and purchased by Henry.

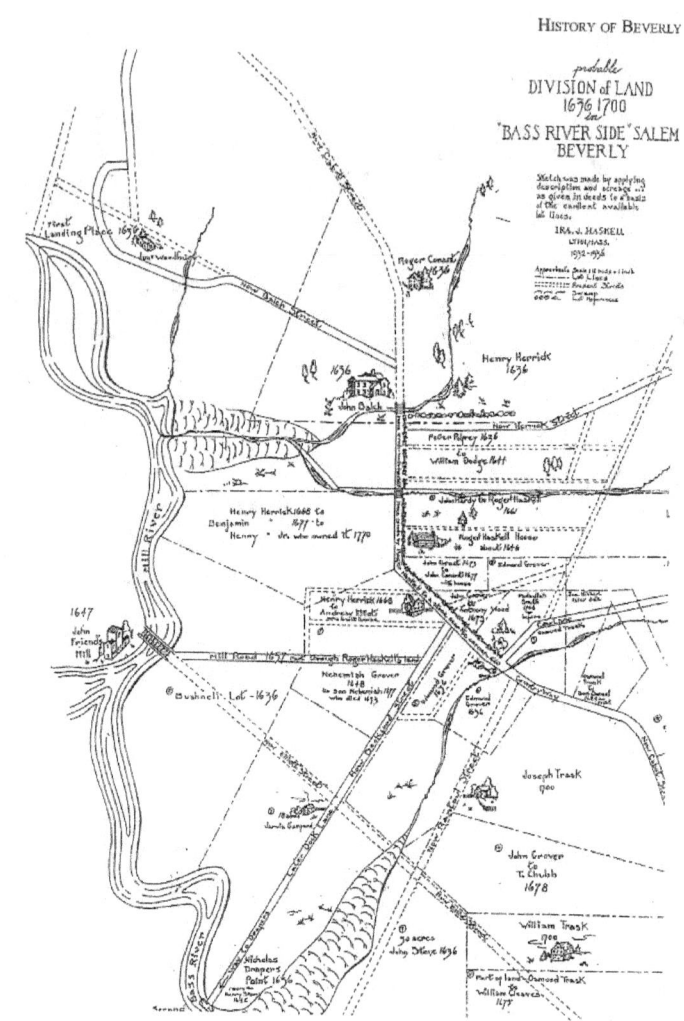

Henry Herrick's land in 1636

CHAPTER 13 — SALEM 1629: STARTING OVER

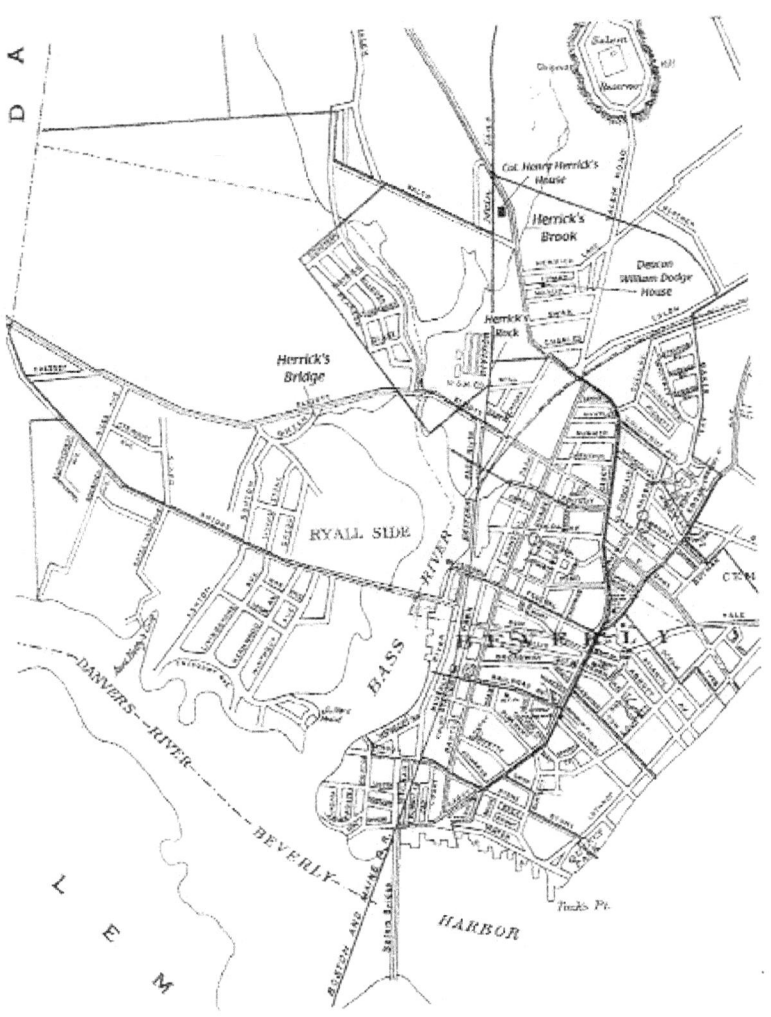

Location of Herrick Rock, Herrick Brook, Herrick Bridge

Beverly in 17th Century

The map above is an ancient map of Beverly prior to major streets. The location of Henry Herrick's 1636 80 acre land grant is in the center of this map. At top left on this map is Allords Hill, near the location where Henry purchased 100 acres in 1653 for three of his sons.

The map below is a detail of the map above, showing a few major streets. It shows two tracts of land granted Henry in 1636. The County Road separating the two tracts is Cabot Street today.

Chapter 13 — Salem 1629: Starting Over

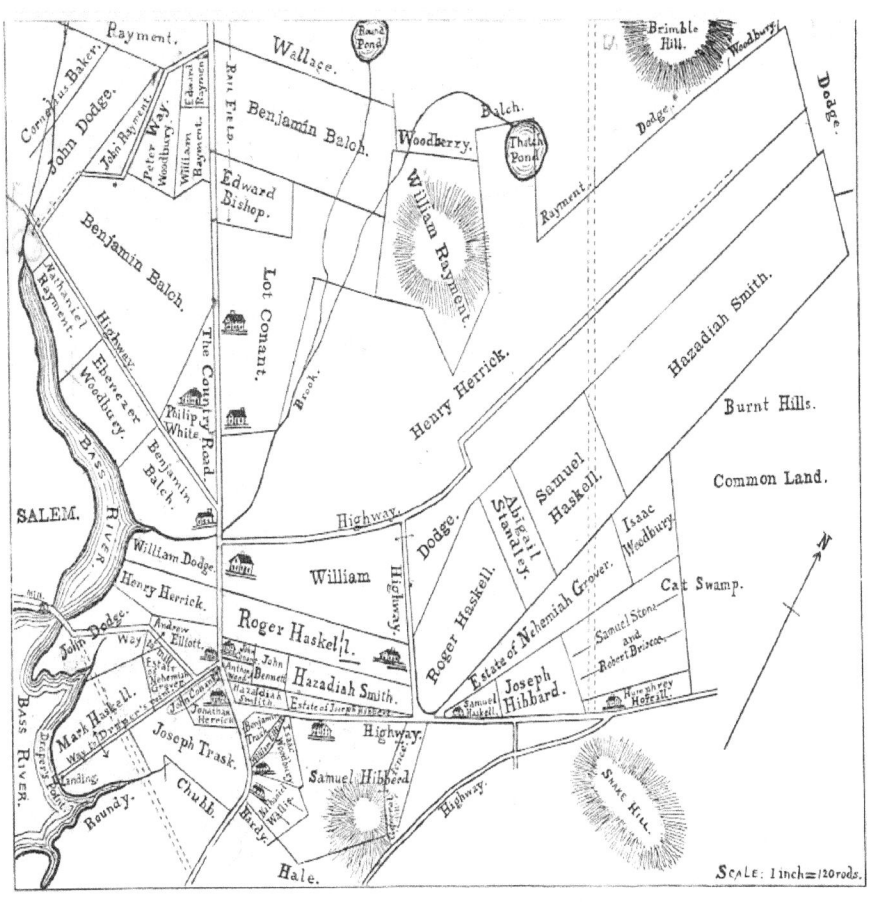

Beverly 1700

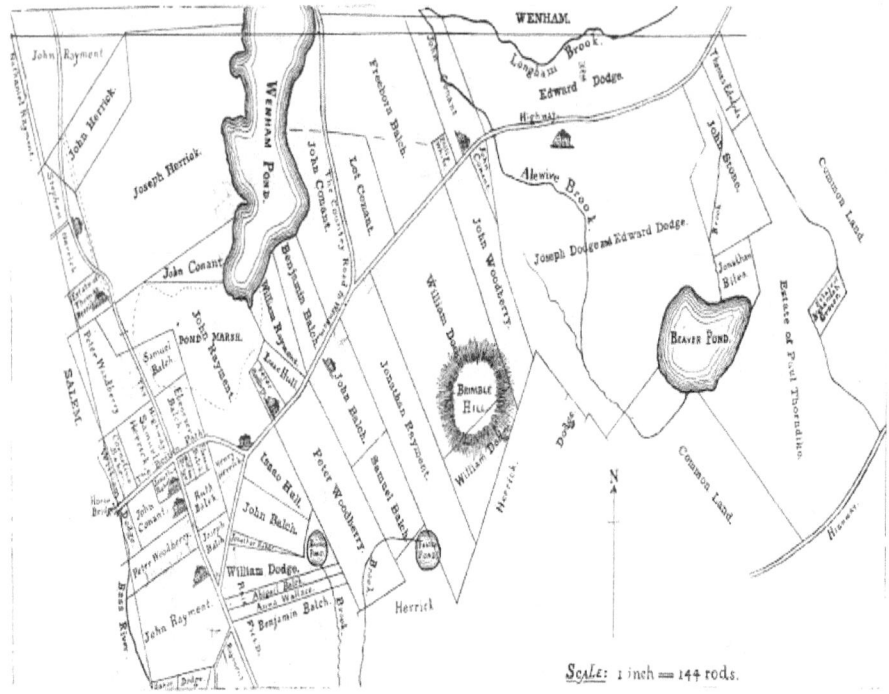

Henry Herrick lands granted to his sons

The map above is another detail, showing the location of Henry's 1636 land grants, located at the bottom of the map. At the top of the map are subdivisions of Henry's 1653 farm purchase, showing locations of parcels inherited by Zacharie, Joseph, John, and Ephraim. Just south of the Joseph Herrick property is the current location of the North Beverly Cemetery, where Joseph was buried and his slate head stone and foot stone still stand.

CHAPTER 13 —SALEM 1629: STARTING OVER

Lands originally leased or granted to Henry Herrick (highlighted) overlaid by current streets

Henry's original two 40 acre parcels are numbered 21 and highlighted in the right center of the map above and extends east of Cabot Street and borders what is now Herrick Street. The land to the north of Herrick Street is Beverly High School today. The United Shoe Corporation is shown on the map and currently occupies some of the land granted to Henry in 1636. The factory can be seen by standing on Herrick Rock, a large rock formation on Henry's land that was used back then to indicate his property boundary.

An understanding of Henry's land grants from the Massachusetts Bay Colony would not be complete without an understanding of the Old Planters. Under the leadership of Roger Conant, the Old Planters initially formed a fishing settlement at Cape Ann near Gloucester. These Old

Planters consisted, in addition to Conant, of the families of William Trask, John Woodbury, Peter Palfrey and John Balch. Conant arrived in Plymouth to settle with the Pilgrims in 1622, but was unhappy with their religious views. Through a grant from the Dorchester Company in England, Conant removed to Cape Ann. However, the settlement failed and then removed again, this time to "a fruitful neck of land" at Naumkaeg, later Salem, in 1626. The settlers, numbering only 15 to 20 men, then abandon fishing and became planters, calling themselves Old Planters to distinguish themselves from the subsequent settlers to Naumkaeg. They claimed and built simple constructed huts for living quarters. This, of course, was a few years before the first arrivals of the setters of the Massachusetts Bay Colony. Although they were first setters in Naumkaeg, the Massachusetts Bay Colony did not recognize the Dorchester Company's presence in the area nor did they recognize Roger Conant's leadership. Consequently, John Endicott was appointed by the Massachusetts Bay Colony to assume leadership of the colony, not Roger Conant. Endicott arrived in Naumkaeg in 1628 on the same ship as Hugh Laskin, Henry Herrick's future father in law.

Antagonisms ensued about land ownerships, religious beliefs, and leadership. Factions between the groups resulted between the Old Planter's Party and the New Planter's Party. However, Roger Conant was not a poor loser in this contest for leadership, as he remained well respected by both the old and new planters. To remain in Naumkaeg, Conant wrote a consolatory letter to John Endicott disclaiming any sinister intentions and offered that "they should be incorporated into the new society and enjoy not only those lands which they had formally 'manured', but such a further proportion as should be judge fit for them." Though John Endicott was the leader of the settlement, it took the minister Francis Higginson to proclaim, "by common consent of all the old planters, all are now combined in one body politique."[48]

---

48 A statue of Roger Conant stands today in Salem as a tribute to his early influence on the village. Descendants of the Old Planters descend from Roger Conant, John Woodberry, William Trask, John Balch, and Peter Palfrey.

CHAPTER 13 — SALEM 1629: STARTING OVER

Statue of Roger Conant on Salem Commons, Salem, MA

By all accounts, Henry must have felt happy and successful, without regrets for the sacrifices he had made by leaving his previous life behind. At last he had freedom from a church that deprived him of his sense of truth and surrounded himself with fellow dissenters. He was able to keep his friendship with Francis Higginson until his untimely death in 1630. It is likely that he continued a friendship with Higginson's son, John, who became a prominent minister in his own right in Salem. Henry was granted and purchased land to become a prosperous farmer, along with a new wife who not only raised Thomas as her own, but also provided him a new home and family.

Historical records in Salem during this time include a glimpse of Henry's day-to-day life. Most official records are court proceedings, and the records show that Henry served as a juror over a dozen times during his life and served twice on the Essex County grand jury, once in 1653 and once again in 1655. He also appeared in court several times in various lawsuits. For example, Henry sued Frances Masters for withholding a cow, evidently for the reimbursement of expenses paid on behalf of Master's son, John. Henry also provided testimony in the case of Edmund Groves, who claimed that his corn had been trampled by Osmond Trask's cows. It appears that cows were important to settlers in 17th century New England. In early New England, stray livestock were brought to the local town pound for holding and the owner would then be required to pay a fine to retrieve the livestock.

The records also reveal that Henry had an indentured servant named Margaret White and perhaps two more between 1642 and 1665. He owned her for what would appear to be seven years for which he was paid by her father, Richard, "small sums to provide her with clothes and sundries." Also, during this time, Margaret White and William Ellatt were presented in court for "uncleanness". She was sentenced to be whipped and be "bound to good behavior". Henry was responsible for paying for the court charges of his servant, Margaret, while Ellatt was discharged.

Henry was listed many times in Salem court records as a witness to lawsuits and various civil offences. For example, in 1666 Mathew Dove was charged for "being disguised with drink two several times." Henry was a witness in this court appearance and provided a deposition that he saw Dove "go along the country way reeling and staggering like a drunken man." However, Henry and his family were not always in court witnessing someone else's trouble. In 1664, Henry's name was entered in the court record when his first born son, Zachary, was fined for "breach of the peace in striking Nicholas Decaine several blows."

When Editha's father died in 1659, Henry was appointed administrator of Hugh Laskin's estate. Clearly, Henry had to appreciate that he was so well thought of by his father in law. There was, however, intrigue in administering the estate. First, Henry had to sue Elias Stileman for taking possession of the estate and preventing Henry from making an inventory of property. Second, Paul Mansfield (second husband of Hugh's daughter in law) had received 2/3 share of the estate for his stepchildren, while 1/3 went to Editha and Henry. Henry sued Mansfield for "breaking up housen" and "taking away the goods and cattle belonging to the estate." Henry won the suit. Additionally, Henry witnessed the Will of John Friend in Salem and conducted the estate

CHAPTER 13 —SALEM 1629: STARTING OVER

inventory for Agnes 'Annis' Balch, both occurring in 1655. Again, this suggests that Henry Herrick was a respected citizen of Salem.

Court records also show that Henry knew Roger Conant, which is not surprising given they both lived in this small community, and in fact lived across the street from one another. In 1661, court records documented that Roger Conant, Henry Herrick and Benjamin Balch "certified that they had measured the highway at the clay pit by Roger Hoscal's hill and found it two poles and five feet in breadth and four poles to the further part of the pit." Apparently the three men were commissioned to do some surveying work for Salem.

The following is an excerpt from The History of Salem by Sidney Pearly.

> Henry Herrick was a husbandman, in easy circumstances, but undistinguished by wealth, or by civil rank or influence in the colony. He was a very good and honest dissenter from the established church, and a friend of Higginson, who had been a dissenting Minister in Leicester. Mr. Herrick and his wife Editha were among the thirty who founded the first church in Salem in 1629; and on the organization of the new parish, on 'Ryal Syde' 1667, they, with their sons and their sons' wives, were among the founders of the first church in Beverly, also. But there are some reasons to suspect that neither Henry, nor his sons were, at all times, and in all things, quite as submissive to the spiritual powers of their day, as they should have been. One the Court records of Essex County is an entry like this: "Henerie Hericke and Edith his wife, are fined 10s. and 11s. for costs of Coort, for aiding and comforting the excommunicated person, contrary to order."

The fines that Henry and Edith inured could have come about from giving "entertaining" to Nicholas Decaine who had not been accepted by the town leaders, despite the fact that he was part of Higginson's church in England.

The Records of the First Church in Salem Massachusetts 1629-1736 indicate that Henry and Editha withdrew from the church in Salem to form a new church across the Danvers River, which would later become Beverly. This was for reasons of convenience, since Henry lived north of the Danvers and the Bass River Side and the church was south of the Danvers River. In 1667, a petition to be dismissed by families and their children from the Salem church was submitted to be a church. The petition was granted, the First Church of Beverly was formed, and Rev. John Hale was ordained to serve the church. One year later, in 1668, the town of Beverly was incorporated.

Entries of H. Herrick and his wife are among the 50 members to withdraw from the Salem church and form the Beverly church on July 4, 1667. The church records cite, "We whose names as underwritten the Brethren and Sisters on Basse Rive Side doe present our desires to the rest of the Church of Salem that with their consent Wee and our children may be a church of ourselves, which we also present unto Mr. Hale desiring him to join with us and be our Pastor with the approbation of the rest of the church". Also, on the list were some of the older children of Henry and Editha, namely Henry Jr., Ephraim, Joseph, and Elizabeth. Their oldest children Thomas and Zachariah did not transfer their membership as children or as adults.

Henry Herrick died sometime after November 24, 1670, which is the date of his Will. His Estate Inventory was dated March 15, 1671. The Will and Estate Inventory for Henry Herrick are found below. His remains are unknown.[49]

Henry Herrick had two lives. The division between those two lives represent a profound sense of courage, hope, faith, and determination. He lived in Leicester, England for 31 years where he grew to adulthood, enjoyed the notoriety of his famous name, became a freeman in his chosen trade, married a woman with family notoriety, and fathered two sons. He also had the courage and gumption to question and stand up for his religious beliefs with the support of his friend and pastor. Then for 42 years, Henry Herrick lived in a strange new land, called the Massachusetts Bay Colony, determined to make a new life for himself. With nothing but his Puritan faith and his young son, he started life over. Giving up a life that he knew for a life unknown. He remarried a woman also facing the unknown in an unknown land. No longer a freeman in the textile trades, he redefined himself as a farmer and landowner and started

---

49 In conversation with a local historian and profiler of local gravesites in Salem and Beverly, it was suggested that Henry Herrick could likely be buried under a parking lot at the First Church of Beverly or under a street adjacent to the current cemetery.

CHAPTER 13 — SALEM 1629: STARTING OVER

life again. With his new wife, Henry Herrick started a new family raising Thomas and seven children of their own. Henry prospered in his new family life, his new religious life, and his new occupation. His children were the beneficiaries of his courage, optimism and persistent hard work.

As noted above, Henry gave much of his land to his children. He gave the western half of his dwelling to Editha and the rest to his son Henry, who would inherit it all at his mother's death. Zacharie received acreage in Birch Plain, while separate farms were willed to Ephraim, Joseph and Benjamin along with animals, pastures and money. His daughter, Elizabeth, received money. As noted earlier, Thomas would only receive a portion of Benjamin's inheritance if he married, which he did only briefly. However, Thomas did receive clothing, money and the land where his house stood. Benjamin died early as a young man and never married.

Below is a copy of Henry Herrick's last Will and his estate inventory. When Henry died, sometime between Nov 24, 1670 and March 15, 1671, he had a house and orchard with 70 acres of land, plus other lands that he did not occupy. According to his inventory, he left 974 pounds (including 413 acres valued at 804 pounds, a musket, sword and a rapier). His inventory also included "four bibles and other books." All in all, Henry was the third largest landowner of his time in Salem. His success suggests wealth, plus skills and capabilities that were suited to the challenges of the early colonial period.

MICHAEL J. HERRICK

HENRY OF SALEM
ADAPTED FROM THE 1885 EDITION AND HFA RESEARCH

The Will of Henry of Salem

"I, HENRY HERICK of the Towne of Beverly in the county of Essex in New England being in a decaying estate of body but in pfect mynd and memorye, through the Lords mercy do heerby make my last will and testament, wherby I commiting my body to the earth, and my Soule to the mercy of god in christ Jesus, I dispose of my estate in order following.

Imps. I give vnto my Deare & loveing wife Edith the westward-most halfe of my now dwelling house, that is the lower roome and leantoo behind it, together with free egress and regress in and out of it, and also the vse of the cellar, well, yard, out houseing & garden, these to haue & injoy Dureing her naturall life. further I giue to my sd wife foure of my best milch cowes & 4 sheepe which shee shall choose and all my house-hold stufe, these to be her absolute free dispose. also I giue vnto my sd wife, the sixt part of the fruits that shall be raysed from the corne lands, & orchard wch I leave with my executor Henry and in the possession of my sonn John Also I give vnto my sonn Thomas all my wearing apparell exsept my best great coate and that 20 Acres of land where his house standeth, with ten pounds to be paid, by my son John wn my executor seeth need to supplye his wants, And if in case he live and dye a single p'son, the lands shall remaine to my sonns Ephraim & Joseph, equally devided & the ten pounds to my sonn Benjamin, if not made vse of to supply him, Also I give my sonn Zackery one hundred Acres of land lyeing in Birch plaine Wch I bought of ffrancis & Henry Skerry of Salem with 5 acres of meadow lyeing in wenham meadow belonging to it, and 16 acres of land more or lesse wheron his house standeth & fenced in by him. Also I give my sonns Ephraim, Joseph and John, that farme I bought of Mr Allford the 20 acres giuen to Thomas being first measured out to him, the rest to be equally devided betweene them three, yet soe that Ephraim & Joseph may inioy what they have improved, and fenct, and John what is improved by Henry, soe as to pay the sixt part of the pduce to my wife before exprest. Also I giue to my sonn John the two lotts I bought of Henry Rennolds of Salem & Richard Kemball of wenham, also my sonn John is to have two acres of meadow in Bounkards meadow, also the bedding he lyeth vpon and my cart and plow with the chaine therof Also I give Ephraim moreover one milch cow & my best great coate and vnto Joseph I giue moreover two ewe sheepe & my timbar chaine, I give vnto my sonn Benjamin all that pasture land, called my english pasture, Wch joyneth on the east syde to Andrew Elliott, lyeing between the countrye high way & the mill River, I say all that land lyeing on the southeast syde of the sd country high way, the Wch pasture land, with the apptenances, my will is shall remaine in the hands of my sonn Henry to improve vntil Benjamin be 21 years of age and in case he dye before he be 21 years of age I giue the sayd land to my sonn Henry, he paying vnto my children Zachry, Ephraim, Joseph & Elizabeth foure pounds a peece Also I giue vnto my daughter Elizabeth forty pounds viz. 14th to be payd by my sonn Henry within three months after the confirmation of my will and the rest to be made vp in 3 cowes & moveables allredy in her possesion, And to John the youngest yoke of stears, and whatsoever I giue to any of my children heerin mentioned by this my will, I giue to them, there heires, executors, administrators & assignes for ever And for the rest of my estate, not aboue mentioned I give it all to my sonn Henry, he paying vnto his mother the sixt part of the increase of the corne land & orchard dureing her life, and p'viding for her the wintering of foure milch cowes 4 sheepe & her firewood redy cut for fire at the dore, for all the yeare long, and liberty to keep 3 swine at the dore, and (I giue my sonn Ephraim one acre of meadow in buncars Joseph 3 acres of meadow in buncars) And to have the p'per vse of the parlour & leanto behind it with free egresse & regresse to housing yards for her necessary occasions as is expresed dureing her life I say these things premised I giue my sonn Henry my dwelling house out houseing orchard tillage land meadows pasture & woodland with my stock & whatever elce within dores & without, not above excepted making this my sayd sonn Henry my sole executor of this my last will

In witness wherof I have set my hand this 24 of November 1670."

In the presents of:/
ROBERT MORGAN, /
NEHEMIAH GROVER /

HENRY HERICK.

Mr John Hale and Capt. Thomas Lathrop chosen as oversees of this will.

Chapter 14
Plymouth

The Puritans in Salem were well aware of the separatists (Pilgrims) who settled nine years earlier and not far away at Plymouth. It is interesting to think that Henry Herrick of Salem was only 65 miles by land from Edward Doty of Plymouth when both started their American family lines. The Herrick line and the Doty line merged 9 generations later.

The Pilgrims struggled to find a spiritual leader that they could rally behind. Without a strong religious leader, they felt a certain religious vulnerability. They knew about the Puritan settlement in Salem and the strong leadership of Francis Higginson. But they were concerned that the strictness of the Puritans, particularly for church membership, may not fit well with the Pilgrim religious norms, which were more relaxed. Francis Higginson was instrumental in achieving peace between the two colonies despite their religious differences. Letters frequently passed between Higginson and Elder William Brewster of the Pilgrims relative to church membership and related issues. In fact, on August 6th, the day Francis Higginson presented is covenant, Elder Brewster, Governor Bradford and few others from the Plymouth colony were invited by the Massachusetts Bay Colony Governor, John Endicott, to attend the covenant reading and ceremony. The day was devoted to fasting, prayer, and the delivery of sermons by Higginson and Brewster, the two ministers from the two settlements.

Governor Bradford and others from Plymouth traveled to Salem by boat but were hindered by cross winds so they missed the first part of the ceremony but arrived later in the day and "gave the right hand of fellowship, wishing all prosperity, and a blessed success unto such good beginnings". Higginson's Confessions of Faith was acknowledged only as a "direction pointing unto that faith and covenant contained in the holy scripture". As a result of the spiritual meeting of the two colonies, "some (from Plymouth) were admitted by expressing their consent to that written Confession of Faith and Covenant; others did answer to questions about the Principles of Religion publicly propounded to them; some did present their confessions in writing, and some did make their confession in their own work and way".

Consequently, the two colonies not only had occasional contact, they had a religious bond as well, despite the strict Puritan Covenant prepared and presented by Francis Higginson. Below is an account from the Pilgrim delegation to Salem for ceremonies and services regarding the covenant.

> They set out from Plymouth by water, but were hindered by cross winds, and so did not arrive before the beginning of the services of the day. They came, however, in season to give the right hand of fellowship, and to wish "all prosperity and, a blessed success unto such good beginnings."[1]
>
> In some points of church discipline, the Puritans did not agree with their friends of Plymouth, but they did agree that the children of the faithful were church members with their parents, and that their baptism was a seal of their being so; only before their admission to fellowship in a particular church it was judged necessary, that they should be examined by the elders, and if approved by them should publicly and personally own the covenant. The fifteen-year-old son of Mr. Higginson, named Francis, "laudably" answered all these requirements, and was then received into the church.
>
> The manner of church services and teaching the people was to be settled by the ministers, and the Company hoped that they would "make Gods word the rule of their accons, and mutually agree in the discharge of their duties." And because their doctrine "would hardly bee well esteemed whose psons are not reverenced," the Company wrote to Governor Endecott that they desired that, both by his "owne example and by comanding all others to doe the like o^r ministers may receive due hono^r."

It is unlikely that a servant of one of the Plymouth settlers, Steven Hopkins a London tanner and merchant, would have attended the ceremonies in Salem. Edward Doty, one of two of Hopkins servants was not even a Pilgrim, but he was one of the 102 passengers on the Mayflower, which arrived at Plymouth in December 21, 1620. Edward was one of 61 passengers who did not come to New England for religious reasons, but for a better, and perhaps a more adventurous, life. The Pilgrims or Separatists were also commonly referred to as "Saints", while those who did not join the Mayflower for religious reasons were referred to as "Strangers".

Although about the same age, Edward Doty and Henry Herrick could not have been more different. Doty was a poor servant from London[50] settling in a Pilgrim (Separatist) community, Herrick a prosperous freeman from Leicester settling in a Puritan community. Doty had no family, Herrick had a family and brought a young child with him to New England. Doty was member of the Church of England, Herrick was a Puritan. Doty was known for his belligerence, Herrick was known for his righteous and industrious manner. Who could imagine that one day the Doty family and the Herrick families would merge. But one day, after 9 generations, they did.

Between 1607-08, English Separatists left England for The Netherlands for religious freedom – first in Amsterdam and then in Leyden. They encountered economic and other problems and finally arraigned travel to America. They set sail on two vessels, the Speedwell and the Mayflower in August, 1620. The Speedwell, however, proved not to be seaworthy, as it was too leaky to survive the trip. Both ships returned to Plymouth, England. On September 6, 1620, the Mayflower set sail alone. Steven Hopkins, his family and his two servants, Edward Lister and Edward Doty, boarded the Mayflower at this time. The Mayflower was 90' long, 15' wide and weighed 180 tons. It arrived on the coast of Cape Cod on November 11, 1620.

Despite being a servant, Doty was still allowed to be one of the 41 signatures to the Mayflower Compact, drafted in the Great Cabin of the Mayflower on November 21, 1620. This invitation to sign the compact indicates that Edward Doty was considered an adult, albeit a youthful servant. Like all other signers of the compact, Edward was allotted a parcel of land in the new settlement. The compact was the first law of the land and needed to be drafted and signed by all in order to settle differences between setters who came for religious reasons and those who came for a better life. The Mayflower Compact has been hailed as

---

50 Edward Doty's English ancestry is unknown, but there is a record of Edward Doty baptized on November 3, 1600 at East Halton, Co. Lincoln, England; the son of Thomas Doty.

"the great charter of freedom" as it was designed to define "just and equal laws" for all in the new colony of Plymouth.

Before the Mayflower actually landed in Plymouth Harbor, Edward Doty was one of 10 volunteers who set out on one of the ship's boats to explore the new land. He was reputedly the largest man among the passengers, which may account for him being the only person selected for all of the many scouting expeditions when looking for a permanent landing site. The scouting party encountered hostile Indians, who discovered the explorers stealing their buried corn and discovering their burial grounds. After escaping the Indians, the explorers found refuge on what is now known as Clark's Island in Plymouth Harbor. Clark's Island was intended to be named after Richard Clark, the Master's mate. But Edward Doty had a different idea. Doty leaped on the island first, wishing to be the first to set foot on the new land, but was severely checked by the others in the party for his forwardness. Therefore, the island should be called Doty's Island.[51]

The scouting party rendezvoused on the island for two days before going to the mainland to check it out. They found the harbor and the mainland to be good for habitation, so they landed and stepped on Plymouth Rock. A few days later, the Mayflower dropped anchor in Plymouth Harbor and the whole party landed and commenced the settlement of Plymouth. This party of volunteers took six weeks to explore the surrounding area for building a permanent settlement. Forty five people died within the first three months of the new settlement.

---

51 This story is told by Joseph Lucas, whose father was a great grandson of Edward Doty.

Chapter 14 — Plymouth

The Mayflower Compact in William Bradford's handwriting

In the name of God, Amen. We whose names are underwritten, the loyal subjects of our dread Sovereign Lord King James, by the Grace of God of Great Britain, France, and Ireland King, Defender of the Faith, etc. Having undertaken for the Glory of God and advancement of the Christian Faith and Honour of our King and Country, a Voyage to plant the First Colony in the Northern Parts of Virginia, do by these presents solemnly and mutually in the presence of God and one of another, Covenant and Combine ourselves together in a Civil Body Politic, for our better ordering and preservation and furtherance of the ends aforesaid; and by virtue hereof to enact, constitute and frame such just and equal Laws, Ordinances, Acts, Constitutions and Offices from time to time, as shall be thought most meet and convenient for the general good of the Colony, unto which we promise all due submission and obedience. In witness whereof we have hereunder subscribed our names at Cape Cod, the 11th of November, in the year of the reign of our Sovereign Lord King James, of England, France and Ireland the eighteenth, and of Scotland the fifty-fourth. Anno Domini 1620.

John Carver	Edward Tilly	Digery Priest
William Bradford	John Tilly	Thomas Williams
Edward Winslow	Francis Cooke	Gilbert Winslow
William Brewster	Thomas Rogers	Edmund Margeson
Isaac Allerton	Thomas Tinker	Peter Brown
Miles Standish	John Rigdale	Richard Bitteridge
John Alden	Edward Fuller	George Soule
Samuel Fuller	John Turner	Richard Clark
Christopher Martin	Francis Eaton	Richard Gardiner
William Mullins	James Chilton	John Allerton
William White	John Craxton	Thomas English
Richard Warren	John Billington	Edward Doten
John Howland	Moses Fletcher	Edward Leister
Stephen Hopkins	John Goodman	

The Mayflower Compact with Signatories

Edward Doty, however, was known for his hot temper. Six months after landing at Plymouth, he got into a sword and dagger fight with Hopkin's other servant, Edward Litster. William Bradford records this fight as Doty's "second" offence, the Clark Island incident presumably being the first. The fight with Litster was the first, and only, dual in Plymouth Colony. What a dubious honor to start a better life! They both succeeded in wounding each other before being separated. The entire colony assembled to decide their punishment. The punishment, ultimately decided by none other than Miles Standish, the military man on the Mayflower, was that the two men have their heads and feet tied together for a period of 24 hours. However, before one hour had passed, they suffered enough to humbly plead their release, which was granted.

Edward Doty was married twice, but nothing is known of his first wife in England, since the only reference to her is from William Bradford's notes, "But Edward Doty by a second wife hath 7 children (at the time of this entry)". It is likely that Edward had an unrecorded marriage some years after arriving in Plymouth. It has not been determined if his first wife was in London or in America. Regardless, Edward married Faith Clarke on January 6, 1635, 13 years after Edward arrived in New England. So, there was plenty of time for a first marriage in America, but the Parish Register of St. Mary's le Strand Church in London lists an Edward Doty marrying Wynefred Waryn on December 12, 1615. If that was the case, he would have been 16 when first married. Nonetheless, Faith Clarke arrived in Plymouth in April 1634 with her parents.

Like Henry Herrick, Edward Doty could have just as easily been involved in the Pequot Wars. Edward, being about the same age as Henry, marrying the second time about the same time, and with the Plymouth colony being equally involved in the Pequot War, the young men could have encountered each other as military allies. Again, it is speculation, but it is possible.

Although a husband and the father of 9, Edward Doty continued his belligerence. He was frequently in court as a plaintiff or defendant. Although most of the law suits that he was involved in were civil disputes, some were complaints lodged against him for trespassing, slandering, assault and battery, debt, and breaking the peace. He lost most of these suits, both civil and criminal, as plaintiff or defendant. In 1633, he was fined for breaking the peace and "drawing blood" from Josias Cooke. In 1636, he was found guilty of a "deceitful bargain" over a lot of land and had to restore the land to George Clarke. Clarke further charged Doty with assault and battery and Doty was fined even further. In 1641, Doty was charged with carelessly allowing cattle to be put in his hands to "break into men's corn" endangering the cattle and other property. For this, Doty was ordered to put his cattle in a "keep". Below is a summary directly from Plymouth Court Records detailing Edward Doty's appearances.

> 1632/3 Sued by Joseph Rogers, failed to pay a contract with six pigs, as had been agreed. Rogers won.
>
> 1632/3 Sued by William Bennet for dealing fraudulently in a trade of bacon for beaver skins. Bennet won.
>
> 1633 Sued by William Bennet for slander. Doty fined 50 shillings.
>
> 1633/4 Sued by his apprentice John Smith to be freed from his 10-year contract. Court agreed and required Doty to give him double payment in apparel for having given so little to his apprentice.
>
> 1633/4 Fined 6 shillings 8 pence for "breaking the peace", and awarded Josias Cooke 3 shillings 4 pence because Doty caused him to bleed during their fight.
>
> 1634 Doty sued Francis Sprague over a debt: Doty won 6 shillings 6 pence, plus a peck of malt.
>
> 1636 Edward Doty and Joseph Beedle sue and counter-sue for "matters being raw and imperfect" and were sent to an arbitrator.
>
> 1637/8 Fined 10 shillings for breaking the peace, by assaulting George Clarke.
>
> 1641 Sued George Allen. Reason and outcome unrecorded.
>
> 1641/2 Sued Thurston Clarke. Doty awarded 12 bushels and 1 peck of Indian corn, and 12 shillings money or an additional 4 bushels of corn, plus 11 shillings for charges. John Jenny then entered an attachment to receive 31 shillings 6 pence from Clarke before it was paid to Doty, of which the court ordered him to then pay Doty five and a half bushels of Indian corn and 3 pence to settle the account.
>
> 1641/2 Court orders Edward Doty to keep his two cows and a steer fenced in during the summer, or pay Thomas Symons for all damage caused by his cows in Symons' cornfield.
>
> 1641/2 Sued George Clark. Doty awarded four bushels of Indian corn.

CHAPTER 14 — PLYMOUTH

1643 Doty ordered to pay five bushels of Indian corn to John Groome, for Manessah Kempton's use.

1647 Samuel Cutbert sued Edward Doty for taking wood from his land. Doty ordered to pay 7 shillings damages plus court fees.

1650 Edward Gray and Samuel Cutbert sue Edward Doty for damage done by his cows to their corn. Doty ordered to pay 1 bushel of Indian corn to each.

After his indenture, Edward Doty prospered. As quoted in Saints and Strangers, "In the matter of worldly goods he had outstripped most of those who had come as freemen, even Captain Standish". Edward purchased land throughout his life but his home for his entire life was at High Cliff, located just north of the Plymouth settlement. He was one of a group of men who purchased land at Dartmouth. He had an apprentice, although an unhappy one. In 1633, the court settled a dispute between himself and his apprentice, John Smith, reducing the time of the apprenticeship from 10 to 5 years. When that apprenticeship ended in 1638, he received another apprentice, William Snow.

Below is an excerpt about Edward Doty from the Doty Genealogy, The Doty-Doten Family in America, by Ethan Allen Doty.

A tall and well-built man, with a strong constitution, a frame well knit together, and arms and limbs evidently used to hard work, active, alert, and full of life, with perhaps a surplus of energy; without school education and yet with an active mind and that knowledge that comes quickly to a close observer from experience; of a kind nature and good intentions, but tenacious of this own to an extent at least of demanding his full rights, and obstinate in obtaining them. Probably when he landed, as a youth, at Plymouth, he did not possess any of the religious feelings which actuated the leading spirits among the Pilgrims, but came soon to admire the inflexible honesty of their dealings and the industry, integrity, and morality of their lives. Perhaps his early association in the family of John Howland helped to curb his unruly spirit. (He lived with the Howlands after first living with Hopkins.) At any rate, from this time on his life appears to have been circumspect, and he seems to be given his energies to the proper support of his increasing family, and with much thrift, to amassing a property and lands. Many of the suits at law which were noted (in Plymouth court records) were evidently brought with no unfriendly spirit, but rather to settle by arbitration disputed claims.

Edward Doty died on August 23, 1655 and was buried at Burial Hill Cemetery where there is still a memorial stone for him. At the end of his life Edward had amassed a sizable estate, the value being 137 pounds. So, in the end, this hot-headed servant had prospered well during his time in Plymouth.

Memorial to Edward Doty in Plymouth

Below is the Last Will and Testament and Personal Inventory of Edward Doty:

May the 20th 1655
In the Name of God Amen

Know all men to whom It may concerne that I Edward Dotten senir: of the Towne of New Plymouth in New England being sicke and yett by the mercye of God in prfect memory and upon matture Consideration Doe by this my last will and Testament leave and bequeath my purchase land lying att Coaksett unto my sons; my son Edward I give a Double portion and to the rest of my sonnes equall alike if they live to the age of one and twenty if they Die before then to bee prted among the rest onely to my wife I leave a third During her life and then after to returne to my sonnes, And unto my loveing wife I give and bequeath my house and lands and meddows within the precincts of New Plymouth together with all Chattles and moveables that are my proper goods onely Debts and engagements to bee paied; As for my Share of land att Punckquetest if it come to anything I give it unto my son Edward; This being my last will and Testament; I Edward Dotten Doe owne it for my Act and Deed before these my loveing ffrinds whoe are Witnesses; and Doe sett my hand to the same; the Day and yeare above written

Witness
John Howland Edward Dotten
James Hurst his Marke
John Cooke
William Hoskins

There being many names besides Coaksett I mean all my purchase land According to the Deed. Att the generall court held the fift of March 1655; faith the wife of Edward Dotten Decased Did give up and make over all her right and enterest she had in the land of Edward Dotten Att Coaksett or places adjacent unto her Children this shee Did in the prsence of the said Court; held att Plymouth yt Day and yeare above expressed;

The abovewritten Will and Testament of Edward Dotten Deceased was exhibited to the Court held att Plymouth the fift of March 1655 on the oathes of

Mr John Howland
James Hurst
John Cooke
and William Hoskins

Chapter 14 — Plymouth

Below is the estate inventory of Edward Doty.

"An Inventory of the Estate of Edward Dotten, lately deceased, taken this 21 of November, 1655, inhabitant of the towne of Plymouth in New England; and Exhibited to the Court held att Plymouth aforesaid the fift of March, Anno. 1656, on the oath of Faith Dotten.

	£.	s.	d.
Imprimis, his dwelling house with his land adjoining	25	00	00
It. three score acres of upland with the meddow adjoining it, lying in the woods	10	00	00
It. the land at Clarke's Island	05	00	00
It. the purchase land lying at Coaksett	20	00	00
It. a yoake of working oxen	12	00	00
It. a cow	04	00	00
It. an heifer of year and vantage	02	05	00
It. 2 calves of this year	01	10	00
It. halfe a calfe of this yeare	00	07	06
It. 2 fatt swine	04	00	00
It. 4 yearling swine	03	00	00
It. cart with Wheels, axltree pins and shakhe	03	00	00
It. a plow with the irons	00	14	00
It. 2 yoakes, a dog yoake and a draught yoake	00	08	00
It. a paire of euples	00	03	00
It. a draught chaine	00	04	06
It. 2 axes att 5s 2 spades att 7s	00	12	00
It. 5 hoes att 10s 1 pot hanger 3s	00	13	00
It. 2 pich forkes at 2s a paire of tonges 1s 6d	00	03	06
It. 3 kittles - a copper kittle and 2 brass-kittles	01	15	00
It. 6 pewter dishes and a candlesticke	00	15	00
It. 2 iron potts	01	00	00
It. Earthen potts and pans	00	06	00
It. a Matchlock Muskett	00	12	00
It. a hay knife and 2 sythes with nibbs & ringes	00	08	00
It. 2 cow bells at 8s - a pound waight 4d	00	08	04
It. a great Wheel and a little Wheel & a paire of cardes	—	11	00
It. 3 paire of hookes and hinges	00	04	00
It. 2 hammers, 2 paire of pincers and a drawing knife	—	05	06
It. 2 andires and a cradle	00	15	00
It. 3 chists	00	18	00
It. 4 wooden trayes, a wooden bowle & straining dish	—	04	00
It. a table and forme	00	03	00
It. a halfe bushell & halfe pecke	00	02	00
It. a half hogshead, a rundlett and sineting trough	—	06	00
It. 2 sickles and a hooke	00	02	00
It. in linnin	03	00	00
It. 30 bushels of rye	05	05	00
It. bed and coverings	05	00	00
It. 10 bushels and an half of peasen	01	18	06
It. 6 bushels of Wheat	01	16	00
It. 4 score bushels of Indian corn	12	00	00
It. 12 load of hay in the woods	03	12	00
It. a watch bill	00	03	00
It. 4 barrells of tar lying in Capt Willetts hands	02	00	00
It. more in rye 7 bushels	01	04	06
It. a steer of two years and the vantage	02	10	00
It. a barrell of tarr	00	10	00
It. a cow hyde	00	07	06
The summe	137	19	06
Debts owing	06	00	02
Paied of this debt	03	13	10

Witnesses   William hopkins
The marke   E. T. of Ephraim Tinkham."

Edward and Faith had six sons[52] and three daughters. Samuel, Edward's fourth son, inherited land in Dartmouth from his father, as did all of Samuel's brothers, which they all immediately sold. The Dartmouth land is referred as Coaksett in his will. Edward's first born son, Edward, received a double share of his brother, Samuel's, portion of the estate.

Samuel was born 1643 at High Cliff and eventually moved to Piscataway, New Jersey. In 1670, at the age of 27, he moved to Piscataway, New Jersey as one of its first settlers. In 1675, Samuel was commissioned Lieutenant of the military company of Piscataway, with Francis Drake as Captain. He married Jane Harmon in 1678 and in 1682 became a freeman. Although he did not grow up in a strong religious family, Samuel was a founding member of the Seventh Day Baptist church of Piscataway, as shown in church records of 1707. Samuel was a farmer all his adult life and died in 1715.

Samuel and Jane Doty had eight children, one of whom was Jonathan. Jonathan married Mary (last name unknown), lived in Piscataway, and later moved to Basking Ridge, New Jersey. They had seven children, one of whom was also named Jonathan. Jonathan was born in Piscataway and moved with his parents to Basking Ridge. He married Patience Sutton and they had six children, one of whom was Zebulon.

Zebulon was born in Basking Ridge (Somerset County) in 1758. Zebulon married three times. His first wife was Sarah Rickey, with whom he had all of his nine children. He served as a private in the Revolutionary War as a minuteman from Somerset County, New Jersey. In his five page declaration of service to receive a war pension, he stated that he enlisted in the army in June 1776 from Somerset County. His regiment marched to New York, where he heard the Declaration of

---

52 Edward's eighth child was Joseph, who is the Doty ancestor of James Duane Doty. James Doty became a close friend of Lewis Cass, governor of Michigan Territory, explored frontiers of Michigan and Wisconsin, and convinced the territorial legislature of Wisconsin to make Madison the new state capital after he purchased the swampy isthmus between Lake Mendota and Lake Monona. He named the new capital after James Madison, fourth President of the United States. He was appointed Territorial Governor of Wisconsin by President John Tyler. In 1861, due to his lifelong concern for Indian affairs, President Abraham Lincoln appointed him Superintendent of Indian Affairs in Utah Territory and later appointed him Territorial Governor.

Independence read. He participated in the Battle of Long Island, where he was injured and taken to a hospital. Once released from the hospital, he returned to his regiment at White Plains, where he was discharged because his five month enlistment had expired. In the winter of 1777, he was drafted back into the army. He served a short period of time and was drafted again in August 1778 for a month. In March 1779, he was drafted once again for a month. He was discharged and drafted twice again for a month each time. During each period of service, he participated in battles or minor skirmishes.

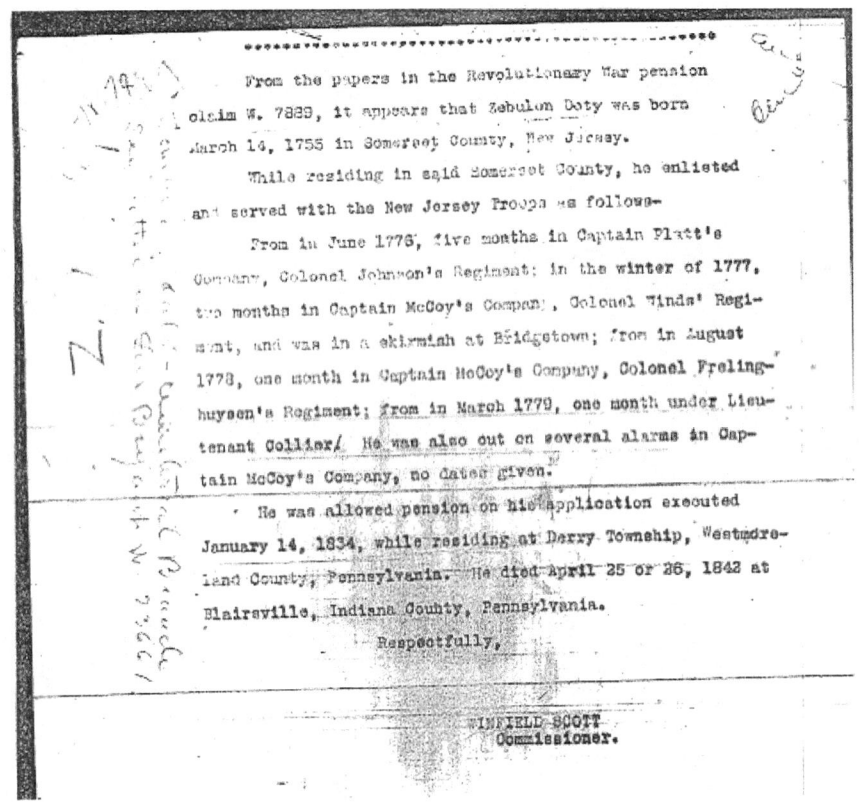

Letter from General Winfield Scott granting
Zebulon Doty Revolutionary War pension

After the war, he moved his family to Derry, Westmoreland County, Pennsylvania near Blairsville, Pennsylvania. One of his nine children was Israel, born in 1785 before the family moved to Pennsylvania. After

Sarah's death, Zebulon married Rachel Colyer and later he married a widow, Jane McWhiston. Zebulon died in Westmorland County in 1842.

Grave of Zebulon Doty, Old Salem Church and Cemetery, Derry, Pennsylvania

Israel married Mary Barnett in 1809 and lived in Westmoreland County, Pennsylvania before moving to Stark County, Ohio where he died in 1856. Israel and Mary had eleven children, one of whom was Zebulon. Zebulon was born in 1815 in Westmoreland County, Pennsylvania and married Frances Elliott in 1835. The westward movement continued from Pennsylvania to Ohio and then to Indiana.

CHAPTER 14 — PLYMOUTH

One of the children of Zebulon and Francs was John Wesley who was born in Elkhart, Indiana in 1860. In 1881, John married Ida (Elizabeth) Garver, also of Elkhart, Indiana. Ida's parent, Lewis and Sarah Garver may have moved from Ohio to Indiana, since Zebulon and Francs also moved from Ohio to Indiana about the same time.

John and Ida Doty moved to the small village of Good Hart, Michigan on the northern shore of Lake Michigan in the early 1890s. John and Ida had six children, one of whom was Ruby Dawn. Ruby was born in Good Hart in 1894 and married Arthur Herrick of the nearby town of Harbor Springs, Michigan in 1914. It took nine generations, but the marriage of Arthur and Ruby merged the Herricks and the Dotys, the Puritans and the Pilgrims, Salem and Plymouth.

Family of John Wesley and Ida Doty with Ruby who is center right, 1904

MICHAEL J. HERRICK

Tree IV : Mayflower Descendants

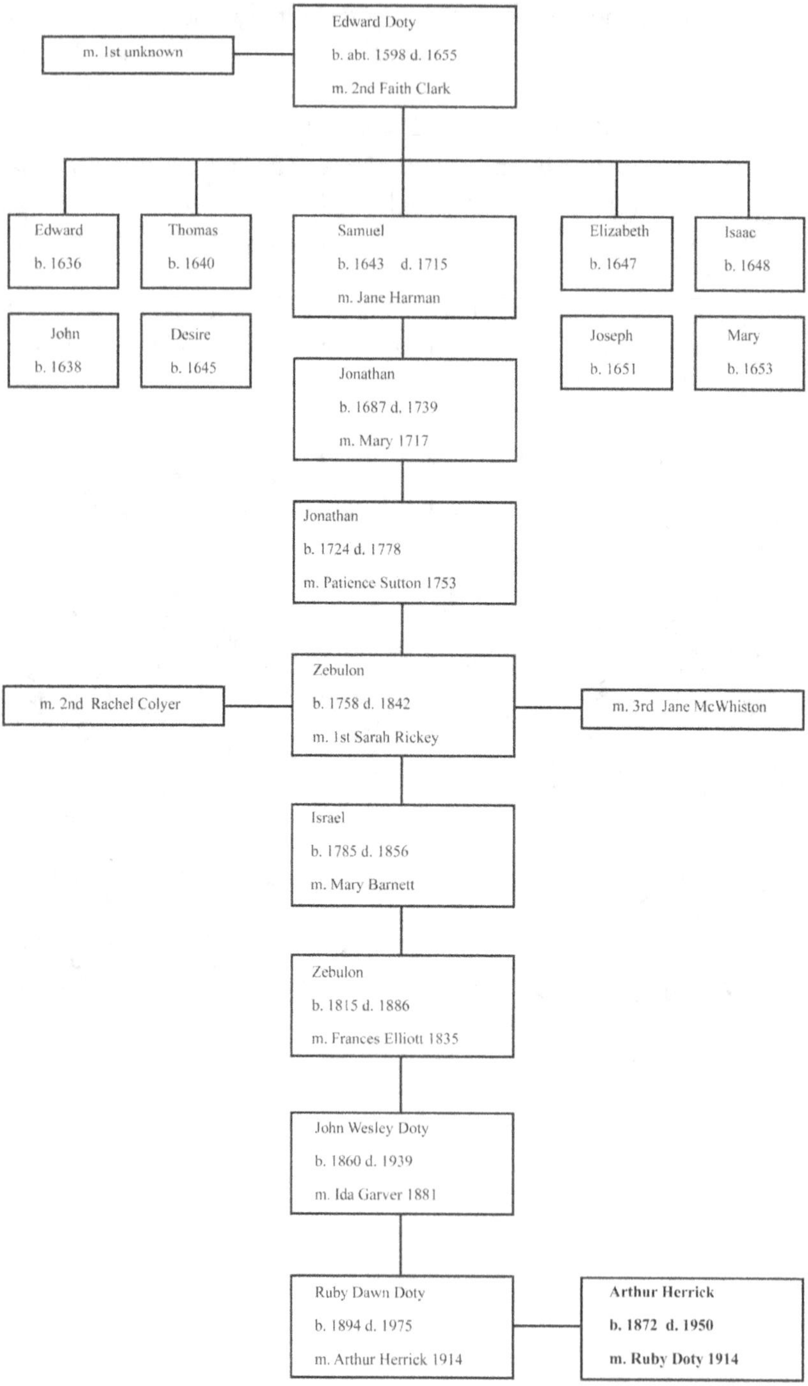

- **Edward Doty** b. abt. 1598 d. 1655
  - m. 1st unknown
  - m. 2nd Faith Clark
  - Children:
    - Edward b. 1636
    - John b. 1638
    - Thomas b. 1640
    - Desire b. 1645
    - **Samuel** b. 1643 d. 1715, m. Jane Harman
    - Elizabeth b. 1647
    - Isaac b. 1648
    - Joseph b. 1651
    - Mary b. 1653
- **Jonathan** b. 1687 d. 1739, m. Mary 1717
- **Jonathan** b. 1724 d. 1778, m. Patience Sutton 1753
- **Zebulon** b. 1758 d. 1842
  - m. 1st Sarah Rickey
  - m. 2nd Rachel Colyer
  - m. 3rd Jane McWhiston
- **Israel** b. 1785 d. 1856, m. Mary Barnett
- **Zebulon** b. 1815 d. 1886, m. Frances Elliott 1835
- **John Wesley Doty** b. 1860 d. 1939, m. Ida Garver 1881
- **Ruby Dawn Doty** b. 1894 d. 1975, m. Arthur Herrick 1914
- **Arthur Herrick** b. 1872 d. 1950, m. Ruby Doty 1914

Chapter 15

Joseph Sr.

Joseph Herrick, unlike his siblings, couldn't seem to stay on the farm. He led a very active and varied life, from farming to volunteer military, to government, travel, and ultimately involvement in the Salem witchcraft trials. Joseph was the fifth child of Henry and Editha, if you include Thomas from Henry's first marriage in England. He was baptized on August 6, 1645 in Salem, presumably at the First Church of Salem where his father was a charter member.

In 1665, at the age of 20, he married Sarah Leach, the daughter of Richard Leach, a prominent man in Salem. Joseph and Sarah settled on a large farm at Cherry Hill just north of Beverly, which was a track of land given to Joseph by his father Henry. Life was good for them, their farm was prosperous, and they began their family. Joseph and Sarah had three boys and one girl in the course of seven years. Then tragedy struck. Not long after their fourth child was born, Sarah died. The year was 1674.

It is not known who took care of the young children, but within a year of Sarah's death, Joseph joined the Massachusetts Bay Colony regiment to fight in King Phillip's War. He was 30 years old.

King Philip, chief of the Wampanoag Indians, took on an English name and title. He lived near what is now Bristol, Rhode Island and united the neighboring tribes to exterminate the English colonists. King Philip led raids killing settlers and burning their homes.

A significant battle at the start of that war was the Narragansett fight, known as the Great Swamp Fight, on December 19, 1675 in what is now South Kingstown, Rhode Island. That battle was significant in that the neutral Narragansett Indians were essentially massacred by the colonists and thus forced the Narragansetts against the colonists and join the Indians lead by King Phillip. The colonists from the Massachusetts Boy Colony and the Plymouth Colony joined forces in an army of

Puritans[53]. Joseph Herrick, a recent widower, participated in that battle under the command of Major Samuel Appleton, who led the militia from Salem and Beverly. These militia in which Joseph fought captured a large Indian fort after which many raids and skirmishes followed. In all, about 600 colonists were killed.

King Phillip's war continued until 1678. It is clear, however, that Joseph left the army to return back to Salem before the end of the war. In 1677 at the age of 32, he married his second wife Mary Endicott.[54] Joseph and Mary continued to live at Cherry Hill and had nine children together. Again, life was good, the farm was prosperous, and Joseph became more politically active. At some time during their 33 year marriage, Joseph acquired the title of Governor. The 'Governor' title came from his work in the Caribbean. Carrying that title, Joseph traveled back to England on family business. It is not clear where in England he went or who he saw, but it is likely that the purpose was related to his business dealings in the Caribbean Islands of Nevis and/or Barbados. Back home during this time he was a representative to the General Court of Beverly for a four-year period.

However, it appears that Joseph was the restless type. Joseph Herrick received a bounty for a 1690 expedition to Canada as part of King William's War[55], which raged from 1689 to1697. King William's War erupted because the French and Indians inhabited lands at the "back door" of the colonies all along the sea coast. Consequently, these inland settlements were subjected to attacks via rivers and streams that allowed the French and Indians to use guerilla tactics to attack farms. Salem, along with Marblehead and Boston, were the main ports at the time. The colonists along the sea coast lived in constant fear of attack, which

---

53 Rev. Nicholas Noyes served as chaplain to the Connecticut troops during the Great Swamp fight in King Phillips War and later as the Pastor at the First Church of Salem where he officiated at the final hangings of those accused of witchcraft. When Noyes asked Sarah Good for a confession, Good's last words to Noyes were, " You are a liar. I am no more a witch than you are a wizard." Joseph Herrick would have known him in both roles.

54 There has been confusion about who Joseph Herrick's second wife was. Some records show his wife as Mary Dodge, because church records were unclear about which Joseph Herrick and which Mary Dodge were getting married. It was finally confirmed through more thorough research that Joseph Herrick married Mary Endicott in 1677.

55 Also known as Sir William Phips War since William Phips was the British commander that led New England in the war.

CHAPTER 15 —JOSEPH SR.

necessitated the vigilance of militia training and preparation. The purpose of the expedition to Canada in 1689-90 was to take the cities of Quebec and Montreal, occupied by the French. One of the ventures of this expedition was conducted in 1690 using the militia from Beverly under the command of Captain William Rayment. Joseph Herrick was part of that invasion force. Shortly after this invasion, an event occurred that forever changed the history and reputation of Salem.

In 1692, a witchcraft hysteria started in Salem Village (now Danvers) and ultimately resulted in accusations, trials, sentencing, and the execution of 14 women and 6 men. Five others died in prison awaiting execution. Joseph Herrick, ever the righteous Puritan and civic minded citizen, was the constable at Salem Village.[56] His job as constable was to arrest those breaking the law, and witchcraft was certainly illegal in Puritan New England.

Witchcraft was a serious phenomenon in England and America. The Puritans in particular believed that the devil was real and could operate in the minds and bodies of people. When evidence of evil or the devil was perceived in another, it was easy to conclude that the individual was possessed by the devil and could therefore afflict others with evil and no good. The solution was often that the devil had to be excised from the body and too often that resulted in killing the person to kill the devil in the person. Such was the hysteria in 1692 Salem.

The witchcraft hysteria lasted 15 months and started when unexplained behavior was experienced by two young girls in Salem Village. In February 1692, Betty Parris age 9, and her cousin Abigail Williams, age 11, the daughter and niece, respectively, of Reverend Samuel Parris, began to have fits described as "beyond the power of epileptic fits or natural disease to effect". The girls screamed, threw things about the room, uttered strange sounds, crawled under furniture, and contorted themselves into peculiar positions, according to the eyewitness account of Rev. Deodat Larson, a former minister in Salem Village.

---

56 Joseph Herrick, the Constable at Salem Village, is not to be confused with George Herrick, the Assistant Sheriff or Marshall of Essex County during the Salem witchcraft trials. As cited in HGR I, George Herrick, although a possible relative of Henry Herrick but no known direct relationship to Henry, came to Massachusetts in 1658.

The first three people accused and arrested for allegedly afflicting Betty Parris, Abigail Williams, 12-year-old Ann Putnam Jr., and Elizabeth Hubbard were Sarah Good, Sarah Osborne and Tibuta Good, who was a homeless beggar known to seek food and shelter from neighbors.

Court records during the trials show that Zachariah Herrick, Joseph's brother, refused to help Sarah Good. Sarah was accused of witchcraft because of her appalling reputation. At her trial, she was accused of rejecting Puritan ideals of self-control and discipline when she chose to torment and "scorn [children] instead of leading them towards the path of salvation". Sarah Osborne rarely attended church meetings. She was accused of witchcraft because the Puritans believed that Osborne had her own self-interests in mind following her remarriage to an indentured servant. The citizens of the town disapproved of her trying to control her son's inheritance from her previous marriage. Interestingly, Zachariah's son, Henry, served as a jurist during the trials.

Tituba, an Indian slave, likely became a target because of her ethnic differences from most of the other villagers. She was accused of attracting girls like Abigail Williams and Betty Perris with stories of witchcraft. Some of these involved tales about sexual encounters with demons, swaying the minds of men, and fortune-telling. These were said to stimulate the imaginations of girls and made Tituba an obvious target of accusations. Each of these women was a kind of outcast and exhibited many of the character traits typical of the "usual suspects" for witchcraft accusations. They were left to defend themselves. Brought before the local magistrates on the complaint of witchcraft, they were interrogated for several days, starting on March 1, 1692, then sent to jail.

In March, others were accused of witchcraft: Martha Corey, a child Dorothy Good and Rebecca Nurse in Salem Village, and Rachael Clinton in nearby Ipswich. Martha Corey had expressed skepticism about the credibility of the girls' accusations and thus drew attention. The charges against her and Rebecca Nurse deeply troubled the community because Martha Corey was a full covenanted member of the Church in Salem Village, as was Rebecca Nurse in the Church in Salem. If such upstanding people could be witches, the townspeople thought, then anybody could be a witch. Church membership was no protection from accusation. Dorothy Good, the daughter of Sarah Good was only four years old, but not exempted from questioning by the magistrates. Her answers were construed as a confession that implicated her mother.

CHAPTER 15 —JOSEPH SR.

As the Constable at Salem Village, Joseph was doing his civic duty by arresting those accused of witchcraft and as such was most certainly under the influence of the witchcraft delusion himself. But records show that he soon thought otherwise and that "his strong and enlightened mind led him out of it." In fact, even as the town Constable, he was one of the petitioners in behalf of an accused person. This was highly dangerous at the time. As the hysteria continued, "he was a leader in the party that rose against the fanaticism and vindicated the character of its victims." However, he did issue warrants and depositions. Below is the deposition of Joseph Herrick accusing Sarah Good of witchcraft.

> Joseph Herrick, Sr. vs. Sarah Good
> The Deposition of Joseph Herrick sen'r who testifieth and saith that on the first day of March 1691/2 I being the Constable for Salem, there was delivered to me by warrant ffrom the Worshipful Jno Hathorne and Jonathan Corwin Esqrs. Sarah Good for me to cery to their majesties Goal at Ipswich and that night I sett a guard to watch her at my own house, namely Samu'l Braybrook Michaell dunell Jonathan Baker and the affore named persons, Informed me in the morning that that night Sarah Good was gon for some time from them both bare foot and bare legde, and I was also Informed that that night Elizabeth Habbard one of the afflicted parsons Complained that Sarah Good came and afflicted her being foot and bare legded, and Samuell Sibley that one of those attending of Eliza Hubbard Strock Sarah Good on the arme as Elizabeth Hubbard said, and Mary Herrick the wife of the abovesaid Joseph testifieth that on the 2th March 1691/2 in the morning I took notis of Sarah Good and one of her Armes was bloody from a little below the Elbow to the wrist, and I also took notis of her Armes on the night before, and there was no sign of blood on them.
> Joseph Herrick sen'r and Mary Herrick appearid before us the Jury for Inquest, and did on oath which they had taken owne this their evidence to be the truth this 28 of June 1692.
> Sworn in Court

Original hand written deposition of Joseph Herrick reporting behavior of Sarah Good used to declare her a witch in 1692

Below is the warrant for the arrest of Tituba and Sarah Osborne who were apprehended and arrested by Joseph Herrick.

Warrant vs. Tituba and Sarah Osborne
Salem febr' the 29'th day, 1691/2

Whereas m'rs Joseph Hutcheson Thomas Putnam Edward Putnam and Thomas Preston Yeomen of Salem Village, in the County of Essex. personally appeared before us, And made Complaint on behalfe of theire Majesties against Sarah Osburne the wife of Alexa' Osburne of Salem Village afores'd, and Tituba an Indian Woman servant, of mr. Sam'l Parris of s'd place also; for Suspition of Witchcraft, by them Committed and thereby much injury don to Elizabeth Parris Abigail Williams

CHAPTER 15 —JOSEPH SR.

Anna Putnam and Elizabeth Hubert all of Salem Village afores'd Sundry times with in this two moneths and Lately also done, at s'd Salem Village Contrary to the peace and Laws of our Sov'r Lord & Lady Wm & Mary of England &c King & Queene

You are there for in theire Maj'ts names hereby required to apprehend and forthwith or as soon as may be bring before us the aboves'd Sarah Osburne, and Tituba Indian, at the house of Lt. Nath'l Ingersalls in s'd place. and if it may be by to Morrow aboute ten of the Clock in the morning then and there to be Examined Relateing to the aboves'd premises --. You are likewise required to bring at the same tyme Eliz. Parris Abigale Williams Anna Putnam and Eliz Hubert or any other person or persons that can give Evidence in the Abodes' Case. and hereof you are not to faile according to this warrant I have apprehended the parsons with in mentioned and have brought them accordingly and have mad diligent search for Images and such like but can find non Salem village this 1. March 1691/92

Dated Salem febr' 29 1691/2
* John Hathorne
* Jonathan. Corwin}Assis'ts
To Constable Joseph Herrick Const' in Salem

The Salem Witchcraft Trials finally came to an end when Sarah Noyes Hale, wife of John Hale the Puritan Pastor at Beverly, was accused of witchcraft. Rev. Hale was a supporter of the witchcraft trials and the court decisions until his wife was accused in November 1692. She along with the ghost of executed Mary Eastey were accused of afflicting her accuser. The accuser was none other than Mary Herrick, the 17 year old daughter of John Herrick, and granddaughter of our Henry Herrick and niece of Joseph Herrick. This accusation is considered to be the one accusation that turned public opinion to end the prosecutions and spurred Rev. Hale to reconsider his support of the trials. Below is the deposition given by Mary Herrick of her accusal of witchcraft of Mrs. Hale.

An Account Received from the mouth of Mary Herrick, aged about 17 yeares having been Afflicted the Devill or some of his instruments, about 2 month, [April]. She saith she had oft been

Afflicted and that the shape of Mrs. Hayle had been represented to her, One amongst others, but she knew not what hand Afflicted her then, but on the 5th of the 9th, [November 5th], She Appeared again with the Ghost of Gooddee Easty, & that then Mrs. Hayle did sorely Afflict her by pinching, pricking & Choaking her. On the 12th of the 9th, [November 12th], she Came again & Gooddee Easty with her & then Mrs. Hayle did Afflict her as formerly. Sd Easty made as if she would speake but did not, but on the same night they Came again & Mrs. Hayle did sorely Afflict her and asked her if she thought she was a Witch. The Girl answered no, You be the Devill. Then said Easty sd & speake, She Came to tell her She had been put to Death wrongfully & was Innocent of Witchcraft, she Came to Vindicate her Cause & she cried Vengeance, Vengeance, & bid her to reveal this to Mr.. Hayle & Gerish, & then she would rise no more, nor should Mrs., Hayle Afflict her any more. Memorand: yt Just before sd Easty was Executed, She appeared to sd Girl, and said I am going upon the Ladder to be hanged for a Witch, but I am innocent, & before a 12 month be past you shall believe it. Sd Girl sd she speake not of this before because she believed she was Guilty, Till Mrs. Hayle appeared to her and Afflicted her, but now she believeth it is all a Delusion of the Devil.

This before Mr. Hayle &
Gerish, 14th of the 9th 1692.
[November 14, 1692].

At the end of the trials, Joseph supported his nephew, Henry Herrick (son of Zachariah), when as a jurist Henry signed a written apology acknowledging the errors and wrongdoing that characterized the witchcraft trials.[57] That apology is below:

---

57 Guilt over the wrongdoings of the trials was pervasive. In 1752 Salem Village was renamed Danvers to distance themselves from the witchcraft trials. Also, the famous author Nathaniel Hawthorne, who grew up in Salem, was so embarrassed by the role his grandfather played in the trials as the presiding judge that he added an 'e' at the end of his name to distance himself.

CHAPTER 15 —JOSEPH SR.

Some that had been of several juries have given forth a paper, signed with our own hands in these words. We whose names are underwritten, being in the year 1692 called to serve as jurors in court in Salem, on trial of many who were by some suspected guilty of doing acts of witchcraft upon the bodies of sundry persons.

We confess that we ourselves were not capable to understand, nor able to withstand the mysterious delusions of the powers of darkness and prince of the air, but were for want of knowledge in ourselves and better information from others, prevailed with to take up with such evidence against the accused as on further consideration and better information, we justly fear was insufficient for the touching the lives of any, Deuteronomy 17.6, whereby we fear we have been instrumental with others, though ignorantly and unwittingly, to bring upon ourselves and this people of the Lord, the guilt of innocent blood, which sin the Lord saith in Scripture, he would not pardon, 2 Kings 24.4, that is we suppose in regard of His temporal judgments. We do, therefore, hereby signify to all in general (and to the surviving sufferers in especial) our deep sense of and sorrow for our errors in acting on such evidence to the condemning of any person.

And do hereby declare that we justly fear that we were sadly deluded and mistaken, for which we are much disquieted and distressed in our minds, and do therefore humbly beg forgiveness, first of God for Christ's sake for this our error. And pray that God would not impute the guilt of it to ourselves nor others. And we also pray that we may be considered candidly and aright by the living sufferers as being then under the power of a strong and general delusion, utterly unacquainted with and not experienced in matters of that nature.

We do heartily ask forgiveness of you all, whom we have justly offended and do declare, according to our present minds, we would none of us do such things again on such grounds for the whole world, praying you to accept of this in way of satisfaction for our offense, and that you would bless the inheritance of the Lord that He may be entreated for the land.

Foreman, Thomas Fisk Thomas Perly, Senior
William Fiske John Peabody
John Batcheler Thomas Perkins
Thomas Fisk, Junior Samuel Sather
John Dane Andrew Elliott
Joseph Evelith Henry Herrick, Senior

In 1694, only two years after the Salem witchcraft trials, Joseph traveled to England again. It is not clear why he made the voyage, who he saw in England, or the nature of his business there. But in most likelihood, his trip to England was business. About the same time, he is recorded to be in the West Indies, most likely Barbados or Nevis, in a government or business capacity such as a command of a military unit of established colony there or trade related business. As mentioned before, he carried the title of Governor during his foreign travels at this time. It makes perfect sense that Joseph and others from Salem would travel to England and to the British West Indies, since Salem was a major commercial shipping port and much of the trading in those days was in the West Indies. Since he was only 49 years old at the time, Joseph still had a wife and large young family. Therefore, it is not clear why he would leave is family and his large farm to pursue interests overseas. Then about 10 years after his overseas business, personal sadness struck again.

In September, 1706, after 33 years of marriage to his second wife, Mary Endicott died. By this time Joseph Herrick and his first and second wives had raised 14 children, the youngest was 16 or 17 by time of Mary's death. Within a few months of her death, Joseph married a third time at the ripe old age of 61. He and his third wife, Mary Folson, were married in January, 1707. Mary Folsom was the daughter of John Folsom and the widow of Caption George March.

During the 10 years of his marriage to Mary Folsom, Joseph continued to be active on his farm, in the community and in his church. In 1713, he was one of the founders of the Second Church of Beverly and was appointed to be on the committee to draw up the plans for the church construction. The Second Church of Beverly is north of town and

CHAPTER 15 —JOSEPH SR.

located near his Cherry Hill farm. Joseph Herrick lived another 5 years after the founding of the church and died in 1717 or 1718 (depending on which calendar was being used) at the age of 72.[58] Mary Folsom survived him and lived another 8 or 9 years after Joseph died.

The Will of Joseph Herrick was proved on February 10, 1717 and is documented below:

Mr. Joseph Herrick
Salem/Beverly, MA
Gentleman
.... Massachusetts Archives
February 10, 1717 Will Proved

In the Name of God, Amen. I Joseph Herrick of Salem in the County of Essex, in the province of Massachusetts Bay in New England, being aged and not knowing how soon my great Change may come, Doe make my Last Will and Testament in forme and manner following.
Impremis: I give up my Immortall Soul to God when he shall please to Call for It, and my Body to Decent burial hoping for a glorius resurrection This . . . of Jesus Christ my Savior and Redeemer- and as for my worldly estate to hath God blessed me . . . dispose of as followeth-
_ I give to my Sons Joseph & John that land I had at Birch Plains which now I now give possession of equally between them; and also land I had of Arthur Leach (Crouch) of Chalmsford to be equally divided between them always provided if they take care of it and Arthur Crouch and his wife foe not suffer for . . . (same? Coain? Waim?)) during their lives.
Item: I also give to my son Joseph two acres approximately (?) in . . . (Harkes? Parker?) meadow. Also a piece of land which he had fenced in which was my brother Thomas Herrick's land only he is to draw back his fence on pole at the north end or

---

58 Joseph Herrick's gravesite with a well preserved a headstone and footstone is in the North Beverly Ancient Cemetery near the Second Church of Beverly.

two rods at south end of it and to allow entry my heirs to carte hay over it as they may have occasion – and my son Joseph is to maintain the division fence between him and my heirs forever.

Item: I give to my son, John one acre of meadow at Birch's (Burkes?) Meadow on the easterly side of the whole length joining to John Herrick (?) his cousin- and my Negro Woman Havia (?) after my wife's decease.

Item: I give to my son Martin that farm where he dwell which I bought of Capt. Rhins (?). I also give him the remainder of the time in my man William Parde (Parle?)

Item: I give to my son Rufus all my home and housing (?) and my land at Larry's (?) farme and all the remainder of my meadow at Sounders (?) Meadow and my wood lott of the Wanha (?) pine swamp.

Item: I give to Mary my beloved wife the aforesaid room in my house the eastward lower room with convenient (?) . . . (?) room and the service of my Negro woman as long as she shall be alive and well at my house and I give herefore to my son Rufus & shall keep her winter and summer, and shall find a house for my wife for her life as thee may be occasion to find her firewood brought to the door, and to find my wife five bushhells of corn a year, and my wife shall have the barn (?) to keep a swine att during winter and use (?) pastures in the summer. _ and my Son Rufus shall find my wife one barrel of sugar a year and to allow her . . . (?) our apple for her use (?) winter or summer, all this to continue so long as my wife shall live and dwell at my house and if she bee caused to remove in lieu of this my son Rufus shall pay my wife forty shillings per year during her life in or as money.

Item: I give to my son Rufus all my personal estate within doors and without and my will is that my son Rufus pay to my daughter Tryphosa Leach ten pounds in or as money. Also, to pay my daughter Tryphonia Traske ten pounds in or as money and also pay my daughter Elizabeth Herrick fifty pounds and also to pay my daughter Edith Porter ten pounds. This my son Rufus shall pay to my . . . (several ?) daughters in household goods as far as it will goe, the rest to be paid in of her pay (?), only my daughter Elizabeth shall have the bed and furniture which stands in the east chamber for part of her fifty pounds,

those several payments to be made within three years of my death.
Item: I give five pounds a piece to my two grand daughters . . . (?) of my daughter Sarah Moulton to be paid them by my son Rufus when they are the age of eighteen years.
Item: I give my common rights to my son William Leach and to my son Benj'm Traske to be equally divided between them, and I give my common rights in Salem to my son Rufus . . . (?) to be understood if without (?) my several children, I give to them and to their heirs and assignees forever.
I so . . . (?) and appoint my son Rufus Herrick the sole executor of this my will.
I also testify (give testimony) that this is my will and testament. I have herewith put my hand and seal this earthly(?) second Day of January, 1717/18.
Signed, sealed and Declared Joseph Herrick Mark
In presence of us
Joseph Herrick
Edward Raymond
Jon'a Putnam
Ex'sor in Ipswich, February 10, 1717.

Before Joseph Herrick, Capt., Edward Raymond and Capt. Jon'a Putnam all personally appeared and made the oath that they were (present?) and saw Mr. Joseph . . . (?) sign and seal and heard him publish and declare the above written instrument to be his last will and testament and when he did he was of good understanding and disposition of mind – and that they all put to said hands as witnesses in his service.

Sworn and attested
Dan Rogers, Regr.
Upon which this will be proved, approved and allowed. The Executor within named approved and accepted the . . . . (task?) and . . . (?) bond to pay all debts and . . . .(?) according to will.
Attest
Dan Rogers, Regr.

It is interesting to note that Joseph's Will indicates that he was a slave owner. He gave one "negro woman" to his son John after his wife's death, and another woman slave to his wife, Mary, for her service for the rest of her life.

The grave and slate headstone and footstone for Joseph Herrick still stands in the North Beverly Ancient Cemetery, across the street from the Second Congregational Church, which he founded; and not far from his Cherry Hill farm. Below is current picture of the headstone and wording on the headstone. By walking through the cemetery and viewing the headstone, one can easily imagine the funeral. His children, including Joseph Jr., were undoubtedly present and his wife Mary would have been there. One can hear them speak in English that is hard to decipher today. Words of praise for his achievements were said, and proclamations of God's will for life eternal, in a Puritan fashion, were surely said on that day.

View of North Beverly Ancient Cemetery in Beverly

CHAPTER 15 — JOSEPH SR.

HERE LYES Y^e BODY
OF Mr IOSEPH HERRIC^k
WHO DIED FEB^R
y^e 4th IN Y^e 73 YEAR
OF HIS AGE 1717

Head stone and inscription of Joseph Herrick in
North Beverly Ancient Cemetery

Chapter 16
Joseph Herrick Jr., Benjamin Herrick

Joseph Herrick Jr., oldest son of Joseph Herrick Sr. and his first wife Sarah, was born in 1667 at Joseph's and Sarah's Cherry Hill farm northwest of Beverly. He was only 7 years old when his mother, Sarah, died and 10 years old when his father remarried. Joseph Sr. and his second wife, Mary Endicott, had nine children, so Joseph Jr. added half brothers and sisters to his family. When he became an adult, Joseph Jr. settled on a farm in Beverly, given to him by his father. He did not stay there long, since he moved to Marblehead where he kept a tavern for a short while, and then moved to Topsfield where he spent the majority of adult life. Joseph Jr. was only 3 years old when his grandfather, Henry Herrick, died. Given the rich details of Henry's life, as no doubt told to him by his father, Joseph Jr. grew up with pride and perhaps in awe in learning what Henry accomplished by risking it all in coming to New England. Coupled with his own father's adventures in war, business, and civic responsibilities, Joseph Jr. must have felt a deep ambition to succeed and contribute.

Joseph married Elizabeth Woodbury of Beverly before 1696 so it is probable that they were married prior to settling in Topsfield. By the time the Salem Witchcraft Trials started in 1692, Joseph Jr. was 25 years old and probably had already settled in Topsfield, as there are no records of his involvement in the trials. Joseph and Elizabeth had five children from 1696 to 1709, all of them born in Wenham. The boundary line between Topsfield and Wenham was close to their property and the line may have been unclear, resulting in their residence recorded in one town and their children's birth in another. Both Joseph Jr. and Elizabeth died in Topsfield – she on September 30, 1748 and he on September 11, 1749.

There are no records that suggest that Joseph Jr. participated in any colonial wars. However, he did benefit from them. As previously mentioned, his father received a bounty or pension for his participation in

King Phillips War and in the Sir Williams Phips expedition to Canada. The History of Topsfield indicates that in 1728 men from Topsfield received land for their war bounty in a town called No. III Souhegan West. That town is now Amherst, New Hampshire. Since Joseph died in 1717, ten years before the bounty was granted, the land was awarded to his heir from Topsfield, who was Joseph Herrick Jr. There is a record of Joseph Jr. claiming the land in Amherst, but there is no record of what Joseph Jr. did with that land.

Despite no apparent war record of his own, it appears that Joseph Herrick Jr. was active in many civic duties in Topsfield. He was often chosen as moderator at meetings, selected as trail jurist, and voted to serve for a number of terms as a Selectman (councilman). In addition he served on various committees for such duties as to survey town boundaries and roads, negotiate annexation of small communities, and choosing a school master. The Town Records of Topsfield indicate that Joseph was an active and respected member of the community. Below is a sample of the meeting notes from the Topsfield town records.

> At a Meeting of the Selectmen of Wenham Aprill 25 1702 they then apointed that our Town bounds between our Town& Topsfield be perambulated & renewed one the 18th day may next Insuing at ten of y clok in fore- noon if it be fair wether but if it be fowle wether then one next fairc day at the Same hour of the day and to meet at the west end of Wenham Causway and Joseph Herrick and Theophelos Rix and Samuel ffiske or any two of them are appointed to meet with such of Topsfield as shall be sent to performe said work order of ye Selectmen Tho fTiske Clark Copia vera atest Sam Stanley Town Clark for Topsfield

> We whose names are under writen being appointed to meet with such of Topsfield as were appointed for to renew bounds betwixt each Town and have renewed the bounds as have bin Renewed according to agreement the 18th of May 1705
> Isaac Peabody Samuel Fiske
> Elisha Perkins Joseph Herrick
> Thomas Town Theophelous Rix

Chapter 16 — Joseph Herrick Jr., Benjamin Herrick

To Mr Joseph Herrick Mr David Commings and Benjamin Towne
Gentlemen you are hereby ordered & fully Impowered to Perambulate & Renew Bounds between the Towns of Salem & Topsfield : And meet with Cap Johathan Putnam Mr Sam Porter Mr John Wolcott and Mr Benj Browne who are appointed by Salem selectmen for service : and you are to meet them at Mr Sam" Porters Dwelling in Salem on Aprill ye 27th Instant at Ten in y Morning:
Dated Topsfield Aprill: 13-1730

April 27-1730 We underwritten by appointment have Met and Renewed the Bounds Mentioned first at Topsfield Line beginning at a white oak Tree Market S W T with a heap of stones Round it Near Wenham Causway and so west south westward unto a black oak Tree & stump with stones between; The Tree mark S T then on to a heap of stones at the Corner of Thomas Dwinels Pasture Near Smiths Hill so called : & so on to a heap of stones Near Nickolses Brook which Seperates Middleton

Jonathan Putnam Sen Joseph Herrick Jqj, Samuel Porter, Benj Towne John Wolcott David Commings Topsfield jnj- Browne Salem A True Copy of order & Return of Perambulation:
Attest Jacob Peabody Town Clerk

To Mr Joseph Herrick Mr David Commings and Benjamin
Towne Gentlemen you are Hereby Impowered to Perambulate & settle bounds Between the Towns of Topsfield & Middleton with such as the selection of Middleton shall appoint and to meet them at house of Mr Nath" Porters in Topsfield on April 2 Instant at one of y Clock afternoon for service April 27 1730

We underwritten by Appointment Met & settled & Renewed the Bounds between Topsfield and Middleton: first begining at Nickolses Brook where Salem & Topsfield Line youst to Crose sd Brook and then as sd Brook Runs and the Northerly branch to the River Called Ipswich River Joseph Herrick Topsfield

John Burton) Middleton David Comniings > Benjamin Knight Benf Towne Committe Ebenezer Nichols) Committe A True Copy of Settlement & Perambulation withMiddleton.
Attest Jacob Peabody Town Clerk

In y year 1729 Mr Joseph Bordman Cap Joseph Gould & Mr Joseph Herrick are Chosen to Discourse with Mr Jacob Towne Refering to the Road Lately Laid out by the Townses house: and when they have heard sd Townses Terms for said Roadand for the Damage he has sustained thereby: sd Committe are to make Report thereof to the Town ; for further Considertion

At A Legal Town Meeting in Topsfield Sep 22nd 1730 Mr Joseph Herrick & Mr Benj Towne are Chosen to serve on the Jury of Tryals at the next Inferiour Court to be holden at Newbery Lieu* Zacheus Gould, Cap John Howlett, & mr Joseph Herrick Mr Benjamin Towne, & Mr Daniel Clark; are Chose a Committee, to Treet with mr Jacob Towne Concerning the way. Lately Laid out between said Townes & Mr Jacob Redingtons. And Said Committe are hereby fully Impowered to agree with said Townes for the s way & damages According to their best Judgment & discretion ; if they think it Convenient: But if sd Committe do not agree with y said mr Jacob Towne, about sd way, & damage he saith he sustains thereby: Then Mr Joseph Herrick, & Mr Benjamin Towne, are Chosen Agents for y Town ; To Implead said Towne and give in y Reasons at y Next Inferior Court to be holden at Newbery why a Jury should not Come to View y said way

At A Legal Town meeting In Topsfield March year 1730-1
Cap* John Howlett Joseph Herrick, John Wildes, Benjamin Towne, & Jacob Peabody are Chosen Selectmen for the year Ensuing Greeting. In his Majesties Name you are hereby Required to Notify & warn all the Freeholders; & other Inhabitants on y North side of River, in Topsfield; Such as are Quallified as y Law directs for Voting: To meet at Meeting house in said Town on Friday fourteenth day of May Currant,

CHAPTER 16 —JOSEPH HERRICK JR., BENJAMIN HERRICK

at three of the Clock in the after noon first To Chuse a Representative.

2 To see if the Town will give order to y Committe that is to Repair the Meeting house; to Draw Money out of y Town Treasurey for said Service.

3 To see if y Town will Chuse a Committe to Petition to the General Court or use any other Lawfull Means to have a fish Corse Cleared up Ipswich River.

4 To allow Bills of Charge 5 To see what the Town will doe with the intrest of their Loan Money

6 To see if the Town will Chuse a Committe to settle bounds with Boxford or doe anything about said Line that y Town shall then think best And Make Return of your doings herein: unto one or more of y Selectmen of said Town one hour at Least before said time of Meeting: as you will Answer the Contrary at y Perrill of y Law John Hewlett

Date Topsfield May 13th 1731
Joseph Herrick John Wildes Benj Towne Jacob Peabody
Selectmen of Topsfield

At A Legal Town Meeting in Topsfield December 14th 1733
Mr Daniel Clark, & Mr Joseph Herrick are Chosen a Committe to Reckon with the Town Treasurer; and mr William Reddington y Clark of the present selectmen is to Assist them in the said service voted And said Committe are to make Report of their doings in that affair: at the annual Town Meeting in March Next

At A Legal Town Meeting in Topsfield March 5th 1733-4
Mr Joseph Herrick Mr Nath Capen & Mr Joseph Peabody are Chosen Surveyers of Highways for the year Ensuing

At a Legal Town meeting in Topsfield March 4 1734-5
Cap Joseph Gould Mr Nathaniel borniau & Mr Joseph Herrick was chosen a committe to supply the Town with a School master for the year Ensuing

At A Legal Town Meeting in Topsfield November the 12: 1734 The Town Allowed one potmd to Mr Joseph Herrick for two Tun of Timber to mend the high ways this year

At a Legal Town meeting in Topsfield March 4th 1734-5
Ens Joseph Dorman philip Town & Mr Joseph Herrick were chosen surveyors of highways sworn Daniel Redington

Robert Perkins & George Bixby were chosen ffence viewers for the year ensuing May 14 1735 the select men approbated Mr William Howlett Schoolmaster for the year Ensuing according as he hath agreed with Capt Joseph Gould m'" Joseph Herrick & Quar Borman a Committie chosen for the End

At a Lawfull Town meeting in Topsfield March 24 1735 or 6
Joseph Herrick & Wm Rogers are chosen to serve on the Jury of Trials

At a Lawful Town meeting in Topsfield March 1st 1736-7
Mr Joseph Herrick, Dea Ivory Hovey & Mr Nath Averill are Chosen a committee to see if our Neghbours in Ipswich farms will agree to the vote of the Town respecting their being laid to us: if they consent thereto then Committee are to take Security of those ghi y the South Side of the River agreable to the vote of the Town and also to joyn with Such as our Neighbours shall choose to agree where & how to state a Line & s'* Committee to make return of their proceeding in the affair to the Town as soon as may be conveint

At A Lawfull Town Meeting in Topsfield March the 23rd 1736-7 voted Mr Joseph Towne, Mr Joseph Herrick, & Mr Benjamin Towne are Chosen a Committe to go to the Neighbouring Towns to See if they will Joyn with us in Trying to Gitt a fish Course Cleard up Ipswich River and if the Neighbouring Towns or the Major part of them which the Said Committee Shall Treat with about the affair Shall See Cause to

Joyn with us as afore the then Said Committe are hereby fully Impowered to use all Proper means as the Law Directs to Git the Same Effected Inasmuch as this Town is very small and there being a Number of our Neighbours in Ipswich farms which are willing to be Laid or set off to this Town Therefore the Town Doe hereby Declare that they are willing to Receive our Said Neighbours into one Township with us and to have them with us in all Civill, and Ecclesiastical Priviledges they paying one half of the Charge of being set off as they agreed to doe : by their Committies Answer to our Towns Committee.

March 14 1736-7 voted Mr Joseph Herrick Enters his Dissent from the Last vote because he would not be at any Cost about a Bridge for our said Neighbours on the South Side of the river

At A Lawfull Town Meeting in Topsfield Sep 23 1737 Mr Joseph Herrick is Chosen Moderator for this meeting Mr Joseph Herrick & Mr Benjamin Towne are Chosen to Serve on the Jury of Tryalls at the Next Inferiour Court to be holden at Newbery

At A Lawfull Town Meeting in Topsfield March 7 1737-8 Mr Joseph Herrick is Chosen Moderator for this meeting Joseph Herrick, Daniel Redington, David Commings, Benjamin Towne and Joseph Perkins: are Chosen Selectmen for the year Ensuing

At a legal Town Meeting in Topsfield March 6 1738-9. Mr Jeremiah Towne, Mr Isaac Estey & Mr Joseph Hirrick Jun are Chosen hogreeves for the year ensuing The Town manifested by a vote that they were willing to recieve our Neighbours in Ipswich farms into Township with us: and Mr Joseph Herrick M George Bixby & M Joseph Towne are chosen a committee to treat with our neighbours in Ipswich farms, to see upon what Terms they will join with us as [a] Township, and make return of their proceedings in affair, to the Town at their next meeting The Town allowed to Mr Joseph Herrick one pound fifteen shillings and to Mr David Cummings three pounds five shillings and to Mr Benja Towne one pound twelve shillings they having paid the afores the Sums to the Glazers that mended the Meeting House Glass last winter

Joseph Jr. wasn't finished in his civic duties as he got older. Towards the end of his life, Joseph deeded a portion of his farm to be used as a community cemetery, known as the South Side Cemetery.[59] The History of Topsfield recorded the following account of that contribution.[60]

On Mar. 13, 1740, Joseph Herrick, who lived on the farm lately owned by William L. Batchelder and now the estate of the late William C. Sills, "in consideration of love, goodwill and affection I bear towards David Cummings, John Cummings, Joseph Towne, Nathaniel Porter, Thomas Dwinell, Benjamin Towne, Samuel Curtis, Aaron Estey, Gideon Towne, Nathaniel Porter, Jr., Amos Dorman, Thomas Dorman, Israel Towne, Daniel Robinson and Joseph Hobbs, deeded to them one-half acre of land in Topsfield on the south side of Ipswich River, known as the burying place, inclosed with a stone wall, to be used as a burying place forever. I furthermore grant a priviledge for said persons to pass and repass across my land to bury their dead.

Joseph Hobbs lived on the William Peabody farm just over the line, in Middleton, and John Cummings lived on the Porter Gould place, also in Middleton. It will be noted that the deed says "known as the burial place," proving that the spot must have been

---

[59] The graves of Joseph and Elizabeth Herrick are not found or recorded at the South Side Cemetery. The exact location of their remains is still a mystery. Upon visiting the cemetery in 2005 in search of their graves, the author only received a bad case of poison ivy.

[60] The South Side Cemetery is situated in the southern part of the town, on Rowley Bridge Street, the highway leading to Danvers. It is on a hill and somewhat removed from the travelled road. A time-stained wall of stone, encloses about an acre of green-sward "where heaves the earth in many a moldering heap. "

CHAPTER 16 —JOSEPH HERRICK JR., BENJAMIN HERRICK

used for burial purposes before 1740. There are no stones to mark the earliest graves and the resting places of only a few of the many Revolutionary soldiers buried here can be identified. There is the grave of Mrs. Esther Estey, who lived to be over a hundred years old, and off in a corner, separated from the other mounds, is a grave with a large tree at its head. There are two traditions relating to this mound, one, that it is the grave of a slave once the property of the Cummings family; another, that it is the grave of an Indian woman named Sarah Tutoo. The late John H. Gould believed in the latter story.[61]

The last Will and testament plus the estate inventory of Joseph Herrick Jr. is below.

Joseph Herrick
Topsfield, MA, Yeoman, Testament
#13159 Massachusetts Archives
September 25, 1749 Will and Probate
October 23, 1749 Inventory

In the name of God, Amen. I, Joseph Herrick of Topsfield in the County of Essex, Yeoman. Being very weak in body, But of perfect mind and memory, thanks be given unto God, therefore calling into mind the mortality of my body and not knowing how soon it may please God to take me out of this world, Do make and Ordain this my last will and testament; that is to Say, principally and first of all I Give and Recommend my Soul Into the hands of God that Gave it and my Body I recommend to the Earth to be Buried in Decent Christian Burial at the Discretion of my Executor, hereafter named, and as touching Such Worldly estate, wherewith it hath

---

[61] In 1814, The Cummings family enlarged the Cemetery by about half as much land as it then contained, the boundary of the old ground being between the Herrick row and the lot of David Towne. The land added in 1814 is now occupied by lots of David and Lorenzo Towne, and the Peterson, Johnson, Cummings, Batchelder and Rea families. The Cummings family also built the wall around the cemetery and the stone gate posts were given by Lorenzo P. Towne.

pleased God to bless Me of in this Life, I give Demise and dispose of the same in the following manner-----

Impremier: I give to my Son Benjamin Herrick my great Bible and five pounds in bills of Creditt of the Old Tenor which make up his full portion of my Estate With what I have given him Before, The said Five Pounds shall be paid by my Executor out of that part of my estate I have hereafter given him.

Item: I give to my Daughter in Law, Hannah Herrick my Negro Boy named Charly, and two cows and three sheep forever; Also I give to my said Daugh'r Hannah, My Negro girl named Lilphen During the said Hannah's life; and I give to the said Hannah the improvement of all my land situate in said Topsfield lying on the west side of the road that . . . . from Nathaniel Porter Jun'r house to Topsfield . . . . Bridge; and the improvements of one half of that piece of meadow I bought of Ebenezer Porter and the improvements of the dwelling house (excepting the new end of till my grandson, Nehemiah Herrick, comes to of age at twenty one years old. I give to my said grandson Nehemiah Herrick and to his heirs all of my said land of situate in Topsfield, lying on the west side of said road as aforesaid and that said half piece of meadow I bought of said Porter; and my said dwelling house excepting the said new end. And forever after he comes to age of twenty one years old. Also I give to the said Nehemiah the bed and what furniture belongs to it which stands in The East room: and my colt and one Iron barr and one half of my timber chain and one draught chain forever And my negro girl named Lilphen forever (after the death of my said Daughter Hannah) And the said Nehemiah after he comes to the age aforesaid shall maintain my said daughter Hannah Herrick During her life, Both in sickness and in health out of that part of the estate I have now given him in and by this will

I give my grandson Gideon Herrick the new end of my house and privilege convenient to bring wood and water to the said new end of my house and one bed and what furniture that belongs to it and one pewter platter and one pewter plate and

CHAPTER 16 —JOSEPH HERRICK JR., BENJAMIN HERRICK

the oak chest forever after he comes of age of twenty one years old.

I give to my grandson Israel Herrick and to my said daughter Hannah Herrick all my household goods Within Doors that I have not disposed of Before and Two cows and four Sheep and two Swine forever To Be Equally Divided Between them; and the said Israel and Hannah shall pay all my funeral charges out of what I have now given them equally between them.

I give to my Grand Daughter Elizabeth Roundey, the Negro girl Named Billah forever.

I give to my Grand Son Joseph Rea, Ten Pounds In Bills of Credit of said old Tenor.

I give to my Grand Daughter, Mary Rea, five pounds in said bills.

I have now given to said Elizabeth. Joseph and Mary is their full portion out of my estate with what I given their mother Before the Legacies that I given said Joseph and Mary Shall be paid by of said Elizabeth Roundy out of that part of my estate. I have given her and by this will.

Item. I give to my Grand Son Israel Herrick (whom I likewise constitute, make and ordain my sole executor of this, my last will and testament) my Negro woman named Deborah forever. Also, I give to said Israel the improvements of said new end of my house and privilege convenient to bring wood and water to said new end of my house till my said grandson Gideon Herrick comes to age of twenty one years old. The said Israel keeping it in good repair as it is in now; Also I give to said Israel and to his heirs forever one half of that piece of meadow I bought of Ebenezer Porter and all the remainder of my estate both real (?) and Personal (that I have not disposed of) where forever it may be found and privilege of using my mill and making cider and a way from said cider mill. ... and the said Israel shall pay all my just debts out of that part of my estate I have now given him: And I do hereby Revoke and Disannual all and every other former testament and wills, legacies and bequests, ratifying and confirming this and no other to be my said will and In witness whereof. I have hereto put My hand and seal on the twenty-fourth of May, A.B. 1749.

Joseph Herrick & seal,

Signed, sealed and declared by said Joseph Herrick at his last will and testament in presence of us: Nathaniel Porter, Hannah Perkins, Elijah Porter.

Essex, Ipswich , Sept. 25, 1749 before the Honorable Thomas Berry Esq., judge of probate of the wills and for the County of Essex. Hannah Perkins and Elijah Porter personally appeared and made oath that they were present and saw Joseph Herrick, late of Topsfield, dec'd sign and seal and heard him ... and declare of within written in to be his last will and testament and whom he said he way of a sound disposing and mind and memory to the best of their discerning. And they together with Nathaniel Porter set to their hand that the same time in his presence as witnesses. Senior Att. Dan'l Appleton, Reg. upon which this will is proved, approved and allowed is appeared and accepted that trust and to give in ... executor. in 30 days Dan Appleton, Reg. , Tho. Berry, J Probate.

A true Inventory of all and singular the land and goods , chattels credits of m. Joseph Herrick late of Topsfield in the county of Essex. Yeoman Dev. taken and apprised in bills of last tenor b us the subscribers being across appointed by the Hon. Tho. Berry Esq. Judge of the Probate of Wills, in and for the County aforesaid. As it was shown to us by the Executor of the last will and testament of the said Joseph Herrick this fifth Day of October A.B. 1749.

Imp: Abt 37 acres of land with a dwelling house situate in said 370.00
Topsfield at 10 pounds per acre
Ten acres of swamp and meadow situate in Salem at 50/ 25.00
Negro woman named Deborah 40 pounds and girl named Bilah @ 50/ 90.00
Negro girl Lilph'n 30 pounds Negro boy Charly 50/ 32.10
The new end of the house given to Gideon Herrick 25.00
1 pewter platter, plate and chest of 10/ 10.00

Chapter 16 — Joseph Herrick Jr., Benjamin Herrick

1 feather bed bolster and spills 116/ and bed pillows/ 6.10
1 covert & blanket and sheets 40/ (curtain vlance, bed 1.4
2.14
The articles mentioned below of new end of said house was given to Gideon
(Carne Aul)
1 horse 50/ 5 cows 15/ 6 Ox 7.10/ 10 steers and 2 heiffers 6.5
41.5
60/ 16 sheep at 7. 1/, some pigs 80/ 14.14
Other swine 9/, colt 6/ wearing apparrial 7/ 19.00
Bible and other books 36/ 1 feather bed and boster and pillow, sheets 6.6 pounds 8.9
Underbed 6/ bed st. 4/ covert and blanket, curtain, valance 40/ 2.10
Feather bed and bed furniture, 100/ 8 pillows 16/ 5.16
5 sheets 75/ a D 15/ 8 D 30/ table linen and towel 8/ 6.8
Chest of drawer 10/chest and 3 tables and trunk 7/6 brass weights 4/ 1.10.6
Money Seal 8/ pewter 5/of earthenware2/ 3.0
Brass kettle and warming pan 5/ iron pott and kettle 12/6 3.2.6
Iron pott 3/ Shilly 10/ Andiron trammel flue and tongs 60/ 3.13
Tub and bottles 7/ chairs 6/ 2 wheels 7/ mors 5/ wood plates 1/6 1.6.6
Beaker glass peper box and salt cellar 1.6 brass /6 flax (flasks?) 15/ .17
Sheeps wool 35/leather 10/loom & stays and barrs 65/ 5.10
40 bushel Indian corn 10 pounds 1 bushel beans, 10/ chest of 21/ 11.11
Churn pail and unil 8/6 hli'd & bb15/ tubs and bear bb....14/ 1.17
Yeicy1/box iron ... 5/ Ipet 5? Trammel and flesh fork 2/ .13
Looking glass 6/ basin 5/ cart wheel hoops 51/ 3.2
Cart wheel tyen 40/ spanshakle & pin 3/curt boxey 2/6 2.5.6
Plow skees 44/ plow and plates 5/ chains 87/6 6.16.6
Pitch fork and .....23/axe 24/ wedges belte and rings 18/ 2.15
Handsaw and shave 6/ shoes 3/old iron 6/ iron barrs 48/ 3.3
Horse tackling 31/ xxx the tackling and grindstone 6/6 1.17.6

About 3 loads of haystalks, and husks 10/ applies and xxx80/ 14.0
Cider mill and wheels 30/ meal bags 5/ 1 bond principle and interest25 L 26.15
Coins silver 1/3 Rasor 1/6 .2.9
Benj'm Town, Nathaniel Porter, Jr, Elijah Porter, Comission Israel Herrick
Thomas Barton ...Judge
Essex: Ipsiwch, October 23, 1749

Then Israel Herrick made an oath to said foregoing inventory and if anyting further appears he would cause it to be added.

Before Thomas Berry, J. Probate.

It is clear from his estate inventory and his will, Joseph was a relatively wealthy man. What is particularly interesting is that Joseph, like his father, was a slave owner. He listed three women and one man, plus their value, as personal property.

As his Will indicates, Joseph Jr. gave his Bible and some money to his son Benjamin. Not mentioned in his Will was a farm in Wenham that apparently was given to Benjamin before he died.

Benjamin was born in 1700 in Wenham and married Lydia Hayward of Beverly in 1720. Benjamin and Lydia had 13 children, 8 of which lived to adulthood. After raising their family, Benjamin and Lydia moved to Gage's Ferry, which is now Methuen. Benjamin and Lydia died in Methuen – he in 1773 and she succeeded him in death. We know little of Benjamin and Lydia, but we do know that Benjamin served as a minuteman for short periods of time, including with Capt. James Mallous' company for only 3 or 4 days in 1768. HGR III indicates that Benjamin carried the military rank of Lieutenant, so it is very likely that he had greater participation in the local militias of Topsfield or Wenham and perhaps participated in some colonial wars, but these have not been verified.[62] Of their five sons who lived to adulthood, three were noteworthy solders in the Revolutionary War.

---

62 Houses and Buildings of Topsfield, MA by C. Lawrence Bond states Benjamin lived on Main street in Topsfield and was a wheel-shop there, which was torn down in 1851. He later moved to Central Street. A small portion of the building on Main street is part of the house that was there as of 1988.

CHAPTER 16 —JOSEPH HERRICK JR., BENJAMIN HERRICK

Their first born, Israel, was a career soldier. Major Israel Herrick served in nineteen campaigns in the French and Indian war and fought in the Battle of Bunker Hill in June 1775, resigning his commission when the army removed to Cambridge after the battle. Ebenezer also fought at the Battle of Bunker Hill where he commanded a company at the Rail Fence where he was killed in the battle. Nathaniel Herrick fought along side his two brothers at the Rail Fence.

Below is Benjamin Herrick's last Will and testament dated October 23, 1773.

Benjamin Herrick
Methuen, Gentleman, Testament
#13115
October 25, 1773
Will Probate and Bond

In the name of God Amen, the twenty third Day of January, Annoque Dominie 1771, I Benjamin Herrick of Methuen in the County of Essex in the Province of Massachusetts Bay in New England, Gentleman, being sick and weak in Body, yet blessed be God of perfect Mind and Memory, and calling to Mind the Mortality of my Body, Do make and ordain this my last Will and Testament that is to say, Principally I give and recommend my Soul into the Hands of God that made it, and my Body I recommend to the Earth to be buried in decent Christian Burial at the Discretion of my Executors here after named with full assurance that at the general Resurrection I shall receive the same again by the mighty Power of God: ---- And as touching such worldly Estate wherewith it hath pleased the Lord to less me in this World I give and dispose of the same in the following Manner and Form.

Imprimis I will and order that all such Debts as I owe at the Time of my Decease and my funeral Charges and Legacies hereafter mentioned be seasonably paid by my Executors hereafter named.

Item I give to my beloved Wife Lydia Herrick all my household goods, and all my Provisions, of all sorts for Eating and Drinking. ____ And having already given Portions to all my children according to my ability and yet in regard of my Parental Love to them.

Item I give to my beloved son Israel Herrick one Shilling lawful money.

Item I give to my beloved grandson Benjamin Herrick, son of my son Edward Herrick

dec'd ten shilling lawful money. ____

Item I give to my beloved son Benjamin Herrick Jun'r all my wearing apparel.

Item I give to my beloved son Nathaniel Herrick one shilling lawful money.

Item I give unto my beloved Daughter Lydia Dodge one shilling lawful money.

Item I give unto my beloved Daughter Hannah Whittier one shilling lawful money.

Item I give all the rest of my Estate to my two beloved sons, namely, Ebenzer Herrick and Thomas Herrick and to their Heirs and assigns even all the Estate which I have or shall have at the Time of my Decease which is not herein before disposed of. I give the whole thereof to my said son Ebenezer Herrick and Thomas Herrick whom I likewise constitute and appoint my joint Executors of this my last Will and Testament hereby disannulling and revoking all former wills and testaments by me heretofore made and confirming this and this only this to be my last will and testament. In testimony whereof I have here unto set my hand and seal the day and year above said.

signed, sealed, pronounced and declared by the above named. Benjamin Herrick the Elder as his last will a testament in the Presence of us.

Nathaniel Messer, Jun'r
Asa Messer
Eben'r Barker
Signed Benjamin (his mark) Herrick (and seal)

CHAPTER 16 — JOSEPH HERRICK JR., BENJAMIN HERRICK

Seal To all People to whom these Presents shall come, Benj'm Herrick Lynde Esq, Judge of the Probate of Wills, etc. in the county of Essex within the Province of Massachusetts Bay in New England sendeth Greeting____

Know ye, That on the twenty fifth Day of October Amno Domini `1773 the Instrument hereto annexed purporting the last Will and Testament of Benj'm Herrick later of Methuen in said County , Gentleman, deceased, was presented for Probate by Ebenezer Herrick and Thomas Herrick the Executors therein named; Then present Nathaniel Messer jun'r and Asa Messer Witnesses thereto subscribed, who made Oath, that they saw the said Testator sign, seal and heard him declare the said Instrument to be his last Will and Testament and that they with Ebenezer Barker subscribed their Names together in Witness to the Execution thereof in the said Testator's Presence, and that he was then (to the best of their Judgment) of sound and disposing mind.

I do prove, Approve and Allow of the said Instrument as the last Will and Testament of the beforenamed decease, and do commit the Administration thereof in all Matters the same concerning, and of his Estate whereof he died said and possess'd in said county unto Eben'n Herrick and Thomas Herrick the before named Executors well and faithfully to execute the said Will and to administer the Estate of the said deceased according thereto; who accepted of their said Trust, and gave Bond to pay all the Debts, legacies and fulfil his Will, and they shall render and Acco't (upon Oath) of Proceedings, when thereunto lawfully required. And Lydia Herrick widow of said dec'd signified her Acceptance of what is given her in said dec'd Will in Lien of her Dower. In Testimony whereof, I have hereunto set my Hand and Seal of Office, the Day and Year above written.

Peter Frye, Reg'r. Signed Benj'm Lynde, J. Prob:
Examined by Peter Frye Reg'r
Essex is: Eben'r Herrick and Thomas Herrick Ex'orsto the last Will and Testament of Benj'm Herrick late of Methuen Dec'd gave Bond with Nath'l Messer jun'r as Sureties to pay the said

Dec'd Debts and Legacies and to fulfill his Will. This 25th Day of October Anno Domini 1773.

Signed Benj'm Lynde J. Probate
Peter Frye Reg'g, Examined by Peter Frye, Reg.

Chapter 17
Nathaniel Herrick

Benjamin and Lydia Herrick had two sons named Nathaniel. The second Nathaniel was named after his brother Nathaniel, who died in 1736 when only 9 years old. Nathaniel was born October 24, 1736 on the family farm in Methuen, Massachusetts, shortly after his brother's death. When he was 23 years old, he married a local girl named Susannah Messer on March 13, 1760. Like his father, grandfather, and great grandfather, Nathaniel served in his local militia and participated for a period of time in the French and Indian War. Which particular conflicts in that war we do not know, but Nathanial's Revolutionary War record is well documented.

As early as 1774, Nathaniel was listed on the records as 1st Lieutenant in Captain John Davis's company in Colonel James Frye's[63] Regiment. Frye's Regiment was part of the Army of Observation with its main purpose to monitor a given area or enemy location in preparation for possible hostilities. Therefore, it is clear that Nathaniel participated in early military conflicts with Great Britain leading up to the Revolutionary War.

---

63 Col. James Frye was from Andover, a short distance from Methuen. He was a career soldier and commanded the Essex County regiment during the early stages of the Revolution. He and his regiment were discharged in December 1775 and he died shortly later in January 1776.

Nathaniel Herrick's enlistment record with James Frye's Regiment, 1775

By the time of his enlistment, Nathaniel had been married for 14 years and had already had started his family. On February 14th, 1775, Nathaniel enlisted as a Minuteman from Methuen in Col. James Frye's Regiment, part of Captain John Davis's company. As mentioned before, the purpose of the regiment was to drill and prepare for anticipated battle with the British.

CHAPTER 17 — NATHANIEL HERRICK

Nathaniel Herrick's Revolutionary War Roll Call, 1775.
Listed in the second column under Lieutenants

Early in 1775, the Continental Congress knew that they needed to store arms and gunpowder somewhere and decided that Concord, a small village away from Boston, would be the site. The British learned about this site, and on the evening of April 18, British troops were ferried across Boston Harbor to start their march on to Lexington and then on Concord to destroy the armaments. To further the British interest in Concord, they received word that two prominent rebel leaders were in Lexington. These two were none other than Sam Adams and John Hancock. So, the idea was to march on Lexington, arrest Adams and Hancock, then proceed to Concord to capture the armaments. Surely this would put an end to the rebellion, or so they thought. As it turned out, it was the beginning of the rebellion. Paul Revere, William Dawes and Dr. Samuel Prescott rode to warn the colonists that the British were coming by land. The alarm was made.

The Minutemen of Col. Frye's Regiment and other local regiments responded and met the British at Lexington. Frye's regiment included the village of Methuen, so this is where Nathaniel Herrick mustered in.

While marching to Cambridge, Nathaniel, together with others in Colonel Frye's Regiment, along with his brothers Israel and Ebenezer, were called to alarm and encountered British soldiers at Lexington at 6:00am and later at Concord's North Bridge on April 19, 1775. The Revolutionary War started here with the "shot heard around the world".

The fighting at Lexington and Concord was fierce once it started, and Nathaniel Herrick may well have been in the thick of it. The Minutemen were ordered not to fire when encountering the British, but the British did fire upon the Colonists. A portion of Frye's Regiment was holed up in the basement of Jason Russell's house at Lexington, and survivors of the initial British attack at Lexington fled for safety at the Russell's house. Russell was killed on his own doorstep, shot twice and stabbed an estimated eleven times by British bayonets in their attempt to capture or kill the colonists. Eight men from Frye's regiment (Nathaniel could have been one of them) hurried into the cellar of the house. By blasting away at any regular (Redcoat) who approached the cellar entrance, they were able to hold off the solders even as they filled the beams of the house with bullet holes that can still be seen today. The militiamen who remained up above in the house were in greatest danger as the regulars poured in. Soon the rooms were filled with the ear-splitting boom of muskets and choking clouds of powder-smoke.

At the end of the fighting in Lexington, the militiamen sustained 17 casualties with 8 dead and the British sustained no casualties.

Chapter 17 — Nathaniel Herrick

Reenactment on Lexington Green of British regulars chasing and killing local militiamen. April 19, 2018

Adams and Hancock escaped, so the Redcoats continued on to Concord with the colonists firing on them all the way. The British and the colonists meet again in Concord at North Bridge, when fighting was intense. After the fighting at North Bridge, the remaining militia, including Nathaniel, started their march from Concord back through Lexington again and on to Charlestown, ambushing the British regulars all along the way. Vicious and bloody fighting occurred at Merriam's Corner, more fighting at Lexington, Hardy's Hill, Watson's Corner, Fiske Hill, Concord Hill, and finally at the village of Menotomy (today Arlington) before their retreat ended at Charleston at sunset. To say the least, it was a long hard day on both sides. The day's total was 273 British casualties with 73 killed, and 95 militia casualties with 49 killed. The British did not capture Adams or Hancock nor did they retrieve the armaments they wanted, but they did learn that the colonists could fight.

The colonial regiments reached Charlestown in May and prepared for one of the most famous battles of the Revolutionary War. Nathaniel Herrick and others in Frye's Regiment were recorded in Cambridge, west of Charlestown, on May 17, 1775. However, it wasn't until June 15, 1775, two months after Lexington and Concord and two days before Bunker Hill, that the Continental Congress formed a real standing army and did away with local militias to continue the war. Thus, the Continental Army was organized and General George Washington was chosen as it's Commander-in-Chief. Washington officially took command of the new Continental Army at Cambridge on July 2, 1775.

What is known as the Siege of Boston began after the Lexington and Concord battles. The Minutemen, including those in Col. Frye's Regiment, were assembled at Charlestown after their long march through Lexington and Concord in order to block the British from land access to Boston. The British were garrisoned in Boston. Then in June 1775, the British attempted to seize control of Bunker and Breeds Hill in order to protect Boston. The militiamen, now the Continental Army, were planning to bombard Boston and drive the British out. So, in preparation for the advance towards Boston, the colonial militia, under the command of William Prescott, attempted to occupy the two hills and constructed a strong redoubt on Breed's Hill, as well as fortified lines across the Charlestown Peninsula. When the British learned of the Continental Army (as they were now known) activities, they attacked them on June 17, 1775. The Continental Army of 1,200 men was made up of regiments of Prescott, Putnam (commanded by Thomas Knowlton) Ebenezer Bridge and James Frye.

CHAPTER 17 — NATHANIEL HERRICK

In order to defend the left flank around these fortifications, the Continental Army built a crude ditch as breastwork and topped it with recently mowed grass and whatever rocks and wood that they could find. This fortification was a good barricade and became known as the rail fence. Under the command of Captain Thomas Knowlton and later reinforced by General John Stark, Frye's Regiment, along with several other regiments, were ordered to position themselves at the rail fence. Soldiers at the fence poked their muskets through the grass on top of the fence to take "deliberate aim" at the enemy. Together on Breed's Hill, Nathaniel and his two brothers, Israel and Ebenezer fought the battle at the rail fence in this manner. Nathaniel was a Lieutenant and his brother Israel was a Major, both serving in the company of their other brother Ebenezer, who commanded the rail fence.

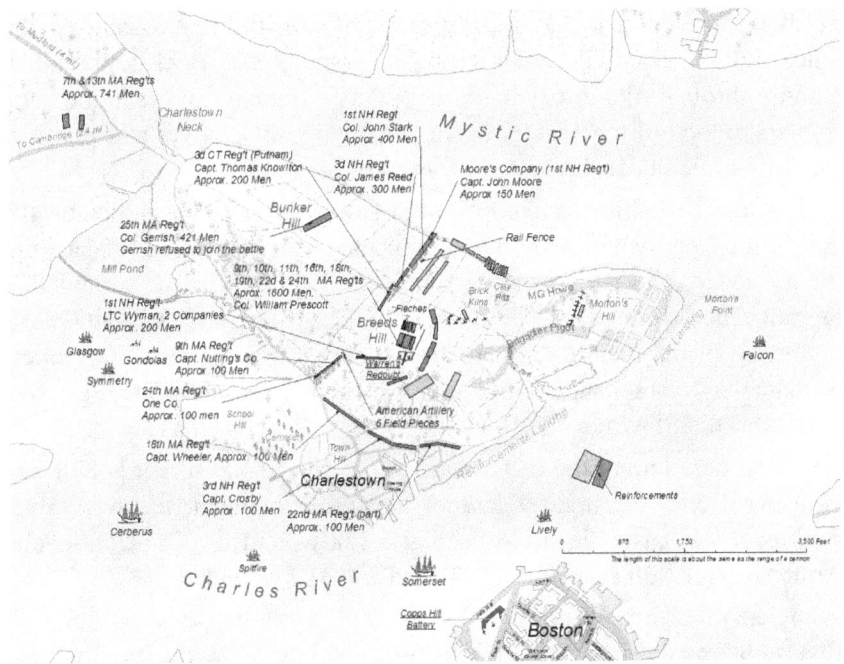

Battle at Bunker and Breed's Hill showing the rail fence
April 19, 1775

The British General, William Howe, had a primary objective going into the battle. That objective was to hit the rail fence hard in order to out flank the colonists. The battle at the rail fence was fierce, and the Herrick brothers had to be scared and nervous when seeing the Redcoats marching towards them as they proceeded along the Mystic River shore to attack the rail fence. But as nervous as they were, they had to wait. It was critical that the first rounds of fire be coordinated, with men alternately firing and loading to keep up a barrage capable of breaking the enemy's charge. Whether or not they were told to hold fire until they saw the "whites of their eyes", the colonialists were told to wait for the order to fire, to aim low, and to pick off British officers. In truth, soldiers at the rail fence were told by General Stark to hold their fire until they "could see the enemy's half gaiters", the heavy linen splash guards that were secured to a British soldier's foot that reached half way up the calf.

As Howe's British Regulars reached the stone wall on the beach, they were met with American soldiers who were not giving up ground. The fire from American musketry and the struggle for the British to negotiate the fences while under fire resulted in the first assault on the fences to be repulsed. After repeated assaults the British prevailed, cutting through the breastwork and over running the redoubt. The soldiers at the rail fence held off long enough to help cover a retreat, but the final scene inside the redoubt was carnage.

Heavy casualties resulted on both sides but more casualties on the part of the Continental Army were prevented by a controlled retreat from the rail fence. The retreat was so successful that most of the wounded at the rail fence were saved. Unfortunately, Ebenezer Herrick, Nathaniel's brother, was not one of them. He died in action fighting at the rail fence. Nathaniel and Israel and the remaining surviving colonials retreated west to Cambridge. It was over.

Despite winning the battle and taking Bunker and Breed's Hill, the British suffered the highest loss of any other battle in the war. They suffered 1,054 casualties (226 dead and 828 wounded). The Continental Army suffered 450 casualties (140 dead and 310 wounded).

General George Washington met his tired and beleaguered troops in Cambridge on July 2nd, two weeks after the battle. Washington had not heard about the battle until it was over. Upon meeting the messenger telling him about the Battle of Bunker Hill, he asked if "the provincials stood the British fire". When assured that they had, he responded, "Then the liberties of our country are safe". The army camped in Cambridge while Washington planned the remaining Siege of Boston. Could it be that Nathaniel encountered George Washington at this time in Cambridge? It was very likely. Would he have been in awe of this giant

CHAPTER 17 — NATHANIEL HERRICK

of a man, his stature, his prominence? Or would he hardly have noticed Washington? Nathaniel was with other survivors of the battle for over two months in Cambridge. During this time, military actions were limited to occasional raids, minor skirmishes, and sniper fire. Then on October 5, 1775, Nathaniel resigned from the militia, which was by then known as the Continental Army, and returned back to his family in Methuen. Why did Nathaniel leave the army? Was he tired of battle? Distraught over the death of his brother? Following his older brother Israel, who resigned his commission as Major due to his age at the same time? Missing Susannah and his family? Or most likely, returning home to see his new son, Nehemiah, born in September, just one month before. Perhaps all of these reasons and more.

Nathaniel Herrick's record of resignation from army, 1775

But his respite from the army did not last long. Enlistments in the army were commonly on a "campaign by campaign" basis, so soldiers were coming and going into the army. But again, we have questions. Was Nathaniel a true patriot willing to sacrifice it all for his new country? Did he feel a sense of personal allegiance to James Frey, who died less than three months after Nathaniel's resignation? All we know is that Nathaniel reenlisted in the Continental Army on December 20, 1776 and served continuously for three years until January 1, 1780, when he was finally discharged. He was no longer a Lieutenant serving in the Methuen militia, but a private from Beverly serving in the Continental Army under the general command of General George Washington. This was indeed serious business. Colonial Frey was dead, so now he served in Captain McNall's company in Colonial Wigglesworth's regiment. During those three years he undoubtedly saw hardship, pain, fear, and loneliness from extended separation from his family. All those emotions and more bore down on him when he served with the army at Valley Forge in the winter of 1777-78.[64] He was on the muster roll at Valley Forge in May 1778. While at Valley Forge, he served in Captain Nehemiah Herrick's company, 3d Essex County regiment. Nehemiah was his 1st cousin from Topsfield. Records also show that Nathaniel, along with many other soldiers at Valley Forge, served as a Commandant's Guard. Aside from protecting General Washington and his baggage, the Guards were also to protect the headquarters which meant its staff and all of the army's records and to select the General's living quarters upon any relocation. The Guard included upwards of 50 men.

---

64 Records from Sailors and Solder's of the Revolutionary War show two Nathaniel Herricks. Francis LaPenna of the Valley Forge Monument, recognized the two Nathaniel Herricks as the same person. Nathaniel's son Nathaniel would have been too young at the age of 10 during Valley Forge to be the second Nathaniel.

Chapter 17 — Nathaniel Herrick

HERRICK, NATHANIEL, Methuen. Lieutenant, Capt. John Davis's co., Col. James Frye's regt.; return of men in camp at Cambridge, dated May 17, 1775; *also*, same co. and regt.; company return dated Cambridge, Oct. 5, 1775; reported enlisted Feb. 14, 1775.

HERRICK, NATHANIEL, Topsfield (also given Beverly). Private, Capt. Joshua French's co., Col. Edward Wigglesworth's regt.; pay abstract for travel allowance, etc., from Albany home; 220 miles travel allowed said Herrick; warrant allowed in Council Jan. 30, 1777; *also*, return of men raised to serve in the Continental Army from Capt. Stephen Perkins's and Capt. Nehemiah Herrick's cos., 3d Essex Co. regt., sworn to in Essex Co., Feb. 18, 1778; residence, Topsfield; engaged for town of Topsfield; joined Capt. Fairfield's co., Col. Wigglesworth's regt.; term, during war (also given 3 years); *also*, Private, Capt. Peter Page's co., Col. Calvin Smith's (late Wigglesworth's) regt.; Continental Army pay accounts for service from Jan. 1, 1777, to Dec. 31, 1779; residence, Beverly; *also*, Capt. Joseph McNall's co., Col. Edward Wigglesworth's regt.; muster roll for May, 1778, dated Camp at Valley Forge; reported mustered by Esq. Cushing; *also*, same co. and regt.; pay roll for Oct., 1778; *also*, same co. and regt.; return of men who were in service before Aug. 15, 1777, and who had not been absent subsequently except on furlough, dated Boston, March 29, 1779; *also*, Capt. Page's co., Col. Wigglesworth's regt.; pay roll for March and April, 1779, dated Providence; enlisted Dec. 20, 1776; reported on command at Boston Neck; *also*, Capt. Fowle's co., Col. Smith's regt.; Continental Army pay accounts made up for the year 1780; reported discharged Jan. 1, 1780.

HERRICK, NEHEMIAH. 2d Lieutenant, Capt. Samuel Cummins's (9th) co., 3d Essex Co.

Entries of two Nathaniel Herricks in the <u>Massachusetts Soldiers and Sailors in the Revolutionary War</u>. It appears that the two Nathaniels are the same but enlisted in the war at two times from two locations under different leadership.

Muster Roll dated Dec. 10, 1777

Chapter 17 — Nathaniel Herrick

Muster Roll dated July 1, 1777

> H | Mass.
> Cogswell's Regiment | Militia
>
> Nathaniel Herrick Jr.
>
> 3 Reg't Mass. Militia
> (Revolutionary War)
>
> Appears on a
>
> RETURN
> of those men that are engaged in the
> Continental Army that belonged to the
> Third Regiment of Militia in the
> County of Essex and list of men hired
> by the town of Ipswich.
>
> List dated. Ipswich, July 30, 1777.
>
> Town to which they belonged before
> they engaged. Topsfield
> Town for which they are engaged
> Topsfield
> Colonel of the Regiment into which
> they are enlisted Wigglesworth
> Captain of the Company into which
> they are enlisted Fairfield
> Time for which they are engaged
> During war or three years
>
> Enlisted or drafted. enlisted
> Remarks:
>
> JWain
> Copyist.

Return of men dated July 30, 1777

CHAPTER 17 — NATHANIEL HERRICK

Pay Roll dated November 1777

Michael J. Herrick

Muster Roll Jan. 6, 1778

CHAPTER 17 — NATHANIEL HERRICK

It is unclear if Nathaniel received a pension for his war service, but it is likely that he did and that his pension was paid via a land grant, as many Revolutionary War veterans were paid. Evidence of a war pension for Nathaniel is found in the pension application of one of his fellow soldiers, Prince Johonnot. Johonnot's pension application documents that Nathaniel Herrick served with him at Bunker Hill under Colonial Frye. In most likelihood, he received a pension of land for homesteading. Sometime after the war, it is not clear exactly when, Nathaniel moved his family to Berwick, York County, Maine[65] and then continued to move north to Vermont, just like Prince Johonnot settled in New Hampshire after the war. Nathaniel, along with most of his family, all except Nehemiah, finally settled in Granby, located in a remote section of northern Vermont. It was here in Granby that he uprooted virgin trees for his home and homes for his grown sons, Joseph and Nathaniel Jr. Could land in Granby, Vermont be is war pension?

---

65 At the time Maine was part of Massachusetts, therefore, his move at the time was to York County, Massachusetts.

Pension declaration of Prince Johonnot's documenting Nathaniel's war experience

CHAPTER 17 — NATHANIEL HERRICK

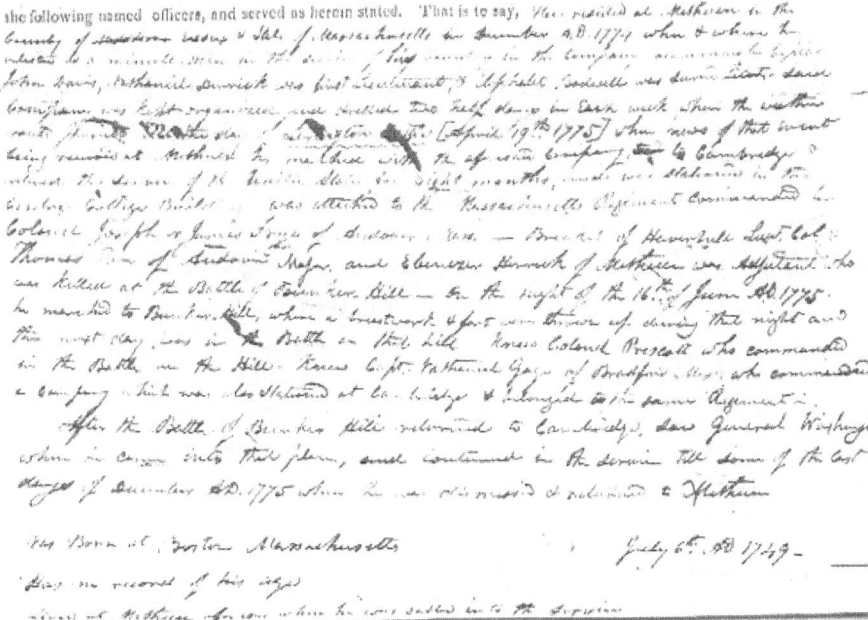

Detail of Prince Johonnot's pension declaration showing reference to Nathaniel and Ebenezer Herrick at Bunker Hill and meeting General George Washington

It was a life changing decision for the entire family. At the ripe old age of 53, Nathaniel, took advantage of his war pension and migrated to northern Vermont, leaving four generations of Herricks in Massachusetts behind forever. His wife, Susannah, and three sons, Joseph, Nathaniel Jr., and Zadock, and two daughters, Susannah and Anna, joined in the arduous trek. Joseph was the oldest at 29 years old and still unmarried. Nehemiah at age 14 stayed in Methuen for unknown reasons for the rest of his life. Zadock, the youngest to make the journey, was only 17 years old. It is highly likely that his oldest son, Joseph, was the leader of this migration north. Joseph was ultimately recognized as one of the founding settlers in Granby.

But first on the route north was Berwick, in York county. The family settled there for an unknown period of time, but it probably was no longer than to regroup with other families to the eventual trip to Granby. It was in the village of Berwick, York County, where he apparently met up with Benjamin Cheney, and the two families most likely journeyed through field, forests, lakes and rivers to a new and hard life.

Once in Vermont, their first settlement was Guildhall, New Hampshire, just over the state border. But how did the Herricks and the Cheneys get to Guildhall? There were only two choices - water routes or land routes. Land routes may have been less likely since they would only have Indian trials to bushwhack through the dense forests, plus they would have had to forge rivers and streams. Winter would have been the likely season for land routes since they could traverse water when frozen over. Regardless of season, water routes were more common at this time either by flat boat with a hollowed out log canoe used to carry family possessions. A flat boat could carry the family plus a cow, perhaps pigs and poultry, and an ox. The ox would be necessary to pull a sled with all family possessions through mud and swamps. A possible water route could have started at the Merrimac River near Newberry, Massachusetts, since that was the ancestral home of the Cheneys. From there they would have traveled up the Merrimac into various lakes in central New Hampshire until they came to the Connecticut River that ultimately leads to the region of Guildhall. Whether they traveled by land or water or in winter or summer, the trip was hard and risky, requiring strength and steely determination.

We don't know how they did it or which route they took, but we know they made it. It is not known exactly when Nathaniel left Methuen or when he left Berwick, but we do know that the Herrick and Cheney families were in Guildhall, New Hampshire (the current county seat) in 1789 to chart plans for a settlement in Granby. On December 8, 1789, a committee was formed in Guildhall, including Nathaniel (probably Nathaniel Jr., his son) and Joseph Herrick, to lay out and complete a road through the town of Granby. In November of 1791, the road was finally surveyed and completed. Joseph Herrick signed the agreement.

Tracts of land, not to exceed 150 acres, were granted to the first 12 settlers who would settle and improve the land. Then on June 14, 1790 in Guildhall, a vote of the grant proprietors gave two lots to Joseph Herrick and Benjamin Cheney, who were, therefore, considered to be the first settlers of Granby. Joseph received lots 7 and 8 in range 5 and Benjamin Cheney received lots 7 and 8 in range 4, "being the lots on which they have begun improvements, provided that each of them pursue and prosecute their improvements as fast as could reasonably be expected."

CHAPTER 17 — NATHANIEL HERRICK

Later Nathaniel Jr. and Zadock also received lots to settle and improve, but no evidence can be found that Nathaniel Sr. and Susannah received lots. Nathaniel may have given his war pension to his sons, while he and Susannah lived out the rest of their lives with one of their sons or daughters. We don't know.

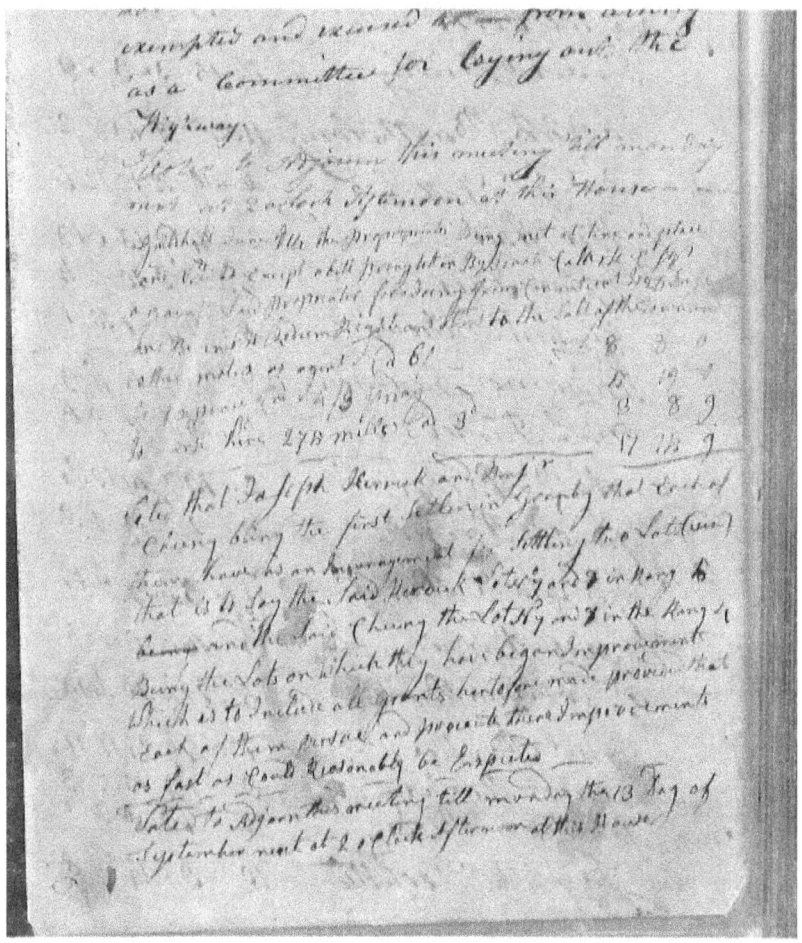

Original notes from June 14, 1790 meeting stating that Joseph Herrick and Benjamin Cheney are the first settlers in Granby

The plot map below shows the locations of Herrick lots in the highlighted areas. Lots 6 and 7 Range 5 are giving to Joseph and Lot 6 and half of Lot 5 Range 4 was given to Nathaniel Jr. The red line through the map is the current day main road called the Granby-Guildhall Road.

The areal map[66] shows the location of the early settler's lots, indicated with yellow dots. The upper left dot is Joseph's farm, the lower middle dot is Nathaniel's farm and the lower right is Zadock's farm. Ben Cheney's farm is in the upper right. The areal map also shows the location of the old Granby Road in the black line that the Herricks helped plan and construct. The road no longer exists but, as the map shows, it runs through the Herrick and Cheney properties.

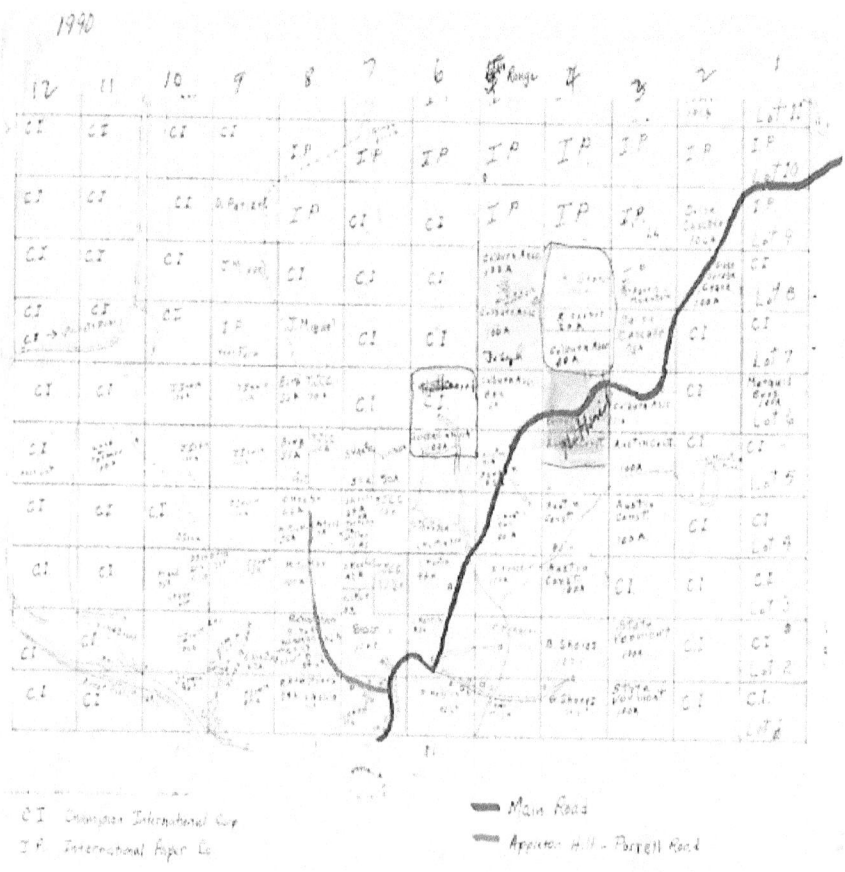

Original plot map of 1790 showing Joseph and Nathaniel Jr. Herrick properties

---

66 Provided by John Irwin, Granby historian

CHAPTER 17 — NATHANIEL HERRICK

Ariel map showing locations of Herrick and Cheney properties. Provided by John Irwin

All of these transactions happened in Guildhall. It wasn't until October 27th, 1795 that the first official meeting in the town of Granby was held, and it was held in the home of Joseph Herrick. At this meeting they voted:

> That, whereas, the proprietors at their meting holden heretofore have given as encouragement to the twelve settlers who shall first settle is said town of tract of public land, not exceeding 150 acres to each, and, whereas, the following persons have made improvement cording to said vote, and are considered as settlers and to hold and to enjoy, to themselves and heirs and assigns forever in fee, the lands as hereafter voted to them respectively, vis.: To Mr. Nathaniel Herrick lot No. 6, range 4th, containing one hundred acres, and the half of lot No. 5 in the same range, adjoining to the other, to him, his heirs and assigns forever.

So, it is clear that Joseph Herrick received his track of land in 1790 and his brother Nathaniel Jr. received his track of land in 1795. Both Joseph and Nathaniel received additional tracks in subsequent years. In the early days of Granby, the Herricks were highly involved as first settlers. In 1795, the first death in Granby occurred. Anna Herrick Pike, the daughter of Nathaniel Sr., died, leaving her husband Robert Pike a widower with their young son, Zadock Pike. That same year Nathaniel Jr. married Sarah Cheney (daughter of Benjamin Cheney). The next year, 1796, Susannah Herrick, Nathaniel's other daughter, married Samuel Hart. Herricks continued to be a prominent family in Granby. Joseph Herrick continued to host town meetings in his home. Nathaniel Sr. was also active in his old age. For example, in a 1798 town meeting, he was chosen to moderate the meeting, while Nathaniel Jr., along with Robert Pike and Benjamin Cheney, were chosen as Selectmen. At this same meeting, Nathaniel Jr. was chosen as the Justice of the Peace, and Zadock Herrick was chosen to be the town constable.

The Herrick family continued their community activities for many more years. For example, six years later in 1804, at a meeting in Joseph Herrick's home the notes indicate that Joseph Herrick was a Selectman and chosen as Town Clerk and Treasurer, Nathaniel Sr. was the meeting moderator, Nathaniel Jr. was made constable, and Zadock was chosen as trustee of the local school district. In 1805, the Essex County Grammar school was Incorporated and located in Guildhall. The Herricks prospered for many years in Granby, as did the entire community. The families from Nathaniel and Susannah began to multiply. In all, 24 Herrick children were born in Granby. But then disaster struck.

Chapter 17 — Nathaniel Herrick

Original notes from 1795 meeting held at Joseph Herrick's home describing settler's land grants

Original notes from 1804 meeting documenting participation
of four Herricks in Granby

After nearly 15 years of extremely hard work and persistence that saw prosperity and success, "the year of no summer" started to set in. If fact it was multiple successive years. Beginning with the "great snowstorm of 1804", the successive winters were extremely cold. Snow

CHAPTER 17 — NATHANIEL HERRICK

was recorded at 4 ½ feet in May, 1807. It got worse every year, and by 1816 it became the coldest year of all. That year the ground never thawed even in the middle of the summer. There was killing frost or ice or snow every month of the year. No crops could be planted. People were starving. This year was known as Eighteen Hundred and Froze to Death.

Truth is stranger than fiction. The account below is from the Danville, Vermont North Star newspaper from June 15th, 1816.

> It was snowing again on June 7 and continued until noon the next day at Waterbury. By that time there was a foot of white on the ground in Montpelier, over 18 inches in Cabot. Many crops and leaves on trees were killed; farmers wearily replanted. Birds which had not taken shelter perished and newly shorn sheep froze to death. July was not much better. Some parts of New England got rain, but Vermont remained dry as a bone. A frost on August 21 killed more beans, potatoes and corn. Farmers burned their hay, sacrificing it to save the corn. By September, frost had killed corn well south into Massachusetts. By September, most of Vermont had seen a full three months without rain. Fires, which swept through parched forest land, filled the air with acrid smoke and a general darkness. Another killing frost struck the final blow on the 10th, wiping out whatever had managed to survive to that point. A meager crop of unripe potatoes was harvested. That winter, cattle starved for lack of hay. There was much human suffering but little starvation, as the more fortunate shared what they had. Fish had become a staple diet, with people in the east operating large nets day and night on the river, and trading fish for maple syrup. Boiled wild foods and porcupines also sustained many. This having been the worst of a string a bad years, many moved west, thinking the weather had turned permanently. Richford was nearly a ghost town, the remaining few barely surviving; Waterford had so few residents that no town meetings were held for several years; Granby's population fell so low that the town gave up its incorporation. Unable to sell their land, they just up and left.

In 1810, there were 12 families in Granby. In 1815, the population was so small that Granby lost its incorporation. By 1817, only 3 families remained.

The Herricks and Cheneys were not among those who remained. It is not known exactly when they left but by 1814 all the Herricks had left Granby. Interestingly, each Herrick family went in a different direction. Joseph Herrick settled in Summit County, Ohio; Susannah and Samuel Hart moved to Lewis County, New York; Nathaniel Jr. settled in Chautauqua County, New York; and Zadock moved his wife and 10 children to Nunda, Livingston County, New York. Given the harsh cold seasons at the time, it is easy to surmise that they traveled in cold and snow, probably with the aid of an ox and sled. The trek from Granby was not dissimilar from the trek they made to Granby only 15 years earlier.

Missing from the mass exodus from Granby was Nathaniel and Susannah. They died on November 7th, 1807. Yes, they died on exactly the same day. What could have happened? Was there an accident that took them both? Was it an illness that made them particularly vulnerable at their advanced age? Nathaniel was 72 at his death and Susannah was 74. Perhaps we will never know.

Below is the hand written Will and testament of Nathaniel Herrick recorded on November 17th and proved on November 19th, 1807.

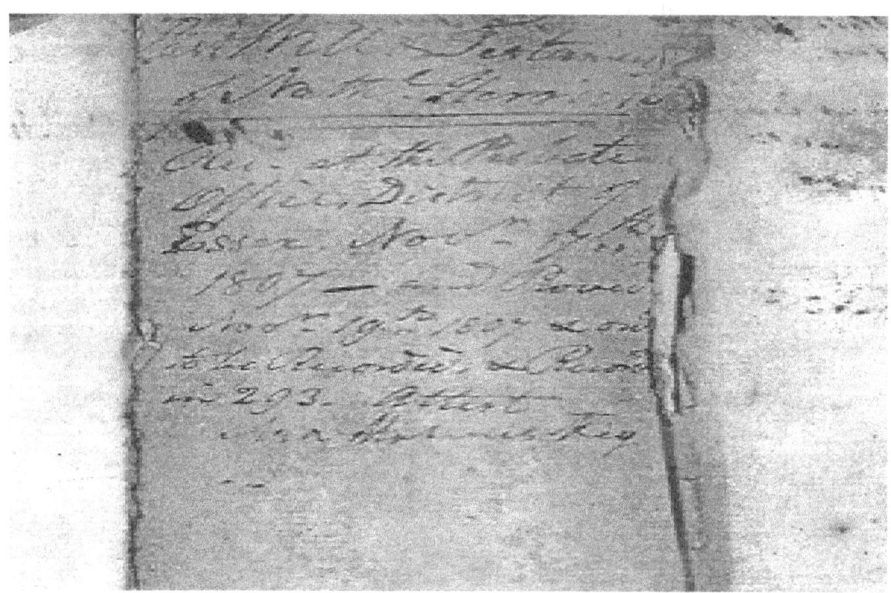

Chapter 17 — Nathaniel Herrick

> State of Vermont }
> District of Essex ss } By the Hon. Daniel Dana Esq.
> Judge of the Probate of Wills &c in &
> for District — To the Heirs & Legatees
> of Nathaniel Herrick, late of
> Granby in sd. District, deceased — Greeting —
>
> The last Will & Testament of the sd. Nathaniel
> Herrick is lodged in the Probate Office of sd.
> District for Proof & allowance by the Court of Probate of sd. District,
> the consideration of which will be on the
> 24th. day of Instant Nov. at the Dwelling
> house of Israel Chase in Guildhall in sd.
> District, at ten O.Clock in the forenoon
> where all persons Interested in sd. Will may
> appear, (if they see cause) and object to the
> Probate of the same — Given under my hand
> at Guildhall this 17th. day of Nov. A.D. 1807 —
> Daniel Dana, Judge of Probate
>
> The Heirs and Legatees aforesd. were notified, excepting Zadock
> &c. as appears to Sworn at the above time
> some were present, no objections to the Will. Witness L. Dana J. Probate

Chapter 17 — Nathaniel Herrick

Original hand written Will and testament of Nathaniel Herrick, 1807

As the above documents make clear, Nathaniel made his youngest son who joined him in Granby his sole executor. Zadock, as part of his responsibility, was charged in paying all his father's debts. In return Zadock inherited his father estate, both real estate and financials. In 1811, Zadock sold the estate he inherited and moved his entire family of 12 to Nunda, New York.

Chapter 18
Move West: Zadock and John

Back in Granby, Zadock met and married Elizabeth (known as Betsy) Pike in 1794, only four years after migrating there from Massachusetts. The Pikes, as well as the Herricks, were respected families in Granby. All the Granby families were close. Zadock's sister, Anna, married Betsy's brother Robert. Of the 10 children of Zadock and Betsy, John was the 5th child and the 2nd son. John and all his siblings were born in Granby. John was born on January 10th, 1805. Below is the handwritten birth record of John Herrick, son of Zadock and Betsy.

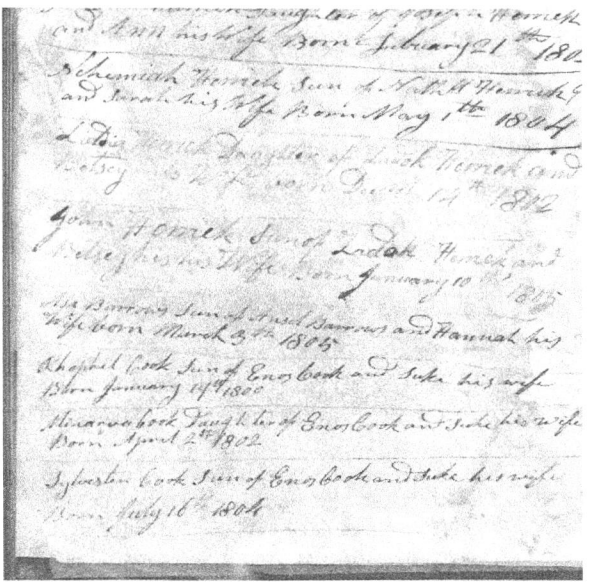

Original hand written birth record of John Herrick, January 10th, 1805

Zadock was 33 or 34 when he moved to Nunda, in southwestern New York state. John was between 6 to 8 years old. The Zadock Herrick family lived there for approximately 43 or 44 years, and by all accounts lived a good and prosperous life. Zadock and Betsy were solid citizens of Nunda, and were charter members of the First Presbyterian Church, which organized on October 6th, 1831. Zadock was one of 14 who established the new church in town and served as Deacon from 1837 to 1839. The new church building was erected two years later in 1833 on the corner of East and Church Streets. In the year Zadock became a Deacon, the church began forming religious classes in cooperation with the Methodists. Since then the church was known as the Methodist Episcopal Church.

During the time Zadock and Betsy lived in Nunda, the Nunda Literary Institute was formed and soon became known as the Nunda Academy. The Nunda Baptists lead the initiative for this school and held classes for children in the Baptist Church, since the church was no longer needed for church purposes. In 1828, it was recorded that 73 children between the ages of 5 and 16 participated in the school, including the school age children of Zadock and Betsy. The school operated for 5 ½ months. One teacher taught the winter months and another teacher taught the summer months.

Before the academy was established, each church had their own school for the education of the youth. So, the congregations of Baptists, Methodists, Presbyterians, Episcopal, and Universalist churches put their theological differences aside and ran the unified school as the Nunda Academy. Trustees were selected on September 28, 1844 and Zadock Jr. (Zadock's son and John's brother) was one of the 13 trustees selected. A month later, another 4 trustees were selected and Lyman Herrick (another son of Zadock and Betsy) was selected. Lyman served until at least 1855, when is father Zadock died.

Zadock died on January 3rd, 1855 at the age of 81, and Betsy preceded him in death. She died in 1849 at the age of 75. Both are buried at the Oakwood Cemetery in Nunda.

Zadock and Betsy's 5th child was also restless. John[67] also migrated west. He and his new wife of one year, Orpha Cookson, who was born and raised in Nunda, New York, left Nunda for Michigan in 1838. John was 33 years old and Orpha was 27 when they moved. Again, there are questions. Why did they move? Was it for economic reasons? Was it a

---

67 Records show his name as John P, but there is no reference as to what the P stands for.

CHAPTER 18 — MOVE WEST: ZADOCK AND JOHN

quest for more land? Why move to Michigan? Or did it have more to do with the adventures of newlyweds? How did they travel? Was it similar to the trek to and from Granby or did they travel exiting trials and roads? Did they travel with ox cart through uncharted woods or by covered wagon along Lake Erie? All of John and Orpha's siblings remained in New York. As in Granby, families in Nunda were close. John's oldest brother, Alpheus, married Orpha's sister, Ann, seven years prior. So, it appears that John and Orpha did not let family tie them down. Whatever the reason for leaving and however the migration occurred, they made their destination shortly after the federal government removed the Indians from southern Michigan.

John and Orpha applied for and received a land patent from the federal government for 80 acres in Carmel Township, Eaton County in south central Michigan in February 1839. Carmel Township was not even organized as a township until a month later. Carmel township is located between Charlotte and Vermontville, Michigan. Then 7 years later in 1846, they received another land patent for 80 acres. Then again in 1853, they obtained yet another parcel of land. The first land grant was in Section 18 of the township and the second grant was in Section 15 of the township. They were farmers and their land purchases suggest that they were doing well.

John and Orpha had nine children, all born in Carmel Township. Five lived to adulthood. John died on October 25, 1868 at the age of 63 and Orpha died June 9, 1852 at the age of 40, only one month after delivering her ninth child. Both are buried in West Carmel Cemetery along with their four children who died in infancy.[68]

---

[68] There are two headstones in the Herrick cemetery lot with no inscriptions. It is surmised that these are the twin grand daughters of John and Orpha and daughters of their son Mahlon.

MICHAEL J. HERRICK

> Georgia Wood
> (Georgia Wood)
> Notary Public, Eaton County State of Michigan
> My commission expires Jan 3 1943
>
> LAND PATENT Received for record this 4 day of April A. D. 1939 at 9:20 A. M.
> United States of America
> to   ───────Register of Deeds
> John P. Herrick
>
> 30¢   THE UNITED STATES OF AMERICA,
> CERTIFICATE)
> No. 9277   ) TO ALL TO WHOM THESE PRESENTS SHALL COME, GREETING:
>   WHEREAS John P. Herrick, of Eaton County, Michigan, has deposited in the GENERAL LAND OFFICE
> of the United States, a Certificate of the REGISTER OF THE LAND OFFICE, At Ionia whereby it appears
> that full payment has been made by the said John P. Herrick, according to the provisions of the Act
> of Congress of the 24th of April, 1820, entitled "An Act making further provision for the sale of
> the Public Lands," for
>   The North half, of the North East quarter, of Section eighteen, in Township two North,
> of Range five West, in the District of Lands subject to sale at Ionia Michigan, containing
> eighty acres,
> according to the official plat of the Survey of the said Lands, returned to the General Land Office
> by the SURVEYOR GENERAL, which said tract has been purchased by the said John P. Herrick
>   NOW KNOW YE, That the UNITED STATES OF AMERICA, in consideration of the premises, and in con-
> formity with the several acts of Congress, in such case made and provided, HAVE GIVEN AND GRANTED,
> and by these presents Do Give and Grant unto the said John P. Herrick, and to his heirs, the said
> tract above described; TO HAVE AND TO HOLD the same, together with all the rights, privileges, im-
> munities, and appurtenances of whatsoever nature, thereunto belonging, unto the said John P. Herrick
> and to his heirs and assigns forever.
>   IN TESTIMONY WHEREOF, I, Franklin Pierce PRESIDENT OF THE UNITED STATES OF AMERICA, have caused
> these Letters to be made PATENT, and the SEAL of the GENERAL LAND OFFICE to be hereunto affixed.
>   GIVEN under my hand, at the CITY OF WASHINGTON, the Fifteenth day of June in the Year of our
> Lord one thousand eight hundred and Fifty four and of the INDEPENDENCE OF THE UNITED STATES the
> Seventy-Eighth
>   BY THE PRESIDENT: Franklin Pierce
>   By H. E. Baldwin Asst Sec'y.
> L. S.   I. N. Granger Recorder of the General Land Office
> 1761899
>
> DEPARTMENT OF THE INTERIOR   GENERAL LAND OFFICE   WASHINGTON, D. C. MAR. 11 1939
>   I hereby certify that this photograph is a true copy of the patent record which is in my custody
> in this office.
>   Evelyn S. Adams
> U. S. G. L. O. Seal   Recorder
>
> EXEMPLIFIED COPY OF LETTERS TESTAMENTARY
> In the Matter of the Estate of Peter Schermerhorn,   Received for record this 4 day of April
>   A. D. 1939 at 9:20 A. M.
>   ───────Register of Deeds

Land Patent from federal government to John P Herrick, 1839

Chapter 18 — Move West: Zadock and John

```
GENERAL LAND OFFICE          I hereby certify that this photograph is a true copy
      SEAL                   of the patent record which is in my custody in this
                             office.
                                              R S Clinton
                                              Chief, Patents Division

                Section 15 -T2N -R5W
                                        Received for Record this 4th day of
United States of America                March A.D. 1946 at 1.10 o'clock P.M.
             To                                     Leonard Marshall
  John P. Herrick                                   Register of Deeds.

      424.
CERTIFICATE)             THE UNITED STATES OF AMERICA,               Ex
No.  3935-  )    TO ALL TO WHOM THESE PRESENTS SHALL COME, GREETING:

WHEREAS John P. Herrick of Calhoun County Michigan has deposited in the GENERAL LAND OFFICE of the
United States, a Certificate of the REGISTER OF THE LAND OFFICE at Ionia whereby it appears that
full payment has been made by the said John P. Herrick according to the provisions of the Act of
Congress of the 24th of April, 1820, entitled "An Act making further provision for the sale of the
Public Lands," for
           the West half of the South West quarter of Section fifteen, in
           Township two North, of Range five West, in the District of Lands
           subject to sale at Ionia, Michigan, containing eighty acres.

according to the official plat of the survey of the said Lands, returned to the General Land Office
by the SURVEYOR GENERAL, which said tract has been purchased by the said John P Herrick
           NOW KNOW YE, That the UNITED STATES OF AMERICA, in consideration of the Premises,
and in conformity with the several acts of Congress, in such case made and provided, HAVE GIVEN AND
GRANTED, and by these presents DO GIVE AND GRANT, unto the said John P Herrick and to his heirs, the
said tract above described: TO HAVE AND TO HOLD the same, together with all the rights, privileges,
immunities, and appurtenances of whatsoever nature, thereunto belonging, unto the said John P
Herrick- and to his heirs and assigns forever.
           IN TESTIMONY WHEREOF, I, John Tyler PRESIDENT OF THE UNITED STATES OF AMERICA, have
caused these Letters to be made PATENT, and the SEAL of the GENERAL LAND OFFICE to be hereunto
affixed.
               GIVEN under my hand, at the CITY OF WASHINGTON, the tenth day of August in
               the Year of our Lord one thousand eight hundred and forty one and
  2094011      of the INDEPENDENCE OF THE UNITED STATES the Sixty Sixth.
    L.S.             BY THE PRESIDENT: John Tyler,
                        By     R. Tyler        Sec'y.
                     Jno S. Wilson, Acting RECORDER of the General Land Office.
                                                              ad interim.

  GENERAL LAND OFFICE
         SEAL                        UNITED STATES
                              DEPARTMENT OF THE INTERIOR
                                GENERAL LAND OFFICE
                              WASHINGTON, D. C.  FEB 28 1946
                        I hereby certify that this photograph is a true
                        copy of the patent record which is in my custody
                        in this office.
                                       R S Clinton
                                       Chief, Patents Division
```

Land Patent from federal government to John P. Herrick, 1846

Carmel Township plot map, Eaton County, Michigan.
John P. Herrick's first two 80 acres highlighted.

Chapter 18 — Move West: Zadock and John

Tree V: Henry's Descendants born in America – To Civil War
1629-1865

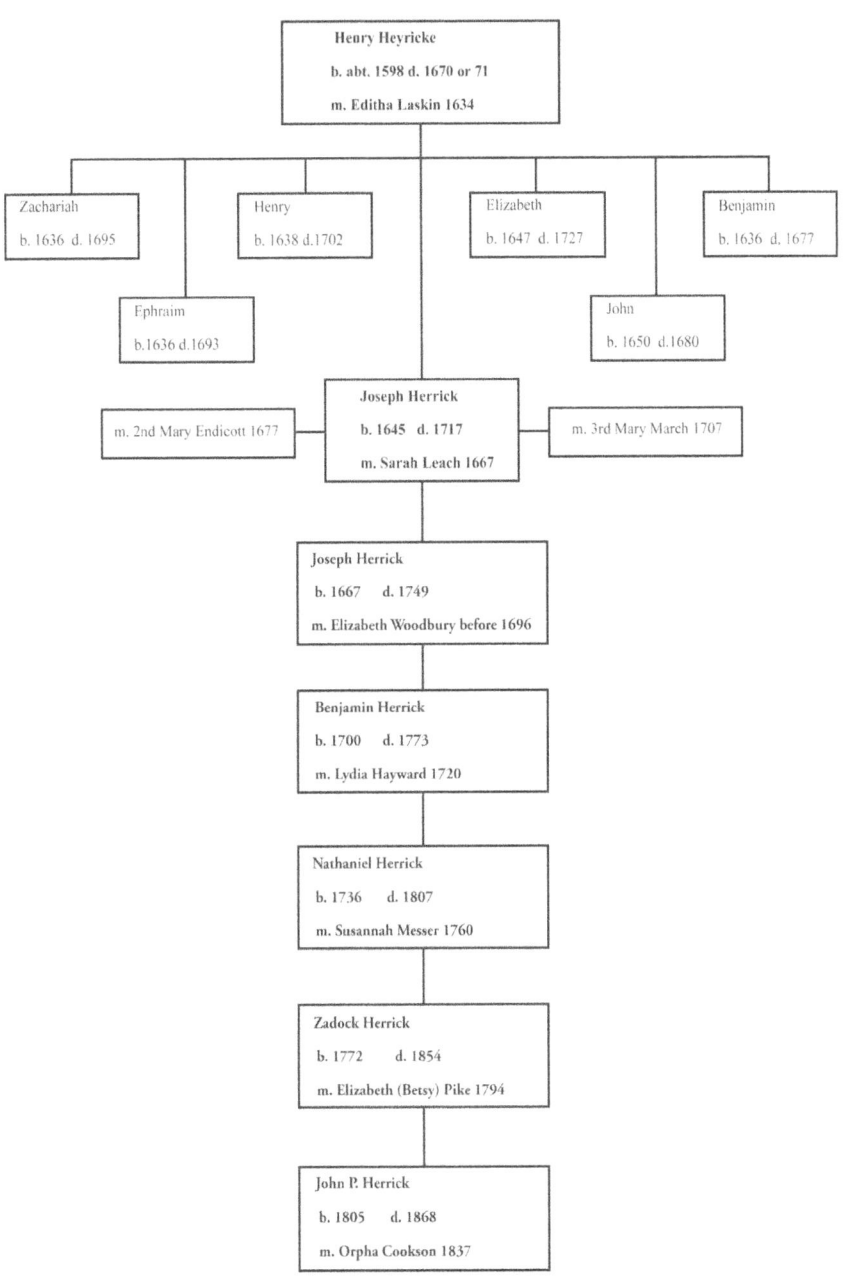

Chapter 19
Beau Manor

At the time that Zadock and John were pushing the western boundaries of America, the Herricks in England were enjoying great wealth. It is undoubtedly true that neither Zadock or John, or perhaps any of the American Herricks, knew much of the English relatives of Beau Manor. Nor, perhaps, did the English Herricks stay in much contact with the American Herricks, or stay tuned into the divisive issues and rebellion in America, except of course the American Revolution. By the mid-19th century, America was heading to a Civil War, but the Herricks of Beau Manor were living a life of wealth and leisure.

But there surely was some contact between the English and American Herricks. It is likely that General Jedediah Herrick made contact with the Beau Manor Herricks in preparation for his 1846 Herrick Genealogical Register (HGR1), the first of three editions of the HGR. Using a collection of New England documents and family member contributions, he concluded (incorrectly) that Henry Herrick of Salem was the son of Sir William Herrick of Beau Manor.[69] Then in 1871, there was correspondence between Edward Herrick and Isabella Herrick James with William Perry Herrick of Beau Manor about the authenticity of Jedediah Herrick's claim about Henry Herrick. So, there was some contact, but the contact seems mostly with the Beau Manor Herricks.

If any of the American Herricks in the 18th and 19th centuries were knowledgeable of the English Herricks, it would have been Sir William of Beau Manor. Sir William, the first of the Beau Manor Herricks, acquired the estate in 1595. He lived there until his death in 1652 at the

---

[69] In her 1937 article in the American Genealogist, "The Alleged Ancestry of Henry Herrick of Salem", Meredith Colket refutes this conclusion by providing convincing evidence that Henry Herrick of Salem could not be the son of Sir William.

age of 96. Beau Manor then came under ownership of a succession of William Herricks. Sir William's eldest son, William II, was the next in line at Beau Manor. Unlike his father and his Uncle Robert, he was not an ironmonger or jeweler, but a lawyer educated at Oxford. But like his father and Uncle Robert, William II was more concerned with court affairs and became the Deputy Receiver of the King's Rents. William II was put in charge of properties of Sir William, including Beau Manor, however, he never lived at Beau Manor, preferring to live in his other house in London. During this time, 1642–1651, the English Civil War erupted and the Herricks supported Cromwell. Due to the war, the Herrick family lost properties and much money in unrecoverable royal debts. Late in the 17th century, Beau Manor was the only property owned by the family and most of the former splendor of the mansion was gone.

William III, son of William II, was the next owner of Beau Manor. Unfortunately, he ran into serious debt and was incapable of managing the estate, and within a few years he conveyed it over to his son, William IV, in exchange for paying off his father's debts. However, William IV seems to have struggled all his life to make ends meet. He took the responsibility to raise his younger brothers and sisters by his father's second marriage in addition to his own young family, plus paying off his father's debts. William IV died before his eldest son William V was of age, so his debts had not been cleared. Consequently, Sir William's original mansion was in deep need of repair and the estate was encumbered with huge debts. William V, who inherited Beau Manor while still a boy in 1705, felt that it would be more economical to build a new house rather than keep patching up the old one. William V managed to build a new Beau Manor on the same land in 1726.

Below is a statement from William IV in 1687 regarding the progression of ownership of Beau Manor.

Sir William Herrick dyed at Beaumanor when he was ninety six years of age. He lived to se his eldest son William Herricke of Beaumanor Esq. and his son's son William Herricke of Beaumanor Esq. These four William Herricks did walk hand in hand all anow together in the Great Chamber at Beaumanor.

CHAPTER 19 — BEAU MANOR

I was the youngest that did write this account and I was when Sir William Herricke dyed three or four years old.

William IV also recorded a glimpse of the old house in 1696, before it was demolished.

A great flood of water that day at Beaumanor the like was never known in any time befoure it began to rain betwixt aleaven and twelve a clock in the fore Noone and thundred and litened veary much and the water came so extrodinary fast from the forest hills that the brooks could not contain the waters within them and it came down the milding yard and through the great gates into the yard all the breadth of the gates and ran into the great moat and into the back moat over the banks as if it had been at a milln ware and over floated all the yard and upon the two bridges of the moat the men when they went out they waded up to the knees and raised the planks upon the bridge coming into the house and some of them swam away with the water and the water came thorough the great gates into the courtyard and all over the fall parlour pantrie kitchen larders and sellers that the hogsheads swam out of the seller to the hall dore and the people went into these rooms up to the knees.

The building of the new Beau Manor began in 1726 and John Westley, a carpenter from Leicester, was contracted to build the new house. The construction was beset by financial problems from the beginning, so much of the building material from the old house was reused for the new house. In fact, the old house did not completely disappear. The dairy and the red chamber above it were retained, the dairy becoming William Herrick's study. The old kitchen and a small part of the adjoining larder were also built into the back of the new structure.

To make matters worse, John Westley had some difficulties and did not complete the work and withdrew from the contract. So, it is hard to tell if the final construction actually met the original plan, but the house was indeed completed.

William Herrick V lived out his life at the Beau Manor that he constructed. His son, William Herrick VI inherited the estate. That adds up to six consecutive direct line generations of William Herricks living at Beau Manor. But that is where it ends. William VI had daughters and no sons, much less a son named William. So, what to do with the estate? As it turned out, William VI, while on his deathbed, turned ownership of Beau Manor over to his nephew, also named William. William was later known as William Perry Herrick.

William Perry Herrick was a fortunate man. Not only did he inherit the Beau Manor estate, but he inherited his own father's property, which was relatively modest compared to yet another inheritance on his mother's side. From his mother's brother, Thomas Perry, William inherited large estates in Wales, including coal and gold mines. It was primarily from the Perry inheritance that William was able to vastly enhance Beau Manor and the surrounding estate.

However, he simply did not like the Beau Manor he inherited from William VI. Although he moved into his inherited mansion in 1832, he decided to demolish the second Beau Manor built by William V and build a new and immensely more costly mansion. He also expanded the surrounding grounds to around 6,000 acres, tripling it in size. That acreage became a park with formal lawns and terraces, a croquet lawn and later, tennis courts. This is the third Beau Manor. Construction began in 1842 and was finished in 1848. It still stands today.[70]

In exchange for this huge inheritance from his mother and Thomas Perry, William was required, in the terms of Thomas Perry's will, to change his name to William Perry Herrick. He was then granted a Perry Herrick Grant of Arms.

---

70 After the death of William Perry Herrick's widow in 1915, the estate left the family, was inherited by the Curzon family, and later was used for military purposes in World War II as a decoding center to break the German code during the London blitz. The decoded messages where sent to Bletchley Park in London. The Nazi code was broken at Beau Manor, the most famous being the Enigma code. The Germans never discovered it. This was made into a movie called The Enigma, staring Kate Winslett..

CHAPTER 19 — BEAU MANOR

William Perry Herrick of Beau Manor

To design his new house, William Perry Herrick chose William Railton, a famous and fashionable London architect. His most well-known architectural project was the design of Nelson's Column at Trafalgar Square in London. From the very beginning William Perry Herrick seemed determined to demonstrate his great wealth. The estimated cost at the beginning of the project in 1842 was 9,723 pounds and in only one year the estimate reached 12,000 pounds. Costs continued to escalate. An army of local tradesmen were employed. A typical workweek in 1846 employed 17 joiners, 14 masons, 4 plasterers, a bricklayer and 11 laborers. The Leicester Journal reported at the time that "it is the wish of Mr. Herrick that his neighbors should have the preference (for employment)." By the time the mansion was completed, the total cost was 37,000 pounds, an astronomical sum in 1848. By comparison, he purchased five cottages in nearby Woodhouse Eaves for just 350 pounds.

William Perry Herrick was 54 years old and still a bachelor when he moved into his new Beau Manor. But he wasn't completely alone. His unmarried sister, Mary Ann, moved into the mansion as well. Mary Ann was known as "The Mistress of Beau Manor". In addition, the 1851 census indicates that 11 "indoor" servants were there to wait on the two occupants. In addition to the indoor servants, there were grooms, coachmen, gardeners, gamekeepers, and other estate workers, some of whom lived in quarters around the stable yard or in cottages on the estate.

One entered Beau Manor by a double door studded with brass and carved with bulls' heads from the Herrick crest. As one continued into the mansion, they would enter the great hall lined with large tapestries. Then one would enter a suite of three rooms, the library, the morning room and the drawing room. Then into the billiard room, the study, and the "papers" room, specially built to hold the large collection of Herrick family records. But the most striking feature of the house must be the great staircase and staircase window, which depicts the coats of arms of the Herrick family and of their connections by marriage from the 16th to the 19th centuries, culminating in the arms of Perry Herrick.

The author in front of present day Beau Manor built by
William Perry Herrick in 1846

Chapter 19 — Beau Manor

Grand Staircase at Beau Manor

Stained glass panels at Beau Manor showing 21 Coats of Arms of five generations of Herricks

Stained glass panel at Beau Manor of Perry Herrick Coat of Arms

There were other interesting relics that dominated Beau Manor during the time of William Perry Herrick. The Great Chair, known also as the Beau Manor Chair, stood in the halls of all three Beau Manors. It is a unique piece of furniture, made of a roughly shaped trunk of a huge pollarded oak, which was felled in the park in 1690. The Beau Manor Coach was also highly used at Beau Manor. This highly elaborate coach was built in 1740 for the occasion of the wedding of William Herrick V and Lucy Gage. The most legendary piece of furniture at Beau Manor, however, is "King Dick's Bed". The bed was acquired by William Perry Herrick, who decorated a special room for it. Allegedly, this is the bed taken from the Blue Boar Inn after King Richard III slept in it the night before he left for Bosworth Field and die at the Battle of Bosworth. All three of these relics still exit and are displayed in museums in and around Leicester.

So, what would a man need when he had unimaginable wealth, a famous name and heritage, and respect from his peers. According the 68 year old, William Perry Herrick, he needed a wife. So, he acquired that too. He and Sophia Christie were married in 1862, she being 38 years younger than himself. William and Sophia were hosts to many foreign dignitaries including an Italian count and Baron de Langen, the attaché to the Prussian Legation. Sophia added much to the life of William. They became noted for their generosity and "good works". Together with Mary Ann, they built and endowed St. Mark's Church in Belgrave and various schools "for the education of children and adults of the laboring and poor classes." They also gave their support to the Leicester Infirmary, Loughborough Dispensary, the Juvenile Reformatory, and the House for Penitent Females in Leicester. Their greatest influence, however, was in the villages of Woodhouse and Woodhouse Eaves, since they owned much of the villages. Woodhouse was almost entirely rebuilt and the cottages and lodges, so distinctive in style, became model residences. Originally, the cottages of Woodhouse were Almshouses (homes for the poor) financed by Mary Ann Herrick. Mary Ann also contributed significantly to St. Mary's in Elms in Woodhouse.

Then in 1876, after 14 years of marriage, William Perry Herrick died. His death was from an accident. While fox hunting on his property, he fell off his horse. He was carried back to the house and died in Sophia's arms. Sophia continued to live at Beau Manor for another 40 years. She continued the tradition of Herrick benevolences, starting the first soup kitchens in the area. She served hot soup from her back door to the poor of the district and in time of distress her soup kitchens expanded to the surrounding villages. In 1915 at the age of 83 Sophia died. Beau Manor, after 322 years and 7 generations of Herricks, passed out of the family.

The year Sophia died, Beau Manor was passed on to William Curzon Herrick. In his will, William Perry Herrick, who had no heir, had provided that after his death and that of his wife, the estate should go to

"Colonel the Honourable Montague Curzon of Garats Hey". However, Curzon died before Sophia, so the estate was inherited by his son, who took the name Herrick in deference to his benefactor. In 1945, the estate passed to a cousin, Lieutenant Colonel Asshely Curzon-Howe-Herrick, who never lived there.

The Loughborough Advertiser
Thursday February 17th, 1876

DEATH OF W. PERRY-HERRICK, ESQ.

It is with deep regret that we have to record in our columns the announcement of the above named gentleman which occurred on Tuesday afternoon last, at his residence, Beaumanor Park, near Loughborough. It is stated the Mr. Herrick was out in the morning, when he went to the meet of the Quorn Hounds, at Woodhouse. He joined the hunt, and a fox being found hard by - at Bawdon Wood - it gave deceased much pleasure. Mr. Herrick was then to all appearance in good health for a gentleman of his age, he being in his 82nd year. When at Bradgate, it is said, he complained of feeling unwell, and his groom (Holland) started for Beaumanor which was duly reached. On arriving at home, Mr. Herrick was assisted to alight from his horse, and on entering the hall he was almost immediately taken worse, and shortly afterwards expired. Medical aid was summoned, but the vital spark had fled, and the public had lost another benefactor whose place it will be difficult to fill.

Mr. Herrick has only survived his sister (the late Miss Herrick) about four years, she having died on Christmas Day, 1871. And death has now cast another heavy cloud of gloom and darkness about Beaumanor, and indeed over the neighbourhood all around. For it is not only at Beaumanor that the loss of Mr. Herrick will be felt; but wherever he was known the tidings of his decease will be received with general lamentation. In him was to be found all that could be looked for in a gentleman of wealth and position; though it is not ours to be able to record the many acts of munificence and liberality to institutions both public and private, which have been performed by him, nor the many little kindnesses and mercies which have held his name in such popular favour with all classes in our midst. But we are confident we are only giving expression to the general feeling when we say that a deep sense of mournful sadness pervades all classes among us.

The painful intelligence of Mr. Herrick's death reached Loughborough with great rapidity, though it was some time before the public could give credence to the report, so heavily were they stricken with sorrow at the sad tidings; and hopes were anxiously entertained that the worst was not true. But so it proved, and the melancholy event may be said to have put the whole neighbourhood into mourning. The villages of Woodhouse, Woodhouse Eaves, &c, present a remarkable appearance, nearly every house having its blinds drawn down. At Loughborough also the same sign of mourning is before us in almost every direction; and in the market place and other of the principal thoroughfares most of the shops have their shutters partially closed.

Mr. Herrick has (like his inestimable sister) left behind him "an example worthy of a lifelong ambition to imitate, and a manner of dispensing benefactions unstained by narrow considerations of sect or party." He also was largely possessed of that grace without which the meretricious advantages of wealth become unworthy of human ambition.

The Loughborough Advertiser
Thursday February 24th, 1876

FUNERAL OF W. PERRY-HERRICK, ESQ.

Which took place at Woodhouse Church, at midday on Tuesday last, was in accordance with deceased's wishes, of a simple and unpretending character in itself; but the desire to shew respect for his memory, was evinced by the great numbers who flocked to witness it. Besides those from the immediate neighbourhood of Woodhouse and Woodhouse Eaves, many were there from Loughborough, the fact of all the principal tradesmen's shops being closed during the time, affording opportunities to many to be there. A number of neighbouring gentry were also present, and many of the tenants of the deceased.

The muffled bell at Woodhouse Church was solemnly tolling all the morning; and at about 12 o'clock the mournful procession left the hall, and proceeded across the park, the body being conveyed on a bier. On reaching the highway, the procession was joined by a large number of gentlemen, who were desirous to shew by their presence, their reverence for the memory of the deceased.

Obituary and Funeral notice for William Perry Herrick

Chapter 19 — Beau Manor

During World War II, Beau Manor was used by the British government for military purposes. It became a highly secret decoding center operating to break the German code and was consequently in continual communication with Bletchley Park in London. After the war in 1946, it was sold by auction. In addition to 4,520 acres, the estate included 28 dairy farms, 6 country residences, 81 houses, cottages and shops in Woodhouse, Woodhouse Eaves and Woodthorpe. The auction also included numerous "small holdings", Beacon Hill, and the 9-hole Charnwood Forest Golf Course. In 1974, the Leicestershire Education Committee decided to buy Beau Manor for a Teacher Training and Conference Center. It was decided that the houses on the property were to be used as residences for school children for environmental studies.

If any stories of the first Beau Manor acquired by Sir William were passed down to his children and grandchildren, however likely, there is no evidence of it. Over the generations in America, from Joseph Sr. to Nathaniel to Mahlon, it is likely the stories of Beau Manor back in England faded from memory. The Herricks in America may have started in Salem with a religious fervor and purpose, but they moved often for land and independence. Theirs was a hard life, pushing west, discovering new places, and meeting unexpected challenges. Had Henry stayed in England, his life would have been vastly different. He would certainly have to compromise his Puritan beliefs but could have continued his prosperous textile trade. He and a new family that he may have had in Leicester would possibly have interacted with their cousins at Beau Manor.

Part III:

The Modern Family

Cast of Characters:

Mahlon Herrick Sr. – As a youth, he was a soldier in the Union Army of the Civil War. Applied and received war disability pensions for the remainder of his life. Moved north to Harbor Springs, Michigan.

Mahlon Herrick Jr. - First Herrick in the family to attend and graduate from college. Entered World War II after Pearl Harbor as a private. Received a field commission as an officer and awarded a Bronze Star. Linked HGRI with his own modern family.

Chapter 20
Civil War and Mahlon Herrick Sr.

While William Perry Herrick was enjoying the new mansion that he built, young Mahlon Herrick from Carmel Township, Michigan was working at his father's farm and growing increasingly restless as the greatest national crisis in America entered its fourth year. Mahlon Herrick was John and Orpha's sixth child and second son, their first son to live to adulthood. Mahlon, whose unusual name is biblical and found in the Book of Ruth, was born August 11, 1847.

At the age of 17, on March 22, 1865, Mahlon enrolled in the Union Army to fight in the Civil War.[71] He was on the muster role at Jackson, Michigan on April 12, 1865. What was he thinking? The war was coming to a close and ended at Appomattox the month after he enlisted. Was it adventure for a young man bored on the farm? Was it stories of war and honor that he may have heard from his cousins back in New York? Or was it nothing more than money for serving as a substitute for a draftee.

Mahlon had four 1st cousins who also fought in the Civil War. All four were from Nunda, New York. His father's oldest brother, Alpheus, had a son William who was Baptist minister serving a parish in Wisconsin. He joined a Wisconsin regiment and was killed in battle at Gettysburg. His father's sister, Mary, had a son, George Hamilton, who served in the New York 33rd infantry during the Civil War but was killed in Cuba during the Spanish-American War. Mahlon's father also had a brother, George B. Herrick, who had a son also named George B (Bell) Herrick. He served with his cousin George Hamilton in the New

---

71 Mahlon had two cousins back in New York who volunteered in the Civil War. George Bell Herrick, son of George Herrick, and Mortimer Herrick, son of Edward Herrick, were in the 33rd regiment of N.Y. volunteers.

York 33rd infantry, as did Mahlon's cousin Mortimer, son of Mahlon's uncle Edward. Mortimer died in battle at Spotsylvania at the age of 21.

But in Michigan, Mahlon, at the young and impulsive age of 17, replaced a local man who was drafted. During the Civil War, a draftee could pay someone else to substitute for them as an army draftee. Mahlon took the bait (and the money) from a draftee named Henry Baker and entered the Fifteenth Infantry for a period of one year from Vermontville, Michigan.

Civil War Muster Roll for Mahlon Herrick

Chapter 20 — Civil War and Mahlon Herrick Sr.

Henry Baker had to be a relatively wealthy man, since only a man of means could afford commutation or substitution. A man whose name was called in the draft lotteries could either pay a commutation fee of $300, which exempted him from service during this draft lottery, or he could provide a substitute, which would exempt him from service throughout the duration of the war. Mahlon saw this new law as a good deal. The war was winding down and, as a young man, he looked to military adventure with a good bounty to boot. With the Enrollment Act 1863, the Civil War truly began to be known as a "rich man's war and a poor man's fight". It is likely that Henry Baker was a local friend of the family, since he was personally identified as the draftee who paid Mahlon to substitute for him. In many cases, middlemen were involved who took a commission for brokering payment for a draftee and paying the substitute, less the brokerage commission. Regardless, such practices were highly unpopular, despite their legality. Below are the lyrics from a song about this practice.

> The well-to-do will hire you to be a substitute. There's others with inferior goods collecting lots of loot. So, what's the crime in getting mine legally to boot by substituting over and deserting from the war. I set up shop in city hall New York it pays me well. I sell exemptions from the draft and business is going swell. I've got runners to bring in patrons who after get to tell by commutation they're exempt from serving in the war.
> —Enlistment Jumpers by Bruce Burnside

Mahlon had his adventure but it didn't last long. On his way to join his regiment, he got sick and ended up in the Fairfax Seminary Hospital in Alexandria, Virginia. He never made it to his regiment, which was located in North Carolina. He did finally get assigned to his unit at Harts Island, New York, but there was no need. He was sick, and the war was over. He was sent back to Michigan and was admitted to Harper Hospital in Detroit on August 28, 1865. Mahlon did have enough military service in the Civil War, however, to be assigned a soldier's uniform, a musket, and enough time to get a painting made of himself.

Mahlon Herrick age 17, Fifteenth Infantry, Civil War 1865

Before Mahlon mustered into service, the Fifteenth Infantry had a notable history. It was organized at Monroe, Michigan in March 1862 with an initial enrollment of 869 officers and men, and lead by Colonel John Oliver of Monroe. The first engagement of the Fifteenth with the enemy was at Pittsburg Landing, Tennessee where the regiment was with the Union forces under General U.S. Grant. The regiment suffered the loss of 2 officers and 31 men. It was tough orientation to battle that the regiment received a complimentary notice from the brigade commander for "conspicuous gallantry". The Fifteenth went on to take part in the battle of Corinth, Mississippi and later engaged the enemy at Vicksburg. After the confederates surrendered Vicksburg, the Fifteenth moved on to reinforce the army of the Cumberland. Then they marched to Alabama where they remained until February 1864. At this time, the regiment returned to Monroe so that soldiers could furlough to visit their families. After a short respite, the Fifteenth regrouped at Monroe and proceeded to Chattanooga, Tennessee. It engaged immediately in the Georgia campaign with General Sherman's army, fighting continuously and leading up to the siege of Atlanta. During the siege, the Fifteenth engaged General Hood's confederates and captured the colors of two confederate regiments and 176 prisoners. After General Hood evacuated Atlanta, the Fifteenth followed him in pursuit. The regiment then returned to Atlanta to participate in the march from Atlanta to the sea. The Fifteenth then marched to the coast through the Carolinas and ultimately into Virginia. By then the war was over.

On May 24th, 1865, the Fifteenth took part in the grand review with Sherman's army in Washington DC. Colonel Oliver was promoted to Brigadier General. The regiment returned to Michigan and disbanded on September 1, 1865.

Since Mahlon mustered into the Fifteenth in March and the grand review in Washington was late May, it is possible that he participated in that ceremony. But it is unlikely, however, given that he was ill and admitted into an Alexandria hospital on May 13th. In all, the Fifteenth suffered 51 killed in action, 24 dying of wounds, 4 dying in prisons, and 182 dying of disease. A total of 286 were discharged for disability (wounds or disease). Mahlon was one of them with 5 months and 6 days of service.

As it turned out, Mahlon did not forget his illness during his 5 months in the army. He was admitted into the Fairfax (Virginia) Seminary Hospital for measles, which he contracted at Fort Hatteras on the way to joining the Fifteenth Regiment. Soon after his recovery from the measles, he developed "bilious fevers", which were diagnosed as Chronic Articular Rheumatism in his limbs. He remained sick until discharged and in August was admitted to the hospital in Detroit. Because the Rheumatism caused such pain in his limbs, he was not able to work up to capacity as a farmer, and consequently he filed for a disability pension through the War Department. His appeals for war related disability continued with the War Department for the rest of his life.

Bed Card from Harper Hospital, Detroit

However, before those appeals began, he met and married Fannie Clements on May 8th, 1870. Fannie grew up in Carmel Township, like Mahlon, but was she born in Tendergall (Six Mile Cross), Tyrone County, Ireland, a small village outside Belfast.[72] She came to Carmel Township with her family as a small child in the 1850s, presumably due to the potato famine in Ireland.

---

72 Belfast is now the capital of Northern Ireland

Chapter 20 — Civil War and Mahlon Herrick Sr.

Discharge papers of Mahon J. Herrick from Civil War

There is no record of any Rheumatism or serious illness that handicapped Mahlon during the early years of his marriage to Fanny. It wasn't until October 2, 1879 that he filed his first claim for a disability pension in probate court of Eaton County – 14 years after his service in the Civil War.

Tintype of Mahlon and Fannie with children Minnie and Arthur, 1875

Mahlon and Fannie, Arthur and Minnie, 1890

Apparently, the federal government didn't see it his way. It took two years, but finally in June 1881, the War Department denied his claim by saying that he "is not entitled to bounty. Substitute for Henry D. Baker (drafted)." A follow up letter from the Adjutant General's Office stated that there was, "No evidence of alleged disease." That decision was supported by an Examining Surgeon's Certificate, which concluded that Mahlon was "not incapacitated for obtaining his subsistence by manual labor from the cause above stated."

Despite this medical determination and War Department denial, Mahlon was given a whopping pension of $2.00 per month effective March 17, 1881. But Mahlon persisted even more. He refilled his claim for "restitution and increase" in the pension through his attorney in May 1882. Plus, he added another surgeon's examination. This exam by another surgeon was conducted in March 1885 and concluded, "We find no physical or rational signs of rheumatism. It is our opinion that he has a weak heart, which is probably the result of fever, which he states he had in the service. We rate for disease of heart ½ total. It is our opinion the disability was incurred in the service as claimed, and that it is not aggravated or protracted by vicious habits. We find the disability as above described to entitle him to a ½ total." This medical statement seemed to be effective, since he received an increase to $8.00 per month effective June 18, 1890.

So, it appears that Mahlon went from measles to rheumatism to heart disease. But it wasn't enough to finally get a surgeon's examination attesting to his claim and to get his attorney to appeal to the War Department. In 1883, Mahlon's attorney took about 25 depositions attesting to his character. All of the character witnesses stated that his reputation was good except one person. That person was his brother-in-law, Berna Kelly, his sister's husband. Kelly's compliant about his reputation is that he is "inclined to be visionary." Perhaps by 'visionary', Berna Kelly was a citing a certain 'persistence' that characterized Mahlon. Below are Mahlon's claims for disability, surgeon statements, a War Department response, and samples of the depositions made by his friends in Vermontville.

MICHAEL J. HERRICK

A.   DECLARATION FOR ORIGINAL INVALID PENSION.   **A.**

To be executed before a court of record or some officer thereof having custody of its seal.

State of Michigan
County of Eaton } ss:

On this 22" day of September A. D. one thousand eight hundred and seventy-nine, personally appeared before me, Judge of the Probate Court, a court of record within and for the county and State aforesaid, Mahlon J. Herrick, aged 32 years, a resident of the Town of Carmel, county of Eaton, State of Michigan, who, being duly sworn according to law, declares that he is the identical Mahlon J. Herrick, who was ENROLLED on the 22" day of March, 1865, in company (_____) of the 15" regiment of Michigan Infantry, commanded by (Volunteers), and was honorably DISCHARGED at Detroit on the 28" day of August, 1865; that his personal description is as follows: Age, 18 years; height, 5 feet 6 inches; complexion, Light; hair, Light; eyes, Hazel. That while a member of the organization aforesaid, in the service and in the line of his duty at Alexandria, in the State of Virginia, on or about the 13" day of May, 1865, he was taken sick with the measles contracted at Fort Hatteras, that soon after his recovery from said measels, he was taken sick with the billius fever and was in a very bad condition, that previous to the breaking up of the said fever, he was taken sick with the Chronic articular Rheumatism in his limbs caused by large doses of calomel and exposure to cold and dampness during his sickness. That he was treated in hospitals as follows: Fairfax Seminary Hospital Alexandria Virginia Ward "VII" _____ under David P. Smith, Surgeon. _____

That he has not been employed in the military or naval service otherwise than as stated above.

That since leaving the service this applicant has resided in the County of Eaton in the State of Michigan, and his occupation has been that of a Farmer. That prior to his entry into the service above named he was a man of good, sound, physical health, being when enrolled a Farmer. That he is now _____ disabled from obtaining his subsistence by manual labor by reason of his injuries, above described, received in the service of the United States; and he therefore makes this declaration for the purpose of being placed on the invalid pension-roll of the United States.

He hereby appoints, with full power of substitution and revocation, Frank A. Dean of Charlotte, State of Michigan, his true and lawful attorney to prosecute his claim. That he has never received nor applied for a pension. That his Post Office address is Charlotte, county of Eaton.

State of Michigan

Claimant's signature: Mahlon J. Herrick

Attest: Charles D. Spofford
Elihu S. Tufts

Mahlon Herrick's original claim for disability pension for Civil War service, 1879

Chapter 20 — Civil War and Mahlon Herrick Sr.

Initial medical exam from Surgeon regarding
Mahlon Herrick's disability claim, 1881

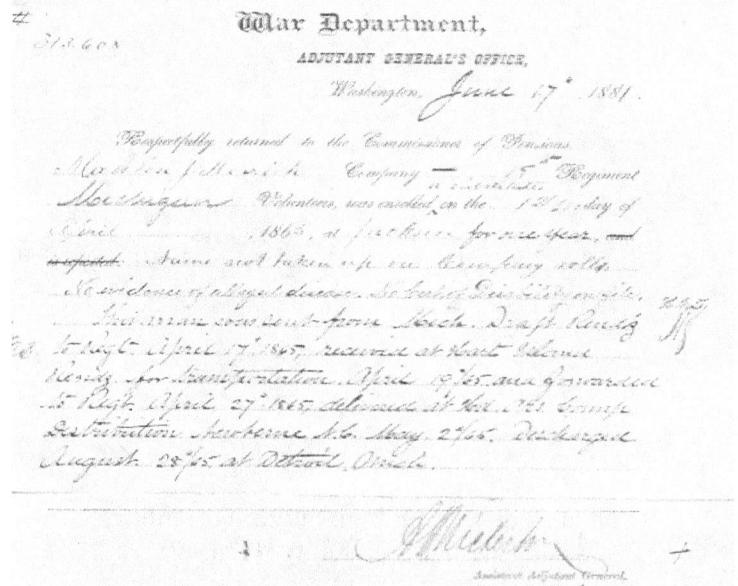

Surgeon General's report to Commissioner of Pensions, 1881

War Department's response to the Commissioner of Pensions, 1881

Chapter 20 — Civil War and Mahlon Herrick Sr.

War Department's denial of disability claim, 1881

Michael J. Herrick

Second Surgeon's Examination, 1885

CHAPTER 20 — CIVIL WAR AND MAHLON HERRICK SR.

Finally, in 1883, sworn depositions were obtained from friends in the Carmel Township area testifying to Mahlon's character and his disability. A total of 25 depositions were made. Below are samples from those sworn written depositions.

Sir,
I have the honor to return herewith the paper in original claim of Mahlon J. Herrick, No. 313608 of Vermontville Eaton Co. Michigan submitted to me for special examination January 17, 1883 with my report of the same. I obtained statement of claimant June 13, 1883 in which he claims at enlistment he was perfectly healthy. Had measles in May 1865, was discharged for disability, was totally disabled for three years after his discharge, has not been able to wear boot or shoes, in 1882-83 was very sick is worse in summer than winter, has had attacks frequently. There is a difference of opinion as to claimant's disability, some claiming him to be truthful others saying he is not. I am inclined to judge from what I saw of him and talking a good deal with him that he is not a truthful person. (unsigned)
—Lansing, Michigan June 25, 1883

Brother-in-law. Was sound before enlistment. Was sick at discharge. Could not work much first year then next year could do labor. Complains of pain in calves of his legs. Has lived about ten miles apart.
—Barna Kelly, 1883

Reputation for truthfulness and judgment excellent. Has known claimant for twenty three years. Was well before enlistment. Understood had a fever at discharge. Never heard any complaints until the last year or so. Able to work hard -----. Has a reputation of being a good worker, never been able to see any difference between claimant and any other man.
—John Shaver, 1883

Has known claimant sixteen years. Yes, before he went into the army – healthy. Has been able to perform manual labor since discharge as any ordinary man.
—Richard Boyles, 1883

Has known claimant since he was born. Lived half a mile from him. Health good before enlistment. Never sick in his life before he went into the army. Sick at discharge. Limbs swollen. Was not able to work for three or four years. Calves of his legs would knot right up and swell. Never has been able to wear any boots in the summer time.
—Samuel Smith, 1883

Below is a sample of sworn verbal statements made by physicians and friends.

<u>Alva A. Nichols, MD</u> says he saw claimant on his return from the army. That he was disabled by rheumatism in his legs so that he was unable to perform his farm work; that he was disabled for nine months in the year for the period of ten years, for performing manual labor, immediately succeeding his discharge from the service; that the rheumatism would come on him in the spring and stay until late in the fall. Say he did not treat him during this period, but he was treated by Dr. Hall of Carlisle, who died about five years ago, since which time (he) has treated him. The disability increases on him every year, and he has been entirely disabled for his farm work by rheumatism in both legs.

<u>Emanuel Ansprocter</u> says that soon after claimant returned home from the service he called upon him and he was disabled with rheumatism in both limbs and unable to walk without crutches; that he went on crutches about four weeks; that he has seen him nearly every day since his discharge; that the rheumatism comes on most severely in the spring of the year, and continues until fall, and that he has been more disabled during the last five years than prior to that time.

Chapter 20 — Civil War and Mahlon Herrick Sr.

<u>James L. Johnson, MD</u> says that in the month of April 1882 the said claimant came to his affiant for medical treatment on account of and for Chronic Rheumatism of the limbs that I could do nothing for him and so advised him and that I gave him no treatment and advised him to --- Physicians alone as in my opinion was that there was no help for him. I made a medical examination of Mahlon J. Herrick on November 15, 1884 and he is not as able for manual labor at present as he was in 1882. In my opinion the said claimant has been disabled one-fourth during the past thirteen years the time that I have known him.

> chronic rheumatism, but at what exact time during such sickness this deponent is unable to say.
> That on or about the 28th day of August A.D. 1865 said Mahlon J. Herrick was discharged from said hospital, and was unable to walk without the aid of crutches, and come to his home in Carmel Township on crutches by reason of said rheumatism.
> And this deponent further says that the said Mahlon J. Herrick was never assigned to any company, that he was assigned at Hart's Island New York to the 15 Michigan Infantry but did not reach his regiment on account of his sickness at Alexandria hospital aforesaid and further says not.
>
> David Horn
>
> Subscribed and Sworn to before me this 18 day of June A.D. 1881
>
> Garry C. Cox
> County Clerk
> Eaton Co. Mich.

Sworn court testimony from a friend David Horn, 1881

Mahlon continued to get medical examinations for his condition from a variety of doctors. Some recommended an increase in disability payments and some recommended rejection of payments. Yet he continued all the rest of his life to apply for increase in pension disability payments.

Chapter 20 — Civil War and Mahlon Herrick Sr.

DEPOSITION A

Case of Mahlon J. Herrick   No. 313608

On this Thirteenth day of June 1882, at Charlotte, County of Eaton, State of Michigan before me John Stilwell, a Special Examiner of the Pension Office, personally appeared Claimant Mahlon J. Herrick, who being by me first duly sworn to answer all interrogatories propounded to him during the Special Examination of his claim for pension deposes and says he is 35 years of age. Farmer P.O. Bermontville, Eaton Co., Mich. Says that he enlisted as a Substitute March 22, 1865, in 15th Michigan Infty. Vols. but was not assigned to any Co. That at time of his enlistment he was 18 years of age, was a strong healthy boy, never had had any disease or sickness except ague before he went into the army. That he was born in Carmel Township, Eaton Co., Mich. and that he had resided there all his life, never had lived any place else previous to going into the army. That he had worked on his Father's farm all his life.

Says that at Alexandria, Va., was taken sick with the Measles on the 13 day of May 1865, contracted at or near Fort Hatteras, N.C., was sent to Fairfax Seminary Hospital Alexandria Va., was in Ward 2, he also had bilious fever in same Hospital, was very low came O.C.R., had a very severe pain in the Calves of his legs. Dr. Lewis P. Smith was Surgeon in charge of that Hospital, which was very severe pain was so severe as to render him unconscious, had a bad Cold at time of discharge which was in August 22, 1865 at Detroit Mich. at Parker Hospital, on account of an order to discharge all men that had no descriptive list. After his discharge came home to Calhoun Eaton County Michigan. Had to use crutches for two or three weeks after his discharge was not able to perform manual labor for three years after his discharge to any extent, could in the winter saw and chop fire wood but in the Summer time and in the Hot weather was not able to do any thing. After the three years spoken of could work some but not very much. Cause worked at all kinds of farm work, but never has been able to work with boot or Shoes on, has to go barefooted, has been years that has not been a Boot or Shoe on from April 1st August, they hurt to wear them, that is on Soft or plowed grounds. When there is any spring to the ground, he is unable to wear a Boot or Shoe. That since his discharge he has been disabled the first three years totally, since then he has been disabled on account of his pain in his Calves totally at times for a week then for a month, but in winter time is able to work, does not feel the pain much unless he walks a good deal in the Snow but is able to work in Winter at all kinds of work. but says that last winter 1882 & '3 he was unable to work all Winter. This Spring has felt first rate has only lost one week since April 1st to the present time. Says that his Mouth was sore at time of his discharge, and that he lost eight teeth in the first two years after discharge and thinks he must have been given Calomel in large doses while in Fairfax Seminary Hospital.

Says that on his return home

Chapter 20 — Civil War and Mahlon Herrick Sr.

after his discharge he lived with his Father and was attended by Dr John Hall of Kalamo Eaton Co Mich. Dr Hall died about seven years ago, was doctoring for the pain in his Calves, does not know what disease that Dr Hall called it, was told by Dr Hall that he would outgrow it, was attended by Dr Alva Nicholes of Charlotte Eaton Co Mich— for seven years past,

9 You have the privilege of being present during the examination of all Witnesses in your case and of crossexamining them either yourself or by an Atty or both. Who do you wish me to see what are their P.O. addresses and what do you expect to prove by them —

a Alma A Nicholes — of Charlotte, as to condition before and since enlistment, David Horn in current of desability his P.O. is Charlotte, Eaton Co Mich. Emanuel Onestocler of Chester Eaton Co Mich condition before and since enlistment. Homer Davis Chester Eaton Co, condition before enlistmt C.S. Spaffard of Carlisle Mich. condition since enlistmt. Peter Sears of Carlisle condition before and since enlistment. Charles Chappell of Charlotte Eaton Co Mich, in current of disability I will be present during the examinations,

Mahlon J Herrick
Deponent.

Subscribed and sworn to before me this 13 day of June 1883, and I certify that the contents were fully made known to deponent before signing.

John Stilwell
Special Examiner.

Deposition of Mahlon Herrick to Special Examiner of the Pension Office, 1883

In 1897, his Declaration for Increase of Invalid Pension cited additional ailments of "disease of rectum, piles, affection of bowels and abdominal viscera resulting from measles and chronic diarrhea contracted in the army." This application got him an increase to $14 per month.

Chapter 20 — Civil War and Mahlon Herrick Sr.

q. What was his physical condition at that time?

a. He was walking with crutches. He was very thin. Do not remember what was the malady said to have Chronic Diarrhoea.

q. How long did he continue in this condition?

a. He gained up some, but do not think that he was able to work for a year or more.

q. Why could he not work?

a. He was sick — said he had Chronic Diarrhoea.

q. Has Claimant had Rheumatism since his discharge?

a. He has claimed that he has pain in the calves of his legs. Cannot tell how long ago he first told me of this but I think he has complained of this ever since he came back. I had an interest in him for he was a substitute for me, and I would ask him how he was getting along and he would say that he had Chronic Diarrhoea and pain in the calves of his legs. He has shown me his legs. They were swollen at times — knotted and swelled up.

q. How much was Claimant disabled from performing manual labor by reason of his Chronic Diarrhoea and pain in the calves of his legs for the first five years after his discharge?

a. For the first two or three years I do not think he did much work. I know he hired to several men and had to quit. Then he bought a twenty acre farm, worked on that partly, cleared it up and worked some for the neighbors. How much he did I cannot say.

> q Haw much labor has Claimant been able to do since 1870.
>
> a Have heard that he could work some and then that he could not work. Three years ago he moved just across the road from m— Church he has been able to work about three quarters of the time since then. Claimant his legs hurt him could not wear shoes had a bad spell last fall. did not work much last winter.
>
> H. H. Baker.
> Deponent.
>
> Sworn to and subscribed before me this 15 day of June 1883, and I certify that the contents were fully made known to deponent before signing.
>
> John Stilwell
> Special Examiner.
>
> Page 76 Deposition 8

Deposition of Henry Baker, 1883

Chapter 20 — Civil War and Mahlon Herrick Sr.

Questionnaire completed by Mahlon Herrick for Bureau of Pensions, 1899

In 1911, Mahlon obtained two more medical exams from two different physicians and an explanation was sent from the Pension Commissioner to the Bureau of Pensions at the Department of Interior, resulting in a letter from the commissioner that "the examinations fail to show that the disability exists is such a degree to warrant a rate in excess of $17 per month." However, he persisted on the basis of documentation from his physicians that "rheumatism in the right shoulder with marked loss of motion . . . impossible for him to raise his right hand to his head." The surgeon's certificate goes on to conclude that "Claimant is so disabled from Rheumatism and disease of heart as to be incapacitated for performing manual labor in a degree equivalent to the loss of a hand or foot and is entitled to $24.00 per month." Mahlon received that increase.

Civil War Division
DEPARTMENT OF THE INTERIOR
BUREAU OF PENSIONS

Washington, D. C. _____, 191__

Dr. _N. H. Rand_, Secretary,
Charlotte,
Co. _Eaton_ _Mich_.

Sir:

Mr. _Mahlon E. Herrick_,
P. O. _Winobatoolla_
Co. _Eaton_ _Mich_.

late a _Pvt_
Co. ___ _15_ Regiment _Mich Vol Inf_
an applicant for _one_
Invalid Pension No. _251,184_
has been directed to report himself to you for examination on account of the disability or disabilities mentioned hereon.

If other causes of disability are found on examination, they should be described. Evidences of the results of vicious habits should be sought in every case and reported on.

Report of Pension Commissioner to Bureau of Pensions at
Department of Interior, 1911

Then in 1918, at the age of 70, Mahlon applied again for an increase in his disability pension. This time the increase was to $30 per month, but not without the involvement of his congressman in the U.S House of Representatives. The letter from the Commissioner of the Civil War Division of Pensions to F.D. Scott, his congressman in the House is below.

Chapter 20 — Civil War and Mahlon Herrick Sr.

```
J McC

Civil War Division
                                November 6, 1918.

Hon. F..D. Scott,
    House of Representatives,
        Washington, D. C.

My dear Mr. Scott:-

        In response to your inquiry of the
25th ultimo, relative to the pension case,
certificate number 251184, of Mahlon J.
Herrick, Unassigned 15th Michigan Infantry,
whose postoffice address you give as Harbor
Springs, Michigan, I have the honor to advise
you that the soldier's claim under the Act of
May 11, 1912, amended by Act of June 10, 1918,
has been allowed at the rate of $30 per month
from July 5, 1918, date of filing claim.

                Very truly yours,

                        G. M. SALTZGABER,

Carbon copy                    Commissioner.
for your files.
```

Letter to Mahlon's congressman in House of Representatives, 1918

Then in 1929, at the age of 81, he got another physical exam and affidavit of a physician for another increase. This time he needed the help of his son and grandson to complete the declaration for a pension increase. On this last request, his son, Arthur, sited "His mind is failing, and he cannot remember a conversation or other talk to exceed one hour at a time. He cannot find his clothes to dress himself and requires watching off and on." This final request boosted his pension to $72 per month. Finally, we're talking about real money.

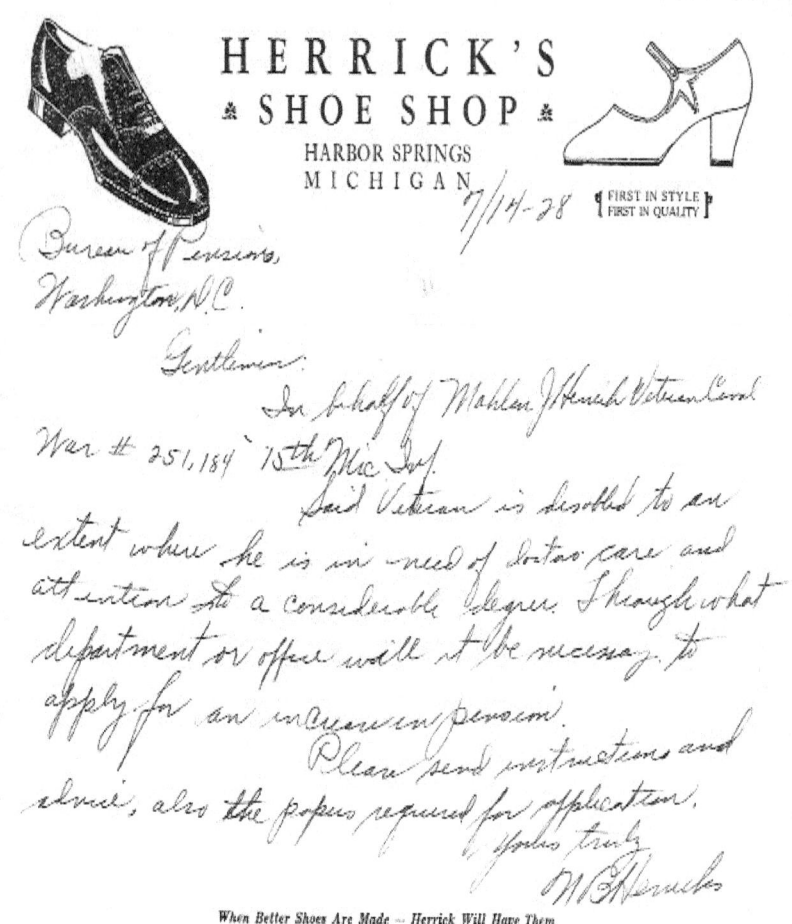

Letter from Mahlon's grandson, Ned Herrick, to
Bureau of Pensions, July 1928. Written on
letterhead of the shoe store that Ned owned.

Mahlon never stopped fighting for what he thought he should get. Although he claimed war related disability all his life, he also worked as a farmer all his life. On his 1918 Declaration for Pension, he cited is occupation as "farmer, also painting, papering and roofing". Clearly, his disability was always in question, but he persisted and received what he thought he was due. He "retired" in 1919 and moved from Vermontville to Harbor Springs, Michigan with his wife Fannie in order to be with his

CHAPTER 20 — CIVIL WAR AND MAHLON HERRICK SR.

son and daughter who had moved previously to Harbor Springs. Fannie died in 1924 and Mahlon died in 1933 at the ripe old age of 86.

Mahlon and Fannie purchased a house on 4th Street in Harbor Springs, Michigan, which stayed in the family for three generations. Mahlon enjoyed his later years despite his physical and mental infirmities, always participating in an annual Civil War veterans parade in Harbor Springs. He was the last remaining Civil War veteran in town. At his death, his total worth was estimated to be $950, which included his Harbor Springs house, his Vermontville house, and 40 acres of cut over land outside of Harbor Springs. The Affidavit Supporting Burial Claim completed by the Erwin Undertaking Co. states that he was "Worth possibly $950 but it wouldn't sell at that."

But that was not enough for the military to pay for his burial expenses. He tried. Even in death, he was denied pension compensation, as the letter below illustrates.

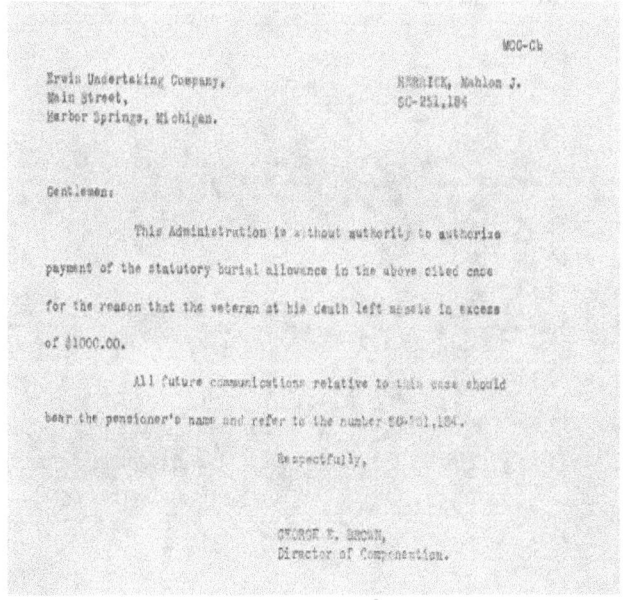

Letter from Director of Compensation to Funeral Home, 1933

Mahlon Herrick Sr. and Fannie, about 1910

Mahlon and Fannie in front of their Fourth Street house in Harbor Springs, Michigan, 1920

Chapter 21

Ireland and Sweden

Ireland

Fannie Clements and two of her three sisters and one of her two brothers came to American from Tendergall (Six Mile Cross), in Tyrone County, Ireland with her parents, Samuel and Margaret, in 1854, The ship that carried Fannie and her parents set sail from Liverpool, England and arrived at New York on May 15, 1854. Fannie's younger brother Samuel was born in Ohio, and her younger sister Minnie was born in Michigan. Economic hardships in Ireland, due probably to the potato famine, caused a rapid increase in Irish immigration at this time. It is not clear what the exact circumstances were for the Clements's immigration, nor is it clear what port of entry they immigrated to, or why they lived in Ohio for a short time, and then ultimately settling in Michigan. But they did settle in Charlotte County, Michigan about 10 to 15 years after the Herricks settled there from Nunda, New York. Presumably, the John Herrick and the Samuel Clements families knew each other and perhaps socialized together. At any rate, Mahlon Herrick and Fannie Clements did, of course, meet and married in May of 1870.

The Clements siblings, 1909 at William Clements farm near Charlotte, Michigan. Fannie Clements with husband Mahlon Herrick are lower left. Fannie's sisters Matilda and Margaret in center, and Minnie is to right of Fannie. Brothers Samuel is second row left and William is second row right.

CHAPTER 21 — IRELAND AND SWEDEN

Tree VI: Fannie Clements and the Irish Connection

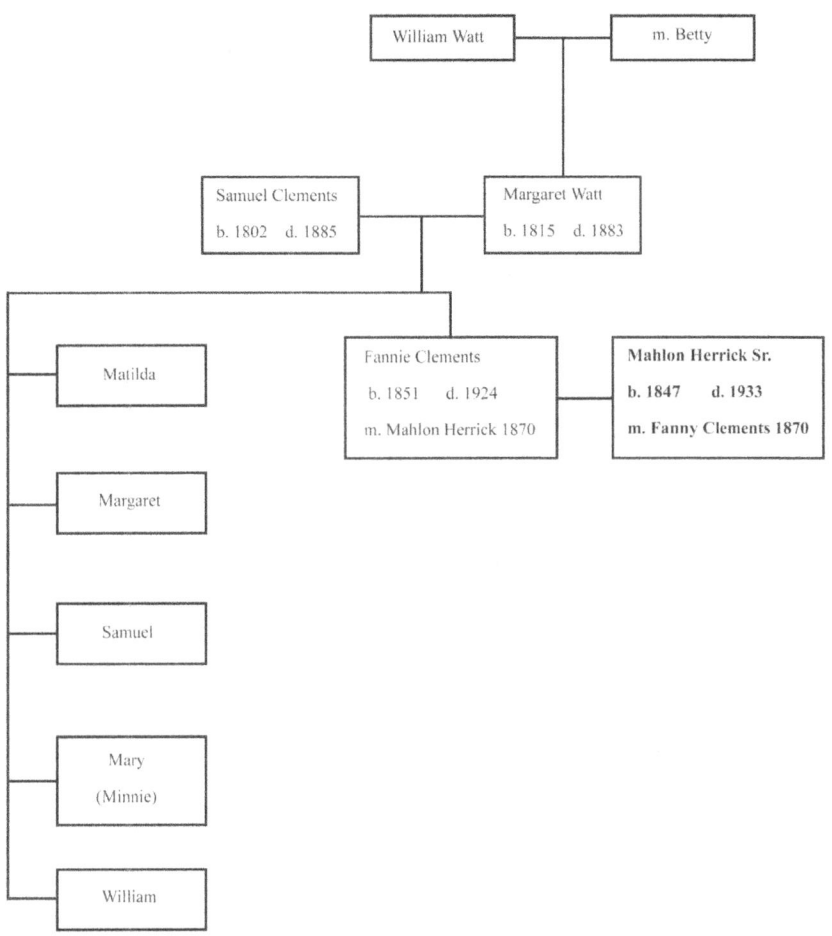

Sweden

The Nels R. Nelson family resided in Melmo, Sweden, at the extreme southern tip of Sweden in the province of Skane. The John Quist family resided at Naset, the name of their farm near Gothenburg in the province of Vastergotland. It took immigration to America in the 1870s for these two Swedish families to unite.

N. R. Nelson was born on March 29, 1846 in Roddinge Parish, located between Malmo and Ystad. N.R. never had a middle name so he took the middle initial of 'R' for his birth parish of Roddinge. He was the son and oldest child of Nels Nelson and Anna Anderson. His father, Nels, died of a farm accident when N.R. was only 10 years old, so his mother had to raise him and N.R.'s three younger siblings, Andrew, Anna and Ingrid. N.R.'s father, Nels, was a farm laborer, living with his family in one of several small cottages on a large farm owned by his employer. After Nels death, the family suffered, and it became difficult to support themselves. Starting at the age of 10, N.R. herded geese for the Parish Pastor, Reverend Cederberg. N.R. made his home with the Pastor and worked as a farm hand for the Pastor until he decided to come to America.

In the spring of 1872 at the age of 26, he immigrated to Minnesota and found work as a laborer building railroad tracks for the Soo Line. When the railroad crew got as far as Eden Valley, Minnesota, N.R. quit his job and came to Green Leaf Township where he found work as a farm laborer for Per Ekstrom, who later became Sheriff of Meeker County. He soon bought a quarter section of land south of the Beckville Church, which became the family home for fifty three years. Then four years after immigrating to American, N.R. married Elsa Kronbeck in 1876, who had immigrated from Sweden with her parents Nels J. and Anna Kronbeck. Soon later, N.R.'s brother Andrew and his sisters Anna and Ingrid also immigrated to America and settled in the Beckville community.

N.R. and Elsa became pillars of the Beckville Lutheran Church and their home was often considered the "second parsonage". N.R. and Elsa had eleven children, ten boys and one girl. Oscar was the first born, Hermas was the youngest, and Joseph was the third oldest, born in 1881. All the children lived to adulthood with the exception of two. Benjamin lived only a year and Hermas died tragically at the age of 6, shot accidentally by his brother Evald.

CHAPTER 21 — IRELAND AND SWEDEN

Below is an excerpt from the 1905 article in the Litchfield Independent Review about the accident;

Hermsas Angorius, the five year old son of Mr. and Mrs. N.R. Nelson was on Thursday noon accidentally shot and killed by his ten year old brother Evald. The story of the shooting is one of the saddest, if not the saddest of the Review has ever been compelled to chronicle. Mr. and Mrs. N.R. Nelson and the other members of the family had gone to Beckville church to attend mission services that morning and the two boys were left at home alone. To pass the time away, the two went upstairs, entered an old truck, and found a revolver of .22 caliber with which they began to play. Suddenly, a shot rang out and the younger boy dropped dead. The accident occurred at about 11:30, as near as the time can be fixed. The family returned from the church at shortly after 12:00 and they had with them as guests for dinner, two ministers and two delegates. Hasty preparations were made for dinner in order that the company might have ample time to drive to Litchfield to catch the afternoon train east. Nothing wrong was suspected. The brother who did the shooting met the family in the yard. Dinner was had, and the guests were about to take leave when the absence of the lad was noticed. On being questioned, Evald told them that Hermas was upstairs. A few minutes later an older brother went upstairs ad found the boy dead. Evald did not know that two of the chambers of the gun were loaded and while playing with it, it accidentally discharged. Coroner Harry Morell drove out to the Nelson farm but deemed an inquest unnecessary.

Despite this tragedy, the Nelson family prospered. N.R. came to America with virtually nothing, looking for a better life. He found the American dream and became a prosperous farmer and highly respected citizen and member of the Beckville church. However, before he died of a stroke at the age of 81 in 1927, he had to bury two other sons in the Beckville cemetery. Eli died at age 27 from a farm accident and Joseph died at age 34 from tuberculosis. N.R. and Elsa are also buried at the Beckville cemetery.

NR Nelson family, about 1891 or 1892 before the birth of Evald and Hermas. Joseph is back row right

Johan Andreasson was born in 1851 on a farm homestead called Naset in Vastergotland near Gotenburg, Sweden. His father, Andreas, built the first farm in the homestead and called it Naset I. Johan and his siblings, August, Hanna and Anders, grew up at Naset I. Later, in 1860, Anders built another farm on the homestead and called it Naset II. Naset is a family farming complex about 50 miles north of Gothenburg and means "a neck of land". This neck of land is a peninsula jutting into Lake Vanderydsvattnet.

In 1880, eight years after N.R. Nelson immigrated to America, Johan Andreasson immigrated to America and also settled in the farming community of Beckville, just a few miles from Litchfield, Minnesota. But there were differences between N.R. and Johan. First, Johan, upon arriving in America, not only anglicized his name to John, but he changed his Swedish surname from Andreasson to Quist. One can understand that a name change would be less confusing in America because there were so many Andreassons and Andersons in the United States, particularly in a Swedish community in Minnesota. But why the new surname of Quist? Perhaps because it was a common part of Swedish surnames such as Lundquist, Bloomquist, Turnquist, Berquist,

CHAPTER 21—IRELAND AND SWEDEN

etc. We don't know for sure, but Quist became the new family name. Another difference between N.R. and Johan is that Johan was married in Sweden. He married Birgitta Andersdotter (or Britta in America) a year or two before they both immigrated to America. Not only did they immigrate as a married couple, but Britta had just given birth to a baby boy only 5 months prior. The young family arrived in New York in July 1880 and quickly made their way to Minnesota.

John and Britta's baby boy was named Karl, but in America he was known as Charley[73]. The family bought a farm just north of the Beckville church and, like the Nelsons, were devout members of the church. After Charley was born, four more children joined the family. Nine years after Charley was born, Alma was born, then Esther, then Hilda, and the youngest was Axel, who was called Elmer.

There is no doubt that the Nelson family and the Quist family knew each other very well. Certainly, the children knew each other very well. In 1909, Joseph Nelson and Esther Quest were married at the Beckville church. Both Joseph and Esther could simply walk across a cornfield to their wedding, since the Beckfield church was located right between their two farms. In the same year, Eli Nelson and Hilda Quist were also married, again at the Beckfield church. Eli and Hilda were married for only 3 years before Eli had a serious farm accident and died of blood poisoning. They had no children.

After Joseph and Esther were married, they moved into a house built by Joseph on land purchased by N.R. on Star Lake just west of the Beckville church. Theirs was a happy marriage. Joseph followed in his father's footsteps and farmed the fertile soil around Beckville, within a mile or two of where they both grew up. He was a hard worker but was cautious not to have an accident like his brother Eli. Joseph and Esther had four daughters, the first three were born on the Star Lake farm. The fourth daughter, Myrtle, was born in Litchfield. The reason for leaving the farm and moving in town was tragic. Around 1916 or 1917, Joseph got sick. He was diagnosed with tuberculosis, a deadly and misunderstood disease at the time. He had to leave the farm since he was too weak to do physical labor. Since tuberculosis is a communicable disease and highly contagious, he was isolated from the family and sent to a TB sanatorium in northern Minnesota, where it was thought that

---

73 Charley Quist married Victoria Chilstrom, who was the aunt of Hebert Chilstrom, first Bishop of the ELCA Lutheran Church in America.

fresh cool air would cure him. It did not. Joseph died in May 1918 at the age of 34, leaving his wife with four daughters to raise, the fourth daughter, Myrtle, was only 9 months old. This is why Myrtle was born and raised in Litchfield.

United States of America,
STATE OF MINNESOTA, District Court 12th Judicial District.
County of Meeker.

John Quist personally appeared before the subscriber, the Clerk of the District Court of the 12th Judicial District for said State of Minnesota, being a COURT OF RECORD, and made oath that he was born in Sweden on and about the year eighteen hundred and Fifty one, that he emigrated to the United States, and landed at the port of New York on or about the month of July in the year eighteen hundred and Eighty: that it is bona fide his intention to become A CITIZEN OF THE UNITED STATES, and to renounce forever all allegiance and fidelity to any foreign Prince, Potentate, State or Sovereignty whatever, and particularly to the King of Sweden & Norway whereof he is a subject.

Subscribed and sworn to this 8th day of Dec. A.D. 1882.

Johan Quist

S. W. Leavitt, Clerk
By T. L. Palisbury, Deputy

John Quist's application for U.S. citizenship, 1882

CHAPTER 21 — IRELAND AND SWEDEN

John Quist's Naturalization papers for U.S. citizenship, 1887

John and Britta Quist and family. Esther is far left.

Joseph Nelson and Esther Quist wedding, May 1909

CHAPTER 21 — IRELAND AND SWEDEN

Joseph and Esther's farm at Star Lake, Beckville, Minnesota, 1910.
Joseph is holding their first born, Edith.

Edith, Evelyn, Esther, Mildred, and Myrtle Nelson
About 1923, 5 years after Joseph died.

Tree VII: Nels Nelson and John Quist and the Swedish connection

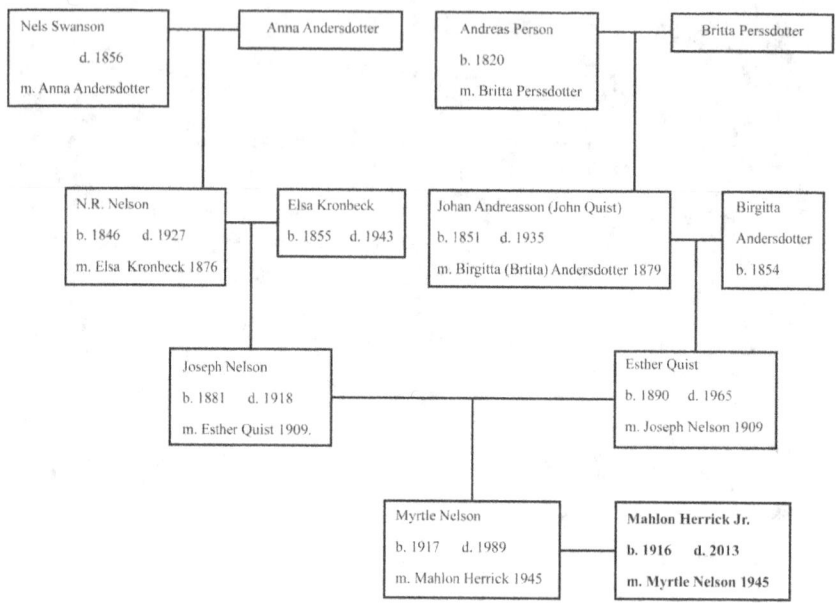

Chapter 22
Move to Harbor Springs

Three generations of Herricks lived in Carmel Township before another move was made. But this time the family stayed in the state and moved to northern Michigan. But why Harbor Springs? At the time Harbor Springs was a quaint little village on the north shore of Little Traverse Bay, about 30 miles south of the straights of Mackinac. The area, then as now, was known for its beautiful and pristine waters, sand dunes between Harbor Springs and Mackinac City, and its deeply forested woodlands along the Lake Michigan shoreline. The soil was sandy and not good for farming, unlike the rich soils of Carmel Township in southern Michigan. But the Herrick move to Harbor Springs was no temporary vacation. It was a permanent move. As it turns out, Minnie, Mahlon's daughter and Arthur's sister, and Theo (Tom) Hewlet, her husband, made the move first. Minnie and Tom, living in Vermontville not far from Carmel Township, decided to leave Vermontville for Harbor Springs around 1910 for health reasons. Minnie had bad chronic asthma and the only treatment for it back then was fresh clean air. Harbor Springs had cool fresh air in abundance, so they moved.

Arthur and Allie

By the time Minnie and Tom moved to Harbor Springs, Arthur had married Allie Ballou, also of Vermontville. They were married in 1894 and their two sons, Ned and Leland, were born in Vermontville. But in 1910 the family of four followed Minnie and Tom to Harbor Springs. The reason that Arthur and Allie followed Minnie and Tom is unclear, but we do know that they bought a house on Fourth Street in Harbor Springs where they lived raising Ned and Leland. Minnie and Tom bought a house "up the hill" but still in town. Arthur did odd jobs around town and became well known and well liked. But for reasons unknown, or unspoken, Arthur and Allie encountered problems in their marriage only a few years after they moved to Harbor Springs. They divorced, and Allie moved out of the house. Soon later, Arthur met Ruby Doty from Good Hart, an even smaller village on the shores of Lake Michigan north of Harbor Springs. They were married in 1914, only four years after Arthur and Allie moved to Harbor Springs. Ned and Leland were 19 and 14 respectively when their father remarried. Ruby was 20 years old when she married Arthur, thus only a year older than Arthur's son Ned.

Arthur and Allie with sons Ned and Leland (Nub), about 1902

Allie continued to live in Harbor Springs for a short period of time, still caring for her young teenage boys. Later she moved to Grand Rapids and remarried. Her second husband was Charles Staldt and they continued to live in Grand Rapids.

In 1916 at the age of 21, Ned registered for the draft, as World War I was raging in Europe, but the U.S. had not yet entered the war. Ned indicated on his draft registration card that he was a "clothier and tailor" living in Harbor Springs. In 1917, Ned married Vivian ReColly and they continued to live in Harbor Springs. About this same time, Ned entered the army and served during World War I, but never was sent to the fighting in Europe. After the war, he came back to Harbor Springs, purchased the Fourth Street house owned by his parents, Arthur and Allie, and purchased a shoe business. He operated Herrick's Shoe Shop, with the moto, "When better shoes are made, Herrick will have them". He successfully ran he business during the 1920s and 30s.

CHAPTER 22 — MOVE TO HARBOR SPRINGS

Ned and Vivian raised four boys and one girl. One of the boys, Dorman, died young at the age of 3. The boys who grew to adulthood were Marvin (Jack), Gerald, and James (Jimmie). The girl in the family was Carol Joy.

Jack married Marjorie Severy and they raised their family in Madison, Wisconsin. Gerry married Viola Miller and they raised their family in Detroit. Jimmie married Joyce Niehaus and they raised their family in Milwaukee. Carol Joy married John Kormash and they raised their family in Ypsilanti. Then relatively late in life, Ned and Vivian divorced and Ned remarried Frances Linchan. Ned died in 1955 at the age of 60.

Ned's brother, J. Leland, took a different path than Ned. His father, Arthur, gave him his nickname, Nub. Mahlon Jr. always called him a "rounder", and his nephew Jack simply called him "irresponsible". By all accounts, he was a fun-loving guy. One story about Nub told by his daughter, Ruth, was that he would love to meet women at the Harbor Bar across the street from the Pier and take them for joy rides in his car. He would sometimes drive out on the pier, rev up the engine, drive as fast as he could on the pier, and at the last minute hit the brakes just before the end of the pier. The women would scream, and Nub would love it.

Nub registered for the draft in 1918 at the age of 18, while living in Grand Rapids with his mother and her new husband. He listed his occupation at the time as a taxi driver for the Black and White Taxi Company. Leland, like his brother, died at a young age of a heart attack in 1949 and the age of 49.

In his short life, Nub was married three times. His first marriage was in 1922 to Margery Johnson. Their only child was Ruth, born in 1924. The marriage lasted 6 years, when Nub married his second wife, Sarah in 1928. They divorced 6 years later in 1934. A year later Nub married Blanche Moser in 1935. Blanche was from Harbor Springs, so they apparently met there between his marriages. Ruth, who was only 4 years old when her parents divorced, lived with her mother in Grand Rapids, even after her mother married Herman Kooistra, who became Ruth's stepfather.

Ruth, who frequently said that "I am my father's daughter", also was married three times. Her first husband was Raymond Huby and they married in 1940, when Ruth was 16. They had one child, Raymond Jr.,[74] who was born in 1943. Ruth and Raymond divorced after about 6 years, and Ruth remarried Lawrence Drake in 1946. Ruth and Lawrence lived in Lansing at the time and by this time Allie had also moved to Lansing. Between her marriages to Raymond and Lawrence, Ruth lived with her grandmother, Allie. But only two years after Ruth married Lawrence, Allie died in 1948. But the marriage between Ruth and Lawrence was not to last. It is not clear when the divorce occurred, but Ruth married a third time to John Schlinkert. They lived in the Port Huron area until John's death in 1985.

Allie on left and Ruth on right. Ned or Nub holding baby. About 1930

---

74 Currently lives in the Los Angeles area, but as of 2008 Ruth had lost all contact with him

CHAPTER 22 —MOVE TO HARBOR SPRINGS

Four generations from right to left: Mahlon Sr., Arthur, Ned, Ned's son Marvin (Jack), 1921

Ned's children: Back row: Jerry, Jack, Carol Joy. Front row: Ned's first wife Vivian, and Jimmy, mid 1990s

Arthur and Ruby

Arthur and Ruby lived in the Fourth St. house after they were married. Two years later they had a son, Mahlon, who was named after Arthur's father. Ruby and her sister-in-law, Minnie, were pregnant at the same time and they had an agreement that whoever had their baby first, and if it were a boy, they would name him Mahlon. Ruby won by two weeks. So, Arthur and Ruby's first born was called Mahlon Jr. Mahlon Jr. was born in the upstairs bedroom of the Fourth St. house on a cold winter's night on January 28, 1916. But they were not to stay there long as Ned wanted the house and Arthur wanted to get back to farming. So, Arthur bought a farm north of Harbor Springs near Stutsmanville. Not long after that, Roberta was born.

Mahlon Jr. and Ruby Doty Herrick, 1916

Chapter 22 — Move to Harbor Springs

Three Generations: Fannie and Mahlon Sr. (center), Arthur (right with mustache), Mahlon Jr. (child front row on right), 1916

Farming may have been Arthur's love, but it was a hard life. The soil was poor and the forest was thick. He worked with a team of horses for all the farming tasks, while Ruby managed the family garden. To make ends meet, Arthur had to seek work off the farm. One of those jobs was working part time at a saw mill. Also, Arthur never got the hang of the horseless carriage. But he did manage to get the funds to buy a Model

T. After getting a brief driving lesson, he attempted to drive the car into the barn. Forgetting which pedal was the break and which one was the accelerator, he promptly drove the car through the back wall of the barn leaving the two front wheels hanging out the end of the barn. Driving wasn't really practical on the farm anyway. The roads were not paved and cars often got stuck in the mud, assuming the tires didn't blow flat. Getting up the steep hill to access the road to the farm was no treat either. The Model T didn't have a forward gear low enough to get up the hill, so the car had to go up the hill backwards in reverse gear to make it home.

Left to right: Arthur, Roberta, Ruby, Mahlon Jr., 1921

Then in 1919, Mahlon Sr. and Fannie decided to leave Vermontville and move to Harbor Springs to be closer to their son and daughter and grandchildren. They purchased a house right across the street from where Arthur once lived and Ned currently lived.

They lived happily in that house on Fourth Street until Fannie died in 1924. With Mahlon Sr. now living along in a big house with advancing age and dementia, Arthur and Ruby and their young family moved in the big house two years later in 1926 to care for Mahlon Sr. Arthur was sad to leave the farm and his horses, but he felt he needed to care for his father. However, his father was driving the family crazy. With his dementia now reaching epic proportions, he was getting lost frequently, meaning someone would have to walk the few blocks into town to find him wandering around not knowing where he was. It was

CHAPTER 22 — MOVE TO HARBOR SPRINGS

even worse when he was at home, since he would just sit in his rocking chair and sing Civil War songs to the sound of his thumping fingers on the armrest. All this ended in 1933 when Mahlon Sr. died. Arthur took over the ownership of the house and he and Ruby had a fourth child, Frances.

Meanwhile, Arthur simply couldn't leave his horses even while living in town. He became a Drayman, driving a team of horses to deliver all kinds of goods on a flatbed wagon to businesses and residences around Harbor Springs. Later, as a retiree, Arthur drove a team of horses pulling a carriage taking residents and guests to and from Harbor Point, an exclusive wealthy resort area where motor vehicles were not, and still are not, allowed. Arthur and Ruby lived a long and happy life in their home on Fourth Street. Like his father 17 years prior, Arthur passed away while living in that same house. While working part time as a janitor at the First Methodist Church in Harbor Springs, Arthur collapsed dying suddenly of a heart attack in February 1950.

Arthur driving a team of horses on Harbor Point, 1940s

Since Mahlon Jr. was the first born of Arthur and Ruby and was born two weeks before his cousin Phil, he was given the "family" name. Roberta was born in 1919, so Mahlon Jr. and Roberta were farm siblings, attending the same one room country school together and having their respective farm chores. As they grew up, they became more dissimilar. Mahlon Jr. had ambitions to attend college as a young adult, while Roberta was content to continue to live in Harbor Springs. Only when she retired from domestic house cleaning and cooking for restorers, did she move to Florida for the remainder of her life. She married Paul Wager in 1945 shortly after World War II ended, where Paul served in the Pacific. They had one child, Ronald, born in 1948. Paul worked in a cement factory in Charlevoix all his life, and finally the dust from the factory got to him and he died of lung cancer in 1964. Roberta remarried Henry (Hank) Olk in 1967. Hank died in 1996 and Roberta died in 2010.

The third child of Arthur and Ruby was Vern. Vern was born in town in 1923, in the Fouth street house, so his early memories were of that house in town. One of Vern's regrets in life was that he never was able to serve in the military like is older brother, Mahlon Jr. or his half-brother, Jack. He was born with a heart murmur, which disqualified him. So, as an adult he became active in leading Boy Scouts, which his three sons enjoyed. Like Mahlon Jr., he married in 1946, only 13 days before Mahlon. His bride was Jean Pabon from Mt. Clemons. Vern never attended college, but started to work for Bell Telephone Company and stayed with them his entire life. He and Jean lived in Port Huron for their early marriage and their four children (three boys and one girl) were born there. They eventually moved to Garden City, a Detroit suburb. Vern's family and Mahlon's family would often get together for vacations, the most memorial were over Thanksgiving in Garden City in the early 1960s, with the highlight being the Detroit Lion and Green Bay Packer football game.

CHAPTER 22 — MOVE TO HARBOR SPRINGS

Arthur and Ruby's children: Vern, Roberta, Frankie, Mahlon, 1970s

Seven years after Vern was born, Frances (Frankie) was born. She may have been a surprise since there were 35 years between Arthur's first born (Ned) and his last born (Frankie). To celebrate the surprise, Arthur bought a new horse in her honor. Frankie, unlike her sister Roberta, did complete high school but like Roberta, stayed in Harbor Springs her entire life and worked as a telephone operator in town. She was fun loving and always enjoyed a good time. In 1968 she married Louis (Louie) Czerkie, who adopted her daughter Roxanne. Prior to that Frankie, Roxanne and Ruby all live together in the Fourth street house. When she married Louie, they moved into a house on Lake street directly across the street from her sister, Roberta. Frankie and Louie had a second daughter, Paulette, shortly after they married and lived in the Fourth street house for a short period of time before moving to Lake street. Of the four children of Arthur and Ruby, Frankie was the youngest and first to pass away in 1998, while Mahlon Jr. was the oldest and last to pass away in 2013.

Arthur and Ruby, mid 1940s

Chapter 23

Mahlon Jr.

Mahlon Jr's early years were on the Stutsmanville farm. Although a hard life since the soil was not that good for farming, Mahlon had fond memories of his early years. He recalled picking wild blackberries not far from the farm house but eating most of them before bringing his bounty back to his mother for blackberry jam. He remembers also the hard work that his father had to engage in, since all the work was done with a team of horses.

Mahlon Jr. playing around the farm, 1918

Mahlon recalled one frightening incident as a young boy when his father, working at the saw mill, seriously cut his arm with a power circular saw. There was no one at the mill to take him to a doctor or a hospital, but word got back to the farm that Arthur was seriously hurt. Since neither Ruby, or Mahlon, or Roberta, could drive the model T, Mahlon was given the task to jump on a horse and ride to town (Stutsmanville) to get a doctor to come the mill. He did that without hesitation, and the doctor came to the mill and saved Arthur's arm. This accident, however, kept Arthur from working at the mill or from farm work for a long time.

But Mahon's most vivid memories are of the one room school house he attended from 1st to 6th grade. The school was located on the southwest corner of Stutsmanville Road and the road to the farm, and was a 2 mile walk from the farm. He made that trek nearly every school day, with exception of heavy snow days. Snow had to be knee deep to be excused from school, since there were no plows or school buses back then. There were about 17-18 children in the school ranging from 1st grade to 6th grade. The one teacher at the school was overwhelmed to teach that many students across 6 grades, teaching different lessons to 6 groups with differing abilities and interests. Mahlon's interests were not exactly on school. His often mentioned school activities were during recess, shooting birds out of trees with his slingshot and playing Annie Over (throwing a ball back and forth over the school house).

Given the challenging learning environment at the country school and the fact the teacher was stretched to meet all student needs, Mahlon received little personal attention in school. However, his favorite subjects were history and geography.

CHAPTER 23 — MAHLON JR.

Mahlon Jr. 5th grade country school, 1926. Mahlon Jr. is front row, forth from the left. Roberta is to his right

After completing 5th grade, the family had had enough of struggling on the farm. Arthur found it very difficult to continue farming with his injured arm from the saw accident, plus Mahlon's grandfather, Mahlon Sr., was not doing well in town. Fannie, his wife, had recently died and Mahlon Sr. was going downhill with dementia. So, the family moved in town and occupied the 4th Street house owned by Mahlon Sr. and Fanny.

Upon moving to town, Mahlon felt that he didn't know much compared to his new school mates, so he was definitely challenged academically in the Harbor Springs schools. Mahlon recalled the embarrassment of "not having a clue" to questions posed by is 5th grade city school teacher when "hands went flying up" all around him to answer questions. Yet his favorite subjects still remained history and geography.

After finishing 5th grade in country school, he was way behind the city kids. The city school teachers talked to his mother, Ruby, about Mahlon's academic difficulties. It was decided that it would be best if he repeated 5th grade, which he did. As an adult, Mahlon reflected that that decision was the greatest break in his life, since he caught up and did well in school from then on.

U.S. history map showing states and territories.
Sixth grade school project by Mahlon Herrick 1928

Mahlon was never an excellent student for the rest of his schooling in Harbor Springs but he was a good and conscientious student, and a very popular one. In fact, by the time he got into high school, he was elected class president his senior year and was an exceptional athlete, playing football, basketball, and baseball on the high school team.

Mahlon had many childhood adventures growing up in that Fourth Street house. One time he was hiding from his mother for some undisclosed reason. He felt that the safest place might be on top of the roof. So up he went. The only thing that his mother could find around the house were the chickens, which were always running around the yard. Mahlon, up on the roof, was safe until he lost his footing moving around.

CHAPTER 23 — MAHLON JR.

His mother almost immediately found him, not on the roof but sprawled on the ground, after falling off the roof. If that wasn't bad enough, he laid squarely on a chicken! The chicken didn't have a chance. His mother, after a bit of scolding, took the dead bird, plucked the feathers and butchered it. The whole family enjoyed chicken dinner that night.

Mahlon also enjoyed camping at Five Mile Creek with friends. Just north of town, Five Mile Creek meandered through dense woods until it emptied into Lake Michigan. This was the site of many camping adventures, picnics and sunsets. Just across Lakeshore Drive[75] was the Five Mile Creek general store. A trip to Five Mile Creek was never complete without loading up at the general store with chocolate bars, marshmallows, and graham crackers for s'mores over a campfire. In these days, it didn't matter that the lakeshore property was private.

Not far from Five Mile Creek was the "old Otis farm." While in high school, Mahlon got to know old man Otis[76] because he was an avid golfer and Mahlon was his favorite caddy. It was on the Harbor Springs golf course nearby that Mahlon made his first $.25 for a round of caddying. After the round, he raced home to show his mother that he was now in big money! Mahlon's love of golf started with caddying, and as he got older he took on wealthy golfers who would come to Harbor Springs by huge ocean liner cruisers that arrived and departed at Harbor Pier. Mahlon and other caddies would carry their client's clubs all the way to the pier for additional tips. Below is the Harbor Pier and a typical cruiser of the 1930s and 40s.

---

75 Now U.S. Highway 119
76 Presumably Charles Otis son of inventor of Otis elevator

Harbor Springs Pier, 1930 or 40s

Mahlon's main job during high school was working at a Harbor Springs grocery store located in the bank building. His job was to transport groceries by horse drawn wagons to resorters on Harbor Point and Wequetonsing. The wealthy resorters would call in their grocery orders and Mahlon would fill baskets with their order, drive the team to the point (where no cars were allowed) or the "Weque" resort, and then carry the baskets to the front door. Mahlon was always fond of the owner, A.J. Faunce, and worked for him for many years during the summer.

Summer was also the time when he was most proud of his namesake, Mahlon Herrick Sr. On each 4th of July and Memorial Day parades through town, his grandfather would march in the parade as an honored Civil War veteran. Mahlon remembers pointing and making sure his friends knew that "hey, that's my grandpa."

Mahlon enjoyed winter sports also. Just walking distance from home was a ski jump enjoyed by local youth. Mahlon had his own skis, basically 8' boards with turned up tips. No broken bones were ever reported. However, close calls came from rope skiing behind cars. This was like water skiing on snow behind a car rather than a boat. The

CHAPTER 23 — MAHLON JR.

constant danger with this was skiing into a tree or a mailbox. The fact that this activity is no longer legal may be due to too many tree encounters.

A favorite hangout for Mahlon and all youth in Harbor Springs was Juillerets, an ice cream parlor and the first soda fountain in northern Michigan. In addition to hanging out with Joe Juilleret, his football friend and the owner's son, Mahlon's favorite recollection was listening to the radio at Juillerets for the play by play of the state basketball championships in 1929 from Lansing. The place erupted when Harbor Springs won the state championship over Flint St. Michael with the score 25-20 in overtime.

He particularly liked football, where he was the team's quarterback. Mahlon was seen by friends and coaches as a leader. He called his own plays in the huddle. After football games, he would often think up completely new plays to tryout. During one game, Mahlon convinced his coach, who was also his math teacher, to try out a play that he had dreamed up the night before. After briefly explaining it to his coach, Mahlon got the go ahead to try it. It required an entirely new offensive formation that no one had ever seen before, so it had a surprise effect. The huddle took longer than usual because he had to explain it to his teammates. The offensive line took an usual formation then after the snap, the entire offense flooded one side of the field. When the defense saw all the action on only one side of the field, they too flood that one side. Then Ace (Asa) Aderling, Mahlon's favorite receiver, bolted from the scrum and Mahlon threw the ball to him for a touchdown.

Mahlon Jr., Quarterback Harbor Springs HS, Fall 1933

However, the football season 1933 was a bittersweet time. The Harbor Springs Rams were undefeated in the conference, under his leadership as quarterback. The day before the last game of the season, his beloved grandfather, Mahlon Sr., died. Mahlon could not decide if he should play the last game of his career or sit it out in honor of his grandfather. He talked to his half-brother Ned, and Ned, without hesitation, said "yes, of course you should play." So, he played, his team won and took home the conference championship.

"I did alright in high school", Mahlon thought. "I was recognized as a good athlete, a leader in my class, but only an average student", he continued to think. But his leadership potential was recognized and he had a stroke of good luck to boot. His high school football coach, and math teacher, saw college potential. He encouraged Mahlon to go to college, but Mahlon knew it would be tough, given that his parents had no money to send him. It was 1934, the depth of the depression. But he did have enough of his own money to attend classes at the University of Michigan extension facilities in Petoskey. But those classes would not even add up to an Associate Degree. Then his football coach came up with an offer he couldn't refuse. He told Mahlon that he had a connection at Eastern Michigan University and he would like to drive him down to Ypsilanti to meet them and other college officials to see what could be done to get him enrolled. Mahlon jumped at the opportunity.

CHAPTER 23 — MAHLON JR.

Mahlon was accepted at Cleary College, the business school of Michigan State Normal School.[77] But he knew right away that this would be just the beginning of his challenges. He came home all excited to tell his mother. He asked his mother to sit down because he had some exciting news. "Mom, I want to go to college" he said. Instead of elation, his mother burst out crying. "You know we can't help you", she said. Mahlon knew that there would be no financial help from home and that he would have to work while attending school in order to afford it. It would be a very tough row to hoe.

And indeed it was. Before he even registered for classes, Mahlon looked for a job. He couldn't have the classes without a way to pay for them. After a short search, he found a job at the Huron Hotel in Ypsilanti. As part of his pay, he was given a room free. He did anything at the hotel that needed to be done, but mostly as a night clerk since he had to go to classes during the day. Not only that, but he had to send money home to his parents who were unemployed and on welfare at the time. He studied whenever he had extra time. He studied when at the check-in desk and studied in his room. He was so tired that he needed a way to read the required assignments and still stay awake. His solution? Standing in the corner of the room facing the wall. This way he wouldn't get distracted and fall asleep while on his feet. It worked. At least for a while.

The candle was burning at both ends. Mahlon was beginning to wonder if he really could manage college with all the financial and work requirements that went along with it. He come up with no answers. No real guidance from home or friends or his supportive high school coach. "Let fate decide", he thought. So, one summer day he walked out to the highway heading north out of Ypsilanti. He carried only two suitcases, so he had to dress himself with his winter coat and put on his winter boots. And it was a warm summer day! He knew he looked silly trying to hitch hike home looking like he had just gone crazy. He wanted that college education, but it proved to be so hard it didn't seem worth the struggle. So, the fates took over. He made a deal with himself. "If my first ride was heading north, then it means I must leave college and go home. If my first ride was heading south, then it means I must continue with the struggles and complete college". He waited and waited for that first ride, at times wondering if even the fates could decide. But then he thought of

---

[77] Now Eastern Michigan University

the way he looked standing on the side of the road with a heavy winter coat, boots, and suitcases in the middle of the summer. "Who would be crazy enough to give this crazy guy a ride" But a car did stop. It was heading south. Decision made. Back to work. Back to college. Relief settled in. At least he knew what he must do.

With renewed determination, he finished college, graduating in 1939, and working all four years at the Huron Hotel. With a Business Education degree, he hit the job market looking for a teaching position. He made it. Now he could make some serious money in a professional career. Not only that, but he felt a degree of satisfaction knowing that he was the only one in his family with a college education, and the first Herrick in his ancestral line to even attend college. In short order, he found a job teaching business and commercial classes at Marlette High School in Marlette, Michigan. Marlette was, and still is, a small rural town in the thumb area of Michigan. It was wonderful.

He loved teaching. He loved helping poor farm kids like himself understand the basics of business and personal finance. Having an affinity for young people and particularly the least likely to succeed, he flourished. With money in his pocket, he honored himself with a major purchase – a nice new black shinny roadster. A 1938 Ford. Life was good. Finally.

Marlette High School Faculty, 1940
Mahlon Herrick back row third from right.

CHAPTER 23 —MAHLON JR.

It was Sunday night, December 7th, 1941. Mahlon was sitting on the floor with a dish of ice cream that his landlady had given him. His lesson plans for the next day were completed. He was listening to the radio, when a news broadcast came on. Pearl Harbor, a large naval base in Hawaii, had just been bombed by a Japanese surprise attack, killing thousands of U.S. servicemen. Stunned, he knew America was now at war and that he would likely be drafted into the army. The next day he listened to President Roosevelt announce that yesterday had been a day that "will live in infamy." Indeed, we were at war with Japan and just a few days later at war with Germany. The United States, and Mahon J. Herrick, had just entered World War II.

The draft board had contacted Mahon for induction into the army. The board gave him the option of induction from Marlette or Harbor Springs. They also allowed him to finish out the year teaching in Marlette. Therefore, he was able to wait until September 1942 to be enlisted. As a draftee, he was enlisted as a private and was mustered in at Camp Custer in Battle Creek. From Camp Custer he was sent to Camp White near Medford, Oregon for basic training.

But wait. A life changing event happened shortly before leaving for basic training. Mahlon was home in Harbor Springs waiting for his orders to leave for Camp White. He decided to pay a visit to his former employer at the Harbor Springs Grocery store. Mr. Faunce was there and was happy to see Mahlon since he was about to leave for the service. As they looked out the store window, Mr. Faunce commented that a new recruit of single ladies had just showed up to teach at the high school. Just then one of those ladies walked by on her way to the school. Mahlon commented that those were the "best looking set of legs" he had ever seen. So, what was a young man to do when finding a pretty young women just about to leave for the army. He got in his shinny (still new) black roadster and drove up the Bluff Drive to the high school. Waiting until the school day was over, he pursued the new teacher and entered her classroom as she was erasing the blackboard from the last lesson of the day. Shocked that there was a young man still around town during the war, the teacher, Myrtle Nelson, enjoyed a conversation with this young solder. As it turned out, the conversation centered around teaching business and commercial subjects, since they both had that in common. He learned that she just arrived from Minnesota, where she taught business classes in McGregor, Minnesota. Mahlon was surprised that she accepted his invitation to take a ride in his car so he could show her around Harbor Springs and the nearby resort community of Wequitonsing, where she was renting a room for the year. They hit it off and agreed to write to each other while he was in the service.

But he was off to Camp White. When he got there, he was assigned to 316th Medical Battalion with a rank of Tech Sargent. A year went by. Mahlon completed his basic training and Myrtle finished the year teaching in Harbor Springs. She went home to Minnesota to live with her mother during the summer months of 1943. The war was still raging, so Mahlon was assigned to serve the 316th Medical Battalion in Italy. But he had a furlough before being shipped overseas, so he went to Minneapolis to see Myrtle. He knew what he was going to do. They walked down to the boat landing at Lake Calhoun. They talked and Mahlon attempted to pop the question. Then Myrtle interrupted and said, "Well, do you want to get married or not?" That did it! They were engaged. But both were pragmatic. They knew what war was and that Mahlon may not return. Mahlon did not want to leave a new wife a widow. So, they delayed marriage until he returned from the war.

Fast forward to spring 1944. On April 12th, 1944, Mahlon and his 316th Medical Battalion landed in Oran, Algeria as a staging site in northern Africa. A month later, on June 18th, they left Oran for Italy. The 316th landed in Naples on June 27, 1944 and was ultimately stationed in Florence as part of the Rome-Arno Campaign of the 5th Army. The war was gruesome in Italy at this time. Tech Sargent Mahlon Herrick was in charge of a unit of medics who retrieved the dead and wounded from the battleground in a motor ambulance company. One of his tasks was to compose letters to the families of deceased soldiers. Not easy.

He proved to be a very conscientious and disciplined soldier. So much so that in only five months he was officially recognized for his work. In September 1944, he was awarded the Bronze Star. The following announcement was made from the 91st Division Headquarters in Italy, "Mahlon J. Herrick of Harbor Springs was awarded the Bronze Star for meritorious services in support of combat operations from 10 July 1944 to 19 September 1944 in the Fifth Army of the Italian campaign." He was further cited for, "his spirit, energy and initiative in the supervision and coordination of the administrative functions of the section."

Chapter 23 — Mahlon Jr.

Mahlon Herrick Has Been Given The Bronze Star

With the Fifth Army, Italy

Technical Sergeant Mahlon J. Herrick of Harbor Springs has been awarded the Bronze Star for meritorious services in support of combat operations on the Fifth Army front in Italy, 91st Division Headquarters announced recently.

Herrick, a personnel sergeant major in a medical battalion of the 91st Division, was cited for his spirit, energy and initiative in the supervision and coordination of the administrative functions of his section.

A teacher in civilian life, Herrick was graduated from Michigan State Normal College in 1939 and has done graduate work at the University of Michigan. He entered the army in September, 1942. *Petoskey Eve. News*

Newspaper account of Tech Sergeant Herrick receiving Bronze Star, 1944

Michael J. Herrick

HEADQUARTERS 91ST INFANTRY DIVISION JFH/swp
UNITED STATES ARMY
A. P. O. 91

AG 200.6   30 September 1944

SUBJECT: Award of Bronze Star Medal

TO   : Technical Sergeant Mahlon J. Herrick, 36401823
         Medical Corps, United States Army

    Under the provisions of Army Regulations 600-45, as amended, you are awarded the Bronze Star Medal for meritorious service in support of combat operations.

CITATION:

    "MAHLON J. HERRICK, (36401823), Technical Sergeant, Medical Corps, United States Army. For meritorious service in support of combat operations form 10 July 1944 to 19 September 1944, in the Italian Campaign. During the period 10 July 1944 to 19 September 1944, Technical Sergeant HERRICK assisted in the supervision of the Personnel Section of his Battalion, demonstrating exemplary initiative and energy in solving the many administrative problems brought about by constantly changing stations. Most of the time the section had been working close to the front lines and under adverse conditions without adequate equipment and facilities. Technical Sergeant HERRICK'S professional and administrative knowledge, courtesy and devotion to duty, gained the respect and gratitude of all whom he served and brought great credit on himself and the United States Army. Entered military service from Harbor Springs, Michigan."

                                                     /s/ Wm. G. Livesay
                                                   WM. G. LIVESAY
                                                   Major General, U. S. Army,
                                                      Commanding

A TRUE COPY:

Mahlon J. Herrick
MAHLON J. HERRICK
2D Lt, MAC

Letter authorizing award for Bronze Star to
Tech Sergeant Mahlon J. Herrick, September 1944

CHAPTER 23 — MAHLON JR.

But the biggest honor was yet to come. Five months later, on February 27, 1945, Mahlon received a field commission near Bologna, a very rare occurrence. Through the Commanding General of the Fifth Army, Lieutenant General McNarney awarded Mahlon the rank of 2nd Lieutenant. He was now an officer. In 2 ½ years in the army, he rose from private, drafted from civilian life, to an officer. Officially, he became an administrative officer whose duties were described as, "Responsible for the administration and control of all records pertaining to enlisted men including service records, pay rolls, special and memorandum orders, immunization, allotments. Has a complete staff of administrative NCO's to supervise and direct in the performance of their duties. Also, responsible for maintenance of statistical reports on their company."

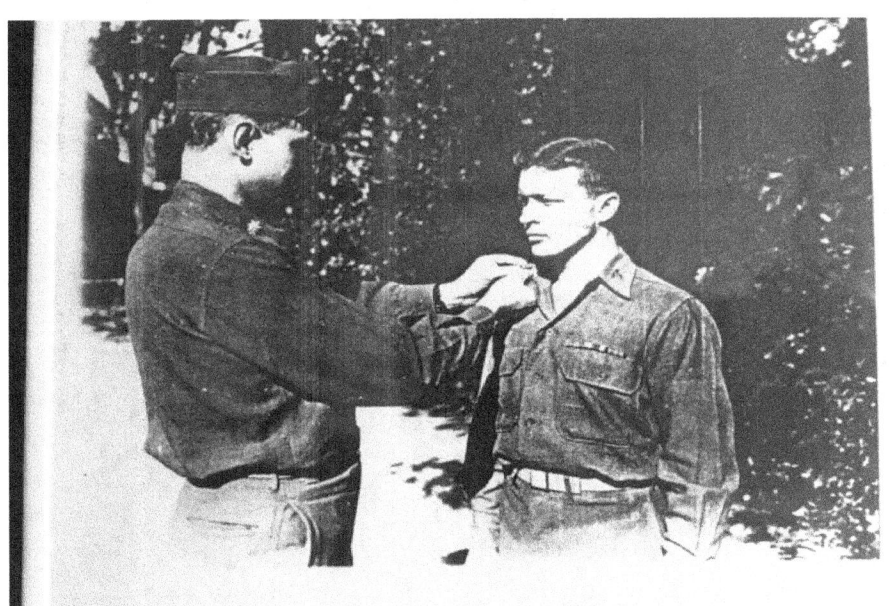

Receiving battlefield commission from Adjutant General Christenberry on behalf of Lieutenant General McNarney, Bologna Italy, WWII, February 27, 1945

Lieutenant Herrick, Bologna Italy, February 1945. With army pals

Memorial brick laid at the D-Day Museum, New Orleans, LA

CHAPTER 23 —MAHLON JR.

Two months later, April 1945, the war in Europe ended. Hitler was dead. America celebrated. Soldiers in Europe, however, wondered what was next for them. Months passed and finally Lt. Herrick and his unit were put on a transport ship with orders that they were headed for Japan. They all knew what that meant. The war in the Pacific was still raging and Japan was not giving up. The soldiers from Europe were being sent to the Pacific to be part of the Invasion of Japan to finally end the war there. But all knew the casualties from the invasion would be very high. Changes were that they would not return home. All of sudden Mahlon the other soldiers heard something on the loud speaker. A loud cheer went up from all of the men. It had just been announced that the ship that they were on was heading to Boston. What had happened? The answer did not take long to discover. A secret bomb had just been dropped on Hiroshima and a second bomb dropped on Nagasaki. One single bomb on each city. One bomb leveled each city. Japan surrendered. The war was now completely over. The ship was now heading to Boston! Now, "How do I get to Lansing", he thought.

Why Lansing? His fiancé, Myrtle, like to move around a lot. After teaching a year in Harbor Springs, she moved to Alpena, Michigan to teach a year there, then she moved to Lansing to teach at East Lansing High School. There were no cell phones, no computers, no way to correspond. Myrtle knew the war had just ended but no idea where Mahon was. He knew she didn't know, so he decided to just get to Lansing and surprise her. He knew her address because of their letter writing, so he was able to find the apartment at 832 ½ East Shiawassee St. Apt. 1. He found it. Now what? She was not there, of course, since she was at school teaching. So, he scribbled a note and taped it to the door of her apartment. It read, "Hi honey, I'm home. Let's get married". And so they did. In a matter of weeks, they were married on September 21, 1945 in Harbor Springs at Zion Lutheran Church in Petoskey.

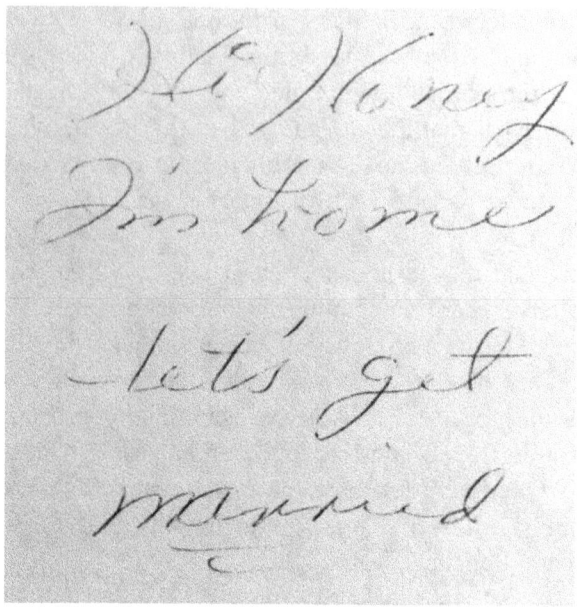

Handwritten note taped to Myrtle's apartment door, Lansing Michigan, September 1945

Mrs. Esther A. Nelson

announces the marriage of her daughter

Myrtle

to

Lieutenant Mahlon J. Herrick

Army of the United States

on Friday, the twenty-first of September

Nineteen hundred and forty-five

Harbor Springs, Michigan

Wedding announcement for Myrtle Nelson and Mahlon Herrick

CHAPTER 23 — MAHLON JR.

It was not the wedding she had dreamed of since she could not get home to Litchfield, Minnesota to be married in her church surrounded by her family and friends. Not even her mother could attend the wedding. But those were the times. The long war was over, he survived, he married the love of his life, and they settled into their first home on Shiawassee St.

Wedding picture Myrtle Nelson and Mahlon Herrick, September 21, 1945

Life was never better. He survived the war with distinction and married his sweetheart. They had no money, but no one coming out of the service and just getting married (a common occurrence in those day) had money. They had a life to build on. Myrtle was teaching commercial classes at East Lansing High School, taking the bus from Lansing since she had no car. "I have a car", Mahlon thought momentarily. And just as quickly, remembered what he did with the shining black roadster he bought back in Marlette before the war. Being the prudent man that he was, he sold it before he went into service, thinking that he couldn't use it while overseas. Now he needed it more than ever. But the automakers had retooled to make tanks for the army, not cars for ex-servicemen. It would be a long wait for a car.

Myrtle's upstairs apartment, first home, Michael's birthplace.
Shiawassee St., Lansing, Michigan

The other challenge for Mahlon was how to get back into the work force. He received GI bill benefits, so he started taking graduate classes at Michigan State University. He also took a job at the Buick assembly line plant in Lansing, just to add to Myrtle's teaching income. He could not teach in the same school as Myrtle since there was a restriction on a husband and wife teaching together in the same school or school district. Plus, their plans for a family had just begun. Myrtle was pregnant. The solution was right in front of them. Mahlon would take over Myrtle's teaching load at East Lansing High School, while she stayed home to care for herself and the new baby. That worked well.

At least for two years. Then Mahlon decided to take a new teaching position in Allegan, Michigan where he was hired to teach commercial classes at the high school. He started teaching in Allegan in September 1947. They decided that it would be Allegan where they would continue raising their family.

CHAPTER 23 — MAHLON JR.

More success and satisfaction awaited Mahlon in Allegan. He was a popular teacher and active faculty member. As he did in previous teaching assignments, Mahlon taught commercial courses at the high school. In addition to his teaching, Mahlon was assistant football coach, refereed basketball games, and was the student council advisor. Also, he and Myrtle were raising a family.[78]

First Allegan house, Adams St., Birthplace of Thomas, Allegan, Michigan

---

[78] Michael was born in 1946 in Lansing. Thomas was born in 1948 and Mary Kay was born in 1952 both in Allegan.

Davis St. house, First house they owned, Birthplace of Mary Kay, Allegan, Michigan

MAHLON HERRICK
Michigan State Normal College, BS
Michigan State College, MA
Business Education

Allegan High School teacher, 1956

CHAPTER 23 —MAHLON JR.

Allegan High School faculty basketball team,
1950. Mahlon is #72 back row far right.

Always interested in sports, Mahlon participated in faculty events like the high school men's basketball league. They played men's high school faculty from neighboring school districts. The women faculty were cheerleaders.

One lasting recognition that Mahlon was awarded was his work as student council advisor. He was the advisor for most of the 10 years that he taught at Allegan High School. In honor of the good work he did as student council advisor, an award was created to recognize one student a year who did the most on student council. It was named the Mahlon J Herrick Student Council Award. Nearly 60 years after he left, that award still hangs in the halls of Allegan High School and awards were still being giving to student leaders each year.

Mahlon J. Herrick holding Mahlon J. Herrick
Student Council Award, 2012

One Sunday afternoon in 1956, after a nice family drive in the country, the Herricks arrived home on Davis street where they saw a mysterious note folded and placed between the front doors. Mahlon opened the note to find that it was from the Director of Admissions at Ferris Institute in Big Rapids. The note indicated that the college had

CHAPTER 23 —MAHLON JR.

found his credentials at Michigan State University[79] and would like to consider him for the position of Registrar at Ferris[80]. Mahlon had never even heard of Ferris Institute, so he went to the library to check into the college. He subsequently called the phone number on note and asked for Harold Wisner, the Admission Director and author of the note. In a matter of weeks, Mahlon and Myrtle drove to Big Rapids, a 2-3 hour drive. Mahlon met with Mr. Wisner and then met with Victor Spathelf, the President of Ferris. During this time, Myrtle drove around town looking for churches with the hope that if Mahlon got an offer, they might find a nice Swedish Lutheran church to attend. Myrtle was extremely excited. She found Immanuel Lutheran, an ALC (Swedish) church. She had missed that in Allegan. When she saw Mahlon leave the administration office where the interviews were conducted, Myrtle, unable to contain herself, said, "Well, did you take the job?" Mahlon smiled, knowing the real source of her excitement, said, "Yes I got an offer and I accepted." And so it was. For the next 23 years the Herricks lived in Big Rapids and Mahlon was the college Registrar, while the college evolved from Ferris Institute to Ferris State College to Ferris State University.

After 5 years in Big Rapids, Myrtle got her Master's Degree at Michigan State University, taught business courses at Big Rapids High School and subsequently taught business at Ferris. Both Mahlon and Myrtle retired from Ferris in 1979.

Myrtle loved Big Rapids not only because of the Lutheran Church, but because of the cultural opportunities available in a college town. Plus, Myrtle was able to use her expertise in business and commercial subjects at the college level. She was respected by students in the high school and at Ferris. Mahlon was also highly regarded as the college Registrar.

In 1989, Myrtle developed severe headaches which was diagnosed as a brain aneurysm. After two surgeries, she died at the at age of 71. Mahlon sold their house in Canadian Lakes, outside of Big Rapids, and lived in their Florida winter residence for another 25 years. He died in 2013 at the ripe old age of 97.

---

79 He received his Master's Degree at Michigan State in the mid 50's
80 Now Ferris State University

Tree VIII : The Modern Family – Civil War to Present

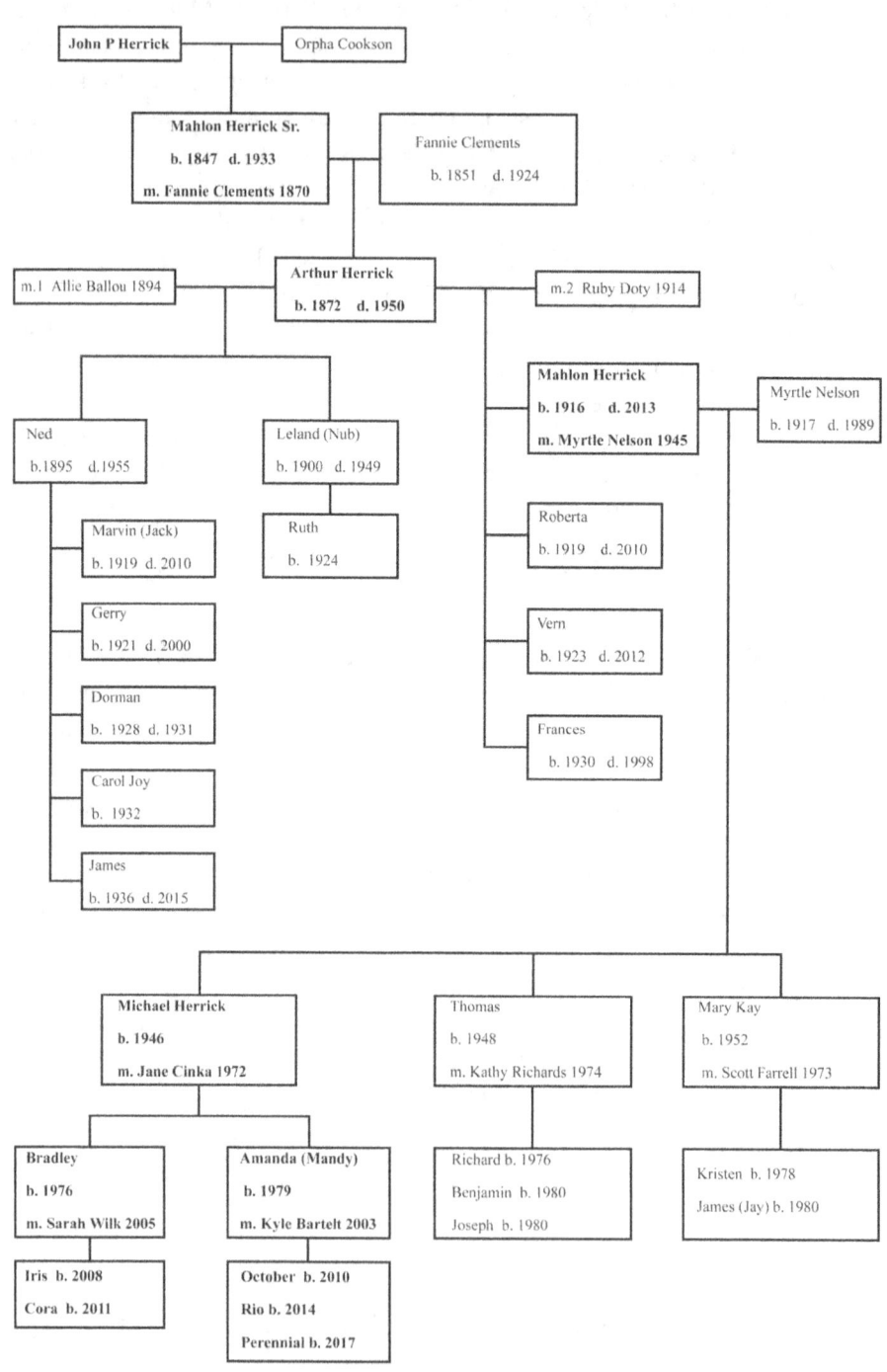

Chapter 23 — Mahlon Jr.

Tree IX: American Ancestial Flow

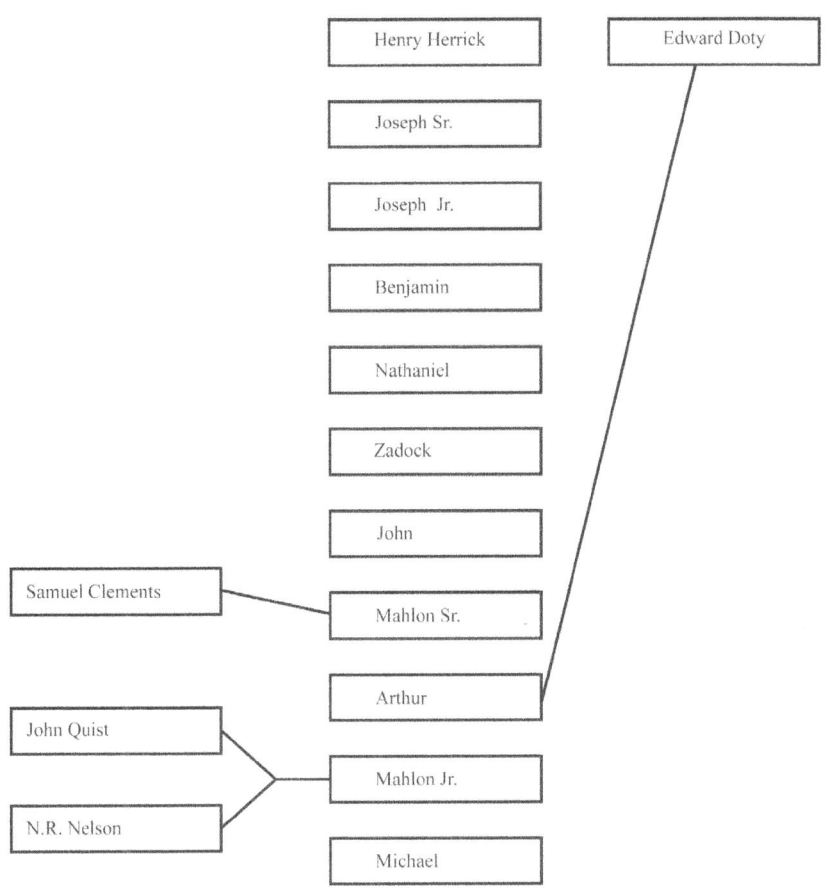

Epilogue

Myrtle and Mahlon Herrick had three children. I was the oldest, born in Lansing, Michigan a year after Mahlon and Myrtle were married. My brother, Tom, followed a year and a half later and my sister, Mary Kay, was born 4 years after that. It was a safe and care free life. We did what most children did growing up in middle America in the 1950s. We tried to please our parents, with occasional violations both knowingly and unknowingly. We enjoyed seeing our grandparents and the stories they told. We enjoyed visits with our cousins and extended family. We aspired to achieve and live within the norms of our family and our community. Allegan and Big Rapids were in many ways ideal small communities to grow up in. We lived and adjusted to the environment we were born into. We had no idea how lucky we were.

But in a broader sense, we were no different than Henry Herrick, or Sir William, or Erik the Forester, or Nathaniel. Across the decades and centuries, the world changes but humans change only to the extent that our environments require it. We do what we must and what we are able. That gives me great hope for my children and grandchildren. They too will adjust and solve problems unimaginable today, just as Henry or Zadock or Mahlon did. Our past generations solved their challenges derived from abuses of political and religious authority, problems of illiteracy, the devastation of the Black Death, and more. Yet they could hardly imagine today's world. Our challenges today are different. This generation and future generations must deal with the serious effects of climate change, over population, environmental pollution, drug and electronic addictions, and much more. I remember a story my father told me about the first time he saw a Model T Ford. His first thought was, "How can they improve on this?" Well dad, they did improve on it, and our future generations will continue to improve on it, as did our ancient generations.

Michael J. Herrick born in 1946 is an amateur genealogist who has worked on Herrick family history for over 20 years, focusing on the Joseph Herrick line in America. He has been an active member of the Herrick Family Association since 2004. Trained in Psychology and Educational Research, he has been employed in various capacities in education, government and business. In 2002, he formed Herrick Research LLC, conducting research and evaluation studies in education. He received his PhD from the University of Minnesota in 2000. He and his wife, Jane, have a son and a daughter, five grandchildren and live on the shores of Lake Superior in Herbster, Wisconsin and in the foothills of Tucson, Arizona.

Bibliography

Anders, Charlie Jane, *The Real-Like Letter Of Apology Written By The Salem Witch Trail Jury*, (https://io9.gizmodo.com/the-real-life-letter-of-apology-written-by-the-salem-wi-1640827487)

Anderson, Robert Charles, *The Great Migration Begins: Immigrants to New England, 1620-1633*, Boston: New England Historic Genealogical Society, 1995

Anglo-Saxon Rulers, *Wikipedia: The Free Encyclopedia. Wikimedia Foundation, Inc.*

Army of Observation, *Wikipedia: The Free Encyclopedia. Wikimedia Foundation, Inc.*

Ashley, Maurice, *Oliver Cromwell and the Puritan Revolution*, New York: Collier, 1958

Baldwin, David, *King Richard's Grave in Leicester*, unpublished article, 1986

Baldwin, David, *Richard III: The Leicester Connection*, London: Pitkin, 2013

Banks, Charles Edward, *The Planters of the Commonwealth*, Boston: Genealogical Publishing, 1930

Barry, John Stetson, *The History of Massachusetts. The Colonial Period*, Boston: Phillip Sampson, 1855

Battle of Bunker Hill, *Wikipedia: The Free Encyclopedia. Wikimedia Foundation, Inc.*

Baxter, Stephen, *The Earls of Mercia: Lordship and Power in Late Anglo-Saxon England*, Oxford: Oxford University, 2008

Beaumanor, *Herrick Family Association* Newsletter Vol. 13. Issue 2

Bishop Robert de Stretton, *The National Directory of Biography*, p. 47, (books.google.com)

Bivans, Steve, *Bones, Burials, and the Viking Great Army in Repton*, (http://www.steveb ivans.com/2014/07/07/bones-burials-viking-great-army-repton/)

Bourough of Leicester: *Charities Under the Management of the Corporation*, Harvard College Library

Boyer, Paul and Nussebaum, Stephen (editors), *Salem Witchcraft Papers*, New York: Da Capo Press, 1977

Brookman, Margot, *The Woodhouse Echo*, Loughborough, England: The Book House, 1979

Brown, David C, (1984). *Guide to the Salem Witchcraft Hysteria of 1692,* Tourist Guide

Burns, William E., *A Brief History of Great Britain*, New York: Infobase, 2010

Burnside, Bruce, (1999). *Enlistment Jumpers, Unsung Stories of the Civil War*, CD recording

Butman, John and Target, Simon, *How the Pilgrims Learned Marketing, New World, Inc.: The Making of America By England's Merchant Adventurers,* New York: Little Brown, 2018

Charlotte Republican, (May 13, 1870), Marriage of Mahlon Herrick and Fannie Clements

Charnwood Forest and It's Historians, Leicester: Leicestershire Archaeological Society

Cheney, Florence Allen, *The History of Guildhall*, Vermont, Benton, 1886

Child, Hamilton, (compiler and publisher,) *Gazetteer of Caledonia and Essex Counties*, VT: 1764-1887, May 1887, pp 444-447

Churchill, Winston, *A History of the English Speaking Peoples*, New York: Skyhorse, 1956

Civil War Soldiers Records, (Ancestry.com)

Collins, Richard, Ancestry DNA and Finding Edward Doty's Parents, *The Pilgrim Edward Doty Society Newsletter*, Vol. 46, July 2015

Dale, Roderick, (personal communication), April 2018.

Danelaw, *Wikipedia*: *The Free Encyclopedia. Wikimedia Foundation, Inc.*

Deposition of Joseph Herrick Sr. and Mary Herrick vs. Sarah Good, *Salem Witchcraft Papers*, Essex County Court Archives, New York: DaCapo Press, 1971

Documentary Archives and Transcription Project, *Salem Witchcraft Papers*, Essex County Court Archives, New York: DaCapo Press, 1971

Doty, Ethan Allen, *The Doty-Doten Family in America*: Descendants of Edward Doty, an Emigrant by the Mayflower, 1620, Vol. 1, Brooklyn: Ethan Allen Doty, 1897

Doty, Samuel, Find a Grave Index, (Ancestry.com)

Doty, Zebulon, Elkhart, Indiana, An Account of the Sale of Personal Property of Zebulon Doty, 1887

Doty, Zebulon, Elkhart, Indiana, *Estate of Zebulon Doty, October 1888, Administrator's Final Account*

Doty, Zebulon, Revolutionary War Pension letter, *United States National Archives*, Washington DC

Doty, Zebulon, *Will of Zebulon Doty, 1842*

Dow, George Francis (compiler), *Early Records of the Town of Topsfield,* Vol 1: 1659-1739, Topsfield, Massachusetts: Perkins Press, 1917

Dow, George Francis, *The History of Topsfield*, Topsfield, Massachusetts: Topsfield Historical Society, 1940

Drinksall, Pamela, *A Brief History of Beaumanor Hall and Park*, Leicester: Leicestershire Education Committee, 1978

Dryden, Alice (editor), *Memorials of Old Leicestershire*, London: George Allen and Sons, 1911

Eaton County, Michigan, Vital Records, (Ancestry.com)

Editor's Union abd Advertisers (May 20, 1864), Casualties in the Companies of the Old 33rd in the 49th New York Volunteers

Edward the Black Prince, *Wikipedia: The Free Encyclopedia. Wikimedia Foundation, Inc.*

Emmet County, Michigan, Vital Records, (Ancestry.com)

Eohric of East Anglia, *Wikipedia: The Free Encyclopedia. Wikimedia Foundation, Inc.*

Eric the Forester, *Wikipedia: The Free Encyclopedia. Wikimedia Foundation, Inc.*

Ericke (or Eohric) King of East Anglia, *Wikipedia: The Free Encyclopedia. Wikimedia Foundation, Inc.*

Essex County *Deeds Office*, Land deeds in Salem, Massachusetts, 1657 - 1668

Essex County *Quarterly Court Files*, Probate Records of Essex County Vol. 1 p. 97

Essex County, Beverly, Massachusetts, Vital Records 1653-1890, (Ancestry.com)

Essex County, Vermont, *Probate Files* 1791-1919

Farnham, George F., *Charnwood Forest: The Charnwood Manors*, Leicestershire Archaeological and Historical Society

Fletcher, W.G.D., Leicestershire Men at the French Wars of 1346-1347, *Leicestershire Archaeological and Historical Society* Leicester

Foster, Jonathan, *A Journal for the Expedition to Canada and the Marches of Capt. Israel Herrick's Company*, (provided by Curt Herrick)

Fox, Levi, Ministers' Accounts of the Honor of Leicester, 1322 to 1324, Leicester: *Leicestershire Archaeological Society*, Series ii, File 337-80

Francis Higginson, *Wikipedia: The Free Encyclopedia. Wikimedia Foundation, Inc.*

Freeman and the Right to Vote in Puritan Massachusetts, *American Creation*, June 12, 2008

Frye, James *Wikipedia: The Free Encyclopedia. Wikimedia Foundation, Inc.*

Gardner, Frank A., Colonel James Frye's Regiment, *The Massachusetts Magazine*, Salem: Salem Press Co., Vol III pp. 246-256,

Gaskill, Malcolm, *Between Two Worlds: How the English Became Americans*, New York: Basic Books, 2014

Godbeer, Richard, *The Salem Witch Hunt: A Brief History with Documents*, New York: St. Martins, 2011

Granby, Vermont, Vital Records, 1720-1908, (Ancestry.com)

Granby, Vermont, Vital Records, 1760-1954, (Ancestry.com)

Great Glen, (https://www.british-history.ac.uk/vch/leics/vol5/), *British History Online*, pp. 102-112

Greenhill, F. A., Seven Leicestershire Wills, Leicester: *Leicestershire Archaeological and Historical Society*

Great Heathen Army, *Wikipedia: The Free Encyclopedia. Wikimedia Foundation, Inc.*

Hale, John, (Beverly minister), *Wikipedia: The Free Encyclopedia. Wikimedia Foundation, Inc.*

Hammond, Fred, Herrick Family Association: Family Reunion, September 22nd-25, 2015, Salem: *Beverly Historical Society*, 2005

Herbert, Albert, *Church of St. Peter*, Belgrave, Leicester: Leicestershire Archaeological Society

Hericke, Thomas, *Will of Thomas Hericke of Belgrave, Weaver, 1621, Early Notices of the Herrick Family*, Leicester: Clarke and Hodgson, 1885 *Herrick Family Association Newsletter,* Vol 10, Issue 2

Herrick, Robert, Alderman (https://www.le.ac.uk/richardiii/history/greyfriars.html), Leicester, *University of Leicester*

Herrick, Curt, (personal communications), October, 2014 to September 2018

Herrick, Curt, The Serendipity Voyage of Herrick DNA Research with the University of Leicester, *Herrick Family Association Newsletter,* September, 2014

Herrick, Curt, Working from the Past to Find Clues of the Movement of Herrick Y-DNA from Scandinavia to Leicester, *Herrick Family Association Newsletter,* Vol. 13. Issue 1

Herrick, Joseph, *Wikipedia: The Free Encyclopedia. Wikimedia Foundation, Inc.*

Herrick, Janet Delana, Application for membership in the Daughters of the American Revolution, (completed application as descendant of Nathaniel Herrick)

Herrick, Jedediah, *Genealogical Register of the Name and Family of Herrick,* 1st Edition, Bangor: Samuel S. Smith (printer), 1846

Herrick, John P., Eaton County, Michigan, Register of Deeds, Department of the Interior, General Land Office, Washington DC: 1839 and 1841

Herrick, John P., West Carmel Cemetery Plots, Eaton County, Michigan

Herrick, John, Vermont Births and Christenings, 1765-1908, Family Search, (Ancestry.com)

Herrick, Lucius C., *A Genealogical Register of the Name and Family of Herrick, 2nd Edition*, Columbus: Higginson (printer), 1885

Herrick, Mahlon J., Award of Bronze Star Medal, Headquarters, *United States National Archives*, September 30, 1944

Herrick, Mahlon J., Headquarters, Mediterranean Theater of Operations United States Army, *United States National Archives,* Feb. 17, 1945

Herrick, Mahlon J., Honorable Discharge from the U.S. Army, Enlistment Records, *United States National Archives,* Vol 16, p. 143, January 2, 1946

Herrick, Mahlon J., Certificate of Battlefield Commission, *United States National Archives*

Herrick, Mahlon J., Certificate of Service, Army of the United States, *United States National Archives,* Vol 14, p. 243, Dec. 14, 1945

Herrick, Mahlon J., Report of Separation Certificate of Service, *United State National Archives*

Herrick, Mahlon J., Separation Qualification Record, *United States National Archives*

Herrick, Mahlon J., World War II Army Enlistment Records, 1938-1946, (Ancestry.com)

Herrick, Mahlon, Civil War Discharge, *United States National Archives,* Washington DC

Herrick, Mahlon, Depositions and Surgeons Reports regarding medical condition of Mahlon Herrick, *United States National Archives,* Washington DC

Herrick, Mahlon, Muster Role, *United States National Archives,* Washington DC

Herrick, Mahon, Civil War Pension Records, *United States National Archives,* Washington DC

Herrick, Mahlon, Claim for Allowance on Burial Expenses, *United States National Archives,* Washington DC

Herrick, Michael J., Lecture notes from trip to Leicester England, September, 2014

Herrick, Michael J., Summary of Robert Herrick Charities, *Herrick Family Association Newsletter* Vol. 11. Issue 3

Herrick, Nathaniel, Muster Rolls Frye's Regiment, Revolutionary War, Pension Records *United States National Archives,* Washington DC

Herrick, Richard Leon (compiler), *Herrick Genealogical Register, 3rd Edition,* Salt Lake City: Family Heritage Publishers (printer), 2008

Herrick, Richard Leon, (personal communication), April 6, 2000

Herrick, Zadock, Church Records 1831-1887, *First Presbyterian Church of Nunda,* New York

Herrick, Zadock, Find a Grave Index, (Ancestry.com)

Heyrick, Robert, 1540-1618 of Leicester, *https://www.historyofparliamentonline.org/volume/1558-1603/member/heyrick-robert-1540-1618*

Higginson, Thomas Wentworth, *Life of Francis Higginson,* first minister in the Massachusetts Bay colony, and author of New England's plantation (1630), Ann Arbor: University of Michigan, 1891

Hollister, C. Warren, *The Making of England: 55 B.C. to 1399,* Lexington, Massachusetts: D. C. Heath, 1992

Hoskins, W.G., *Further Notes on the Anglican and Scandinavian Settlements of Leicestershire* Transactions web archive, Leicestershire Archaeological and Historical Society

Hoskins, W.G., *Wigston Magna Lay Subsidies 1327 to 1599*, Leicestershire Archaeological and Historical Society

Hoskins, William George, *Leicestershire*, London: Faber and Faber, 1970

Hoskins, William George, *The Midland Peasant: The Economic and Social History of a Leicestershire Village*, London: St. Martins, 1957

Howarth, David, 1066: *The Year of the Conquest*, New York: Penguin, 1977

Higginson, John, *Wikipedia: The Free Encyclopedia. Wikimedia Foundation, Inc.*

Ingraham, Susan, (Oct. 20, 2013), *Henry Herrick and Editha Laskin*: Little is Known, Diversions

Inquisition p.m. Roger Wigston, Taken 21 September 7, 1609, Leicester: *Leicestershire Archaeological Society*, Series ii, File 337-80

Irwin, John, (personal communications), September 2016 to October 2018

Jenkins, Simon, *A Short History of England*, London: Profile, 2011

Johnson, Shirley, *Witchcraft at Salem Village,* New York: Random House, 1956

Join Our Search for Henry Hericke in England?, *Herrick Family Association Newsletter* Vol. 12. Issue 3

Jonasson, Bjorn, *Vikings: Information Guide,* Iceland: Gudrun Publishing, 2018

Jones, Dan, *The Plantagenets: The Warrior Kings and Queens Who Made England*, New York: Penguin, 2012

Jones, Dan, *The War of the Roses: The fall of the Plantagenets and the Rise of the Tudors,* New York: Penguin, 2014

Jones, Michael, Bosworth *1485: The Battle that Transformed England,* New York: Pegasus, 2015

Jones, Michael, *The Black Prince*, New York: Pegasus, 2018

Jones, Terry, *Medieval Lives*, London: BBC Books, 2004

Kingdom of East Anglia, *Wikipedia: The Free Encyclopedia. Wikimedia Foundation, Inc.*

Kendrick, T.D., *A History of the Vikings*, New York: Fall River, 2013

Kennedy, Maev and Foxhall, Lin, *The Bones of a King: Richard III Rediscovered,* Leicester: Wiley, 2015

Kings and Queens of England, (poster), *Weststar Publications,* 2013

Kirby, D.P., *The Earliest English Kings,* London: Unwin Hyman, 1991

Lambert, Tim, *Life in 16th Century England* (http://www.localhistories.org/tudor.html), A World History Encyclopedia

Langel, Susan, The Mayflower Voyage, Pelgrim Edward Doty Society Newsletter, Vol. 39, Number 4, Autumn 2018

Langley, Michael, Philippa and Jones, The Search for Richard III: The King's Grave, London: John Murray, 2013

Lapham, Alice Gertrude, *The Old Planters of Beverly in Massachusetts and The Thousand Acre Grant of 1635*, Salem: Beverly Historical Society, 1930

Leicester Castle and Manor, Leicester: Leicestershire Archaeological Society

Leicester Castle, Leicester: Leicestershire Archaeological Society

Leicester Herrick Home, *Herrick Family Association Newsletter* Vol. 11. Issue 1 (originally published by the Leicestershire Architectural Society)

Liddle, Peter, (personal communication), University of Leicester, April 21 2018

Life in a Medieval Village, (http://www.medieval-life-and-times.info/medieval-life/life-in-a-medieval-village.htm)

List of Monarchs of East Anglia, *Wikipedia: The Free Encyclopedia. Wikimedia Foundation, Inc.*

Lyon, H.R., *The Vikings in Britain,* New York: St. Martins, 1977

Lyon's Whelp, *Wikipedia: The Free Encyclopedia. Wikimedia Foundation, Inc.*

MacCulloch, Diarmaid, *Christianity: The First Three Thousand Years,* New York: Penguin, 2009

Maguie, Robert J., (October, 1965). Hand's Cove: Rendezvous of Ethan Allen and The Green Mountain Boys for the Capture of Fort Ticonderoga, *Vermont History,* Vol. 23 No. 4, pp. 417-437

Martin, R.E., *The Legends, Forklore and Dialect of Leicestershire* with an Introduction on the General History of the County, Leicester: Leicestershire Archaeological Society

Massachusetts *Soldiers and Sailors in the War of the Revolution,* Boston: Massachusetts Secretary of the Commonwealth, 1896

McKinley, R.A., *Parishes in the Ancient Borough: All Saints, Leicester: City of Leicester,* (originally published by Victoria County History, London, 1958)

Michigan Volunteers, *1861-1865: Fifteenth Infantry, Record of Service of the Michigan Volunteers in the Civil War* Vol. 11, 1861-1865, Lansing: Legislature of the State of Michigan

Michigan, Eaton County, *1840 United States Census,* John Herrick

Michigan, Eaton County, *1845 Michigan State Census,* John Herrick

Michigan, Eaton County, *1850 United States Census,* John Herrick

Michigan, Eaton County, *1860 United States Census,* John Herrick

Michigan, Eaton County, *1880 Michigan State Census,* Mahlon Herrick

Michigan, Eaton County, *1880 United States Census,* Mahlon Herrick

Michigan, Eaton County, *1890 United States Census,* Mahlon Herrick

Michigan, Eaton County, *1910 United States Census,* Arthur Herrick

Michigan, Eaton County, *1920 United States Census,* Arthur Herrick

Michigan, Eaton County, *1930 United States Census,* Arthur Herrick

Michigan, Vital Records 1867-1950, (Ancestry.com)

Milhorat, Edith Herrick, *The Herrick Family in England and America*, Baltimore: Gateway, 1984

Minnesota, Meeker County, *1900 United State Census,* John Quist

Minnesota, Meeker County, *1900 United State Census,* N.R. Nelson

Minutes and Records, *1831-1875 History of the First Presbyterian Church of Nunda*, Nunda, NY: Nunda Historical Society

Morris, Marc, *The Norman Conquest,* New York: Pegasus, 2012

Morris, Mathew and Buckley, Richard, *Richard III: The King Under the Car Park*, Leicester: University of Leicester Archaeological Services, 2013

Morris, Mathew, Buckley, Richard, and Codd, Mike, *Visions of Ancient Leicester*, Leicester: Leicestershire Archaeological and Historical Society, 2011

Narragansett Campaign and the Great Swamp Fight, *Wikipedia: The Free Encyclopedia. Wikimedia Foundation, Inc.*

Nicholas Noyes, *Wikipedia: The Free Encyclopedia. Wikimedia Foundation, Inc.*

Nelson, Wendell, (July 17, 1966), *Descendants of N.R. Nelson and Elsa Nelson: Family History*, Handout for Nelson Family Reunion

New York Passenger Lists, 1820-1957, (Ancestry.com)

New York, Nunda, *1840 United States Census*, Zadock Herrick

New York, Nunda, *1850 United States Census,* Zadock Herrick

Noble, Ruth S., *Thru the Woods Down the River Over the Hill*: Granby, VT, Granby, Vermont: Granby Historical Group, 1990

North Star, Danville, Vermont (June 15, 1816), *Eighteen Hundred and Froze to Death*

North, Thomas, *A Chronical of the Church of St. Martin in Leicester, During the Reigns of Henry Viii, Edward VI, Mary, and Elizabeth, With Some Account of Its Mopnor Altars and Ancient Guilds,* Sydney: Wentworth Press: 2016

North, Thomas, *The Letters of Alderman Robert Heyricke of Leicester 1590-1617,* Transactions of the Leicestershire Architectural and Archaeological Society

Notestein, Wallace, *A History of Witchcraft in England from 1558 or 1718*, New York: Crowell, 1968

Old Leicester Gaol, Leicester.webarchive, Curiouser and Curiouser, University of Leicester

Oliver, Neil, *The Vikings*, New York: Pegasus, 2014

Parishes In The Ancient Borough All Saint, webarchive, British History Online

Payson, Huldah Smith, *Museum Collections of the Essex Institute,* Salem: Essex Institute, 1978

Pennsylvania, Westmoreland County, *1810 United States Census,* Zebulon Doty

Perley, Sidney, A History of Salem Massachusetts, Vol. 1, Salem: Sidney Perley, 1924

Petoskey Evening News, (September, 1944), Mahlon Herrick Has Been Given The Bronze Star

Philbrick, Nathaniel, *Bunker Hill*, New York: Penguin, 2013

Philbrick, Nathaniel, *Mayflower*, New York: Penguin, 2006

Pierce, Calvin P., *Ryal Side From Early Days of Salem Colony*, Salem: Beverly Historical Society, 1931

Pierce, Richard D. (editor), *The Records of the First Church in Salem Massachusetts 1629-1736,* Salem: Essex Institute, 1974

Pilgrim Edward Doty, What a Troublemaker, *Pilgrim Edward Doty Society Newsletter*, Spring 2018, Vol. 39. Number 2

Pill, David H., *The English Reformation 1529-58*, Totowa, New Jersey: Rowman and Littlefield, 1973

Pitts, Mike, *Digging For Richard III: The Search for a Lost King*, London: Thames and Hudson, 2014

Platt, Colin, *Medieval England: A Social History and Archaeology from the Conquest to 1600 AD*, New York: Scribner, 1978

Portrait and Biographical Album of Barry and Eaton County, *Eaton County Genealogical Society*

Quist, John, Application and Acceptance for U.S. Citizenship, Twelfth Judicial District Court, Meeker County, *Minnesota, Minnesota Historical Society*

Quist, John, Naturalization papers, Twelfth Judicial District Court, Meeker County, Minnesota, *Minnesota Historical Society*

Readman, John, Doughty, Richard, Arkansas, Joe, Doty, Jerry, Doughty, Sue, Stapp, David, Doty-Doughty DNA Project Update, December 3, 2016, *The Pilgrim Edward Doty Society* Newsletter, Vol. 38, Number 1, February 2017

Redmonds, George, King, Turi, and Hey, David, *Surnames, DNA, and Family History*, Oxford: Oxford University, 2011

Reynolds, Alice, (2007) *Henerie Hericke: Search for His English Ancestry; Facts, Clues, References*, Candidates, Assumptions and Research Directions, Handout for Herrick Family Association Annual Meeting

Reynolds, Alice, (January, 2009) *Herrick Timeline: England and United States*, Handout for Herrick Family Association

Reynolds, Alice, (January, 2014) *Herrick Timeline: England and United States*, Handout for Herrick Family Association

Reynolds, Alice, (January, 2014) *Herrick: English Family Trees 1-12*, Handout for Herrick Family Association

Reynolds, Alice, *Herrick Patriot Index*, Handout prepared for Herrick Family Association Annual Meeting, January, 2010

Reynolds, Alice, Herrick, Karen, Yoe, Dale, and Turlington, Irene, *In Search of Henry Hericke of Salem*: Research Trip Report, Leicester, England, (unpublished), Report to the Herrick Family Association, April 2009

Reynolds, Alice, *Herricks at Various Battles in Northern States*, Handout prepared for Herrick Family Association Annual Meeting, January, 2010

Reynolds, Alice, *Herricks in the Revolution - Lineage Chart*, Handout prepared for Herrick Family Association Annual Meeting, January, 2010

Reynolds, Alice, (January 2011). *In Search of Henry Hericke: Roots in England*. Handout for Herrick Family Association Annual Meeting

Reynolds, Alice, *Henry Herrick of Salem - Ancestors Found?* Handout for Herrick Family Association Annual Meeting

Robotii, Frances Diane, *Chronicles of Old Salem: A History in Miniature*, Salem: Newcomb and Gaus, 1948

Rosenthal, Bernard, (General Editor), *Entries from Records of the Salem Witch-Hunt*

Ross, Charles, *Richard III*, Los Angeles: University of California Press, 1981

Ross, David (editor), *Dissolution of the Monasteries,* (https://www.britainexpress.com/History/Dissolution_of_the_Monasteries.htm), Britain Express,

Ross, David, *Medieval England - Daily life in Medieval Towns,* (https://www.britainexpress.com/History/Townlife.htm), Britain Express

Ruppert, Bob, His Excellency Guards, *Journal of the American Revolution,* August 18, 2014

Reynolds Alice (personal communication), January 2008 to September 2018

Robert de Stretton, *Wikipedia: The Free Encyclopedia. Wikimedia Foundation, Inc.*

Shears, Jon (personal communication), University of Leicester, September 17, 2018

Siege of Boston, *Wikipedia: The Free Encyclopedia. Wikimedia Foundation, Inc.*

Successful Vermonter, (1904). *A Modern Gazetteer*, East Burk, Vermont: Historical Publishing

Salem Quarterly Court Records and Files, Salem: *The Essex Antiquarian*

Sawyer, Peter (ed.), *The Oxford Illustrated History of the Vikings,* Oxford: Oxford University, 1997

Schiff, Stacy, *The Witches: Salem 1692,* New York: Little Brown, 2015

Sharlene Thuma, (personal communication), *Eaton County Genealogy Society*, October 4, 2007

Skidmore, Chris, *Richard III: England's Most Controversial King,* New York: St. Martins, 2017

Skidmore, Chris, *The Rise of the Tudors: The Family that Changed the English History,* New York: St. Martins, 2013

Skillington, S.H., *Beaumanor and Its Lords and Their Connexions,* Leicester: Leicestershire Archaeological Society

Smith, Lacey Baldwin, This Realm of England: 1399 to 1688, Lexington: D. C. Heath, 1992

St. Nicholas: *Leicester's Oldest Place of Worship*, Tourist Guide Book, Leicester: 2011

Strange, Daniel (complier), *History of Eaton County*, Michigan: Carmel Township, Pioneer History of Eaton County, 1833-1866

Stretton Magna deserted village, two fishponds and moated site Historic EnglandStretton Magna, Leicestershire Genealogy

Sweden, Skane, 1854 Census, N.R. Nelson, *LDS Family History Library,* Salt Lake City

Sweden, Vastergotland, 1854 Census, Britta Andersdotter, *LDS Family History Library,* Salt Lake City

Sweden, Vastergotland, 1854 Census, Johan Andreassen, *LDS Family History Library,* Salt Lake City

Sweden, Vastergotland, 1866 Census, Johan Andreasson, *LDS Family History Library,* Salt Lake City

Sweden, Vastergotland, Immigration papers 1880, Britta Andersdotter, *LDS Family History Library,* Salt Lake City

Sweden, Vastergotland, Immigration papers 1880, Johan Andreassen, *LDS Family History Library,* Salt Lake City

Sweden, Vastergotland, Immigration papers 1880, Karl Johansson, *LDS Family History Library,* Salt Lake City

The High Cross, *Leicester Chronicler,* City of Leicester:

The Kings of East Anglia, *Britannia,* Retrieved from (http://www.britannia.com/history/monarchs/eastang.html)

T.Y. Cocks (personal communication), Leicester Cathedral, April 16, 1997 (provided by Mary Kay Farrell)

The Anglian and Scandinavian Settlement of Leicestershire, Leicester: Leicestershire Archaeological Society

The Anglo-Saxon Chronicle, Original Introduction to Ingram's Edition 1823, Online Medieval and Classical Library Release #17

The Anglo-Saxon Chronicle: Part 1: A.D. 1 - 748, Online Medieval and Classical Library Release #17

The Anglo-Saxon Chronicle: Part 2: A.D. 750 - 919, Online Medieval and Classical Library Release #17

The Anglo-Saxon Chronicle: Part 3: A.D. 920 - 1014, Online Medieval and Classical Library Release #17

The Anglo-Saxon Chronicle: Part 4: A.D. 1015 - 1051, Online Medieval and Classical Library Release #17

The Anglo-Saxon Chronicle: Part 5: A.D. 1052 - 1069, Online Medieval and Classical Library Release #17

The Anglo-Saxon Chronicle: Part 6: A.D. 1070 - 1101, Online Medieval and Classical Library Release #17

The Anglo-Saxon Chronicle: Part 7: A.D. 1102 - 1154, Online Medieval and Classical Library Release #17

The Freemen of Massachusetts Bay 1630-1636, The Winthrop Society

The Herrick Manuscripts, Leicester: Leicestershire Record Office

The Heyricke Letters, Illustrating The State of Leicester in the Reigns of Elizabeth and James The First, Leicestershire Archaeological and Historical Society

The Heyricke Letters, Leicester: Leicestershire Archaeological Society

The High Cross, Leicester Chronicler

The History of Beaumanor Hall and Park, Tourist Guide

The House That Herick Built, ULAS News, March 16, 2015

The Longsborough Advertiser (February 17, 1876), Death of W. Perry-Herrick, Esq.

The Longsborough Advertiser (February 24, 1876), Funeral of W. Perry-Herrick, Esq.

The Old Planters of Beverly, Beverley: Beverly Historical Society, 2016

The Old Town Hall of Leicester, Leicester: Leicestershire Archaeological Society

The Vermontville Echo (1930), Clements Reunion

Thompson, James, *The History of Leicester: From the Time of the Romans to the End of the Seventeenth Century*, London: W. Pickering, 1849

Towne, George Warren, *South Side Cemetery Inscriptions,* Topsfield Historical Society

Thatcher, Wendy, (personal communication), Topsfield Library, Sept. 16, 2006

The Name of Herrick, *Wikipedia: The Free Encyclopedia. Wikimedia Foundation, Inc.*

Turlington, Irene (personal communications), October 12, 2014 to October, 2018

Valerie Griffing (personal communication), *Nunda Historical Society*, June 18, 2018

Vermont, Granby, Official Town Meetings, 1790-1810

Vermont, Granby, Essex Co., *1790 United States Census*, Nathaniel Herrick

Vermont, Granby, Essex Co., *1800 United States Census*, Nathaniel Herrick

Vermont, Granby, Essex Co., *1800 United States Census*, Zadock Herrick

Viking Sherwood, The Friends of Thyngowe, (http://www.thynghowe.org.uk/VikingSherwood.html) ,

Vital Records of Topsfield Massachusetts to the End of the Year 1849, Topsfield: *Topsfield Historical Society*, 1903

William Herrick (MP), *Wikipedia: The Free Encyclopedia. Wikimedia Foundation, Inc.*

William I, 1066-1087, *Wikipedia: The Free Encyclopedia. Wikimedia Foundation, Inc.*

Wauda, Nathan H., James Duane Doty, *A Tale of Twin Cities*, Neenah Historical Society, 1993

Weir, Alison, *Mary Queen of Scots and the Murder of Lord Darneley*, New York: Random House, 2003

Weir, Alison, *The Life of Elizabeth I*, New York: Random House, 1998

Welch, C.E., *An Ecclesiastical Dispute at Woodhouse,* Leicester: Leicestershire Archaeological and Historical Society

Wells, Loomis, Granby, *Vermont Historical Magazine*, pp. 987-995

Wessel, Caroline, *Beaumanor War and Peace*, Leicester: Caroline Wessel, 2018

Wessel, Caroline, *Nichols' History of Leicestershire: A Bicentenary Celebration 2015, Leicester*: Leicestershire Archaeological and Historical Society, 2015

Wessel, Caroline, *Portrait of Beaumanor*, Leicester: Beaumanor Society, 1988

Wessel, Caroline, *Robert Herrick 1591-1674: Poet and Cousin of the Herricks of Beaumanor,* Leicester: Caroline Wessel, 2012

Willison, George F., *Saints and Strangers,* New York: Reynal and Hitchcock, 1945

Wood, Michael, Doomsday: *A Search for the Roots of England*, London: BBC Books, 1986

Yoe, Dale (complier), Annotated index of research articles on the Herrick Family, *Phillips Library* and *Massachusetts Historical Society,* Sept. 2018

Index

100 Years War 53, 55, 56
Alfred the Great ... 3, 35, 40, 41
All Saints Church ... 14, 22, 23, 24
Allegan, MI 304, 305, 306, 307, 309, 313
Anglo-Saxon Chronicles ... 37, 39, 43, 48
Anglo-Saxons, ... 5, 13, 37, 39, 45
Ballou, Allie 273
Battle of Bosworth 10, 80, 83, 84, 86, 223
Battle of Hastings 3, 14, 46, 47, 48
Battlefield Commission .. 299, 323
Beaumanor 21, 33, 55, 63, 64, 65, 66, 67, 68, 69, 70, 71, 72, 78, 80, 82, 89, 215, 216, 217, 218, 219, 220, 221, 222, 223, 225, 318, 320, 333, 335, 336
Beaumont, Henry 67
Beaumont, John 67
Beaumont, William 67
Beckville, MN . 264, 265, 266, 267, 271

Belgrave ... 4, 9, 14, 23, 29, 59, 60, 97, 223, 322
Beverly, MA 151
Big Rapids, MI ... 308, 309, 313
Black Death 53, 56, 313
Black Prince 3, 53, 55, 56, 320, 325
Blue Boar Inn .. 10, 14, 83, 86, 223
Bradford, William 123, 127, 128, 129
Brewster, William 123, 128
Bronze Star 227, 296, 297, 298, 323, 330
Bunker Hill 97, 170, 180, 182, 191, 193, 317, 330
Carmel Township ... 1, 97, 209, 212, 229, 234, 243, 273, 333
Charnwood Forest 66, 225, 318, 320
Cheney, Benjamin 194, 195, 198
Church of the Annunciation 86
Civil War, England 216
Civil War, US .. 215, 227, 229, 230, 231, 232, 235, 236,

238, 256, 258, 281, 290, 318, 319, 323, 327
Clark, George............ 129, 130
Clark, Richard 126
Clarke, Faith 129
Cleary College 293
Clements, Fanny 234, 261, 262, 318, 335
Cnut 42, 45
Conant, Roger 30, 99, 104, 105, 107, 116, 117, 119
Concord, MA 97, 177, 178, 179, 180
Danelaw.... 37, 38, 40, 42, 45, 46, 50, 319
Despenser, Hugh................ 67
Doomsday Book ... 39, 48, 66, 67
Dorchester Company 105, 116
Doten 128, 131, 319
Doty, Edward .. 123, 124, 125, 126, 128, 129, 130, 131, 132, 133, 319, 326, 330, 331
Doty, John Wesley 139
Doty, Jonathan................. 136
Doty, Samuel 319
Doty, Zebulon... 137, 138, 319, 330
East Anglia...3, 35, 36, 37, 38, 39, 42, 43, 45, 46, 320, 326, 327, 334
East Lansing High School... .... 301, 303, 304
Edward III 3, 53, 55, 67
Edward the Confessor 46, 48, 50
Endicott, John.... 30, 99, 105, 107, 116, 123, 142, 150, 157

Erick the Forester .45, 46, 47, 50
Eyrick, Nicholas 57
Eyricke, Nicholas 3
Eyricke, Sir William 4
Eyryk of Stretton 50, 51
Eyryk, Robert or Robert de Stretton..................... 56, 57
Eyryk, William or Sir William...55, 56, 57
Ferris Institute 308
First Church of Beverly.... 120
First Church of Salem...30, 97, 100, 103, 104, 141, 142
Five Mile Creek 289
Folsom, Mary 150, 151
Free Grammar School... 4, 10, 11, 13, 14, 16, 78
Frye, James ...5, 176, 180, 321
Godwinson, Harold............ 46
Good, Sarah...... 142, 144, 145, 146, 319
Granby, VT 11, 329
Great Stretton or Stretton Magna 3, 50, 51, 52, 53, 55, 56, 57, 58
Great Swamp Fight... 141, 329
Great Viking Invasion or Great Heathen Invasion... .... 35, 36, 37, 38, 39
Grey, Lady Jane 68
Greyfriars 13, 16
Guildhall.... 13, 75, 76, 77, 80, 82, 194, 196, 197, 198, 318
Guthrum.... 37, 38, 39, 42, 43
Hale, John 120, 147
Harbor Point 281, 290

Harbor Springs 139, 227, 258, 260, 273, 274, 275, 278, 280, 281, 282, 283, 287, 288, 289, 290, 291, 292, 295, 296, 301
Hastings, William 67
Henry VIII...15, 16, 17, 36, 68, 79
Hericke, Thomas....... 60, 322
Herrick Genealogical Record 1, 42, 43, 44
Herrick, Arthur 139, 328
Herrick, Benjamin .. 159, 160, 162, 163, 164, 165, 170, 171, 172
Herrick, Carol Joy.... 275, 277
Herrick, Ebenezer 172, 173, 182, 193
Herrick, Editha Laskin ... 105, 107, 108, 118, 119, 120, 121, 141, 325
Herrick, Ephraim....108, 109, 114, 120, 121
Herrick, Frances (Frankie)... 283
Herrick, George.....................7
Herrick, George Bell 229
Herrick, Henry or Henry Heyricke. ...5, 7, 8, 9, 10, 11, 12, 13, 14, 18, 21, 22, 23, 27, 29, 30, 31, 32, 99, 100, 104, 105, 106, 107, 108, 109, 112, 114, 115, 116, 117, 118, 119, 120, 121, 123, 125, 141, 144, 147, 148, 313
Herrick, Israel...137, 138, 164, 166, 167, 169, 170, 171, 178, 181, 182, 183, 321

Herrick, Jerry................... 277
Herrick, Jimmy................ 277
Herrick, John............147, 152
Herrick, Joseph Jr. 2, 154, 157, 158, 161, 162, 163, 170, 194, 195, 197, 198, 199, 202
Herrick, Joseph Sr...141, 142, 143, 145, 146, 147, 150, 151, 153, 154, 155, 157, 225
Herrick, Leland...273, 274, 275
Herrick, Mahlon Jr. 1, 225, 227, 275, 278, 279, 280, 281, 282, 283, 285, 287, 288, 290, 292, 295, 296, 298, 302, 304, 307, 308, 309, 313, 323, 330
Herrick, Mahlon Sr...227, 229, 230, 231, 232, 233, 234, 236, 273, 277, 278, 279, 280, 281, 287, 292, 318, 323, 328
Herrick, Marvin (Jack)... 275, 277
Herrick, Mary.. 145, 147, 148, 319
Herrick, Mary Ann...........223
Herrick, Michael J. 315
Herrick, Myrtle or Myrtle Nelson 295, 301, 302, 303, 304, 305, 309, 313
Herrick, Nathaniel... 175, 176, 177, 178, 180, 183, 191, 197, 202, 205
Herrick, Ned 257
Herrick, Nehemiah . 166, 183, 184, 191, 193
Herrick, Robert the Poet ...89

Herrick, Roberta 278, 280, 281, 282, 283, 286, 287
Herrick, Ruby Doty.. .... 139, 274, 278, 279, 280, 281, 282, 283, 284, 286, 287
Herrick, Ruth 275, 276
Herrick, Samuel 136
Herrick, Sir William ... 3, 4, 8, 11, 13, 16, 21, 53, 55, 57, 59, 60, 63, 64, 65, 66, 68, 69, 72, 75, 78, 82, 84, 85, 89, 90, 142, 215, 216, 225, 313
Herrick, Sophia 223, 224
Herrick, Thomas .... .152, 172, 173
Herrick, Tobias.................. 11
Herrick, Vern........... 282, 283
Herrick, William II... 215, 216
Herrick, William III 216
Herrick, William IV.......... 216
Herrick, William Perry..... 68, 70, 215, 218, 219, 220, 222, 223, 225, 229
Herrick, William V ... 216, 218
Herrick, William VI...217, 218
Herrick, Zacharie 114, 121
Herrick, Zadock...... 198, 207, 329, 336
Heyrick, Joan 21
Heyricke, Nicholas .57, 60, 61
Heyricke, Robert or Robert Herrick... 63, 76, 78, 80, 82
Heyricke, Thomas...3, 7, 9, 10, 23, 29, 30, 32, 57, 59
Higginson, Francis...4, 18, 21, 22, 23, 25, 27, 29, 30, 31, 97, 99, 100, 101, 103, 105, 116, 117, 123, 124, 321, 324
Hopkins, Steven 124, 125
Houghton on the Hill......... 51
Ironmonger 5, 8, 11, 30, 57, 60, 61, 63, 64, 82, 89, 95, 215
Jewry Wall.............. 13, 14, 26
King James or James I... ....4, 17, 18, 21, 63, 66
King Phillips War.... 107, 142, 158
King Richard III or Richard III 12, 10, 13, 14, 50, 80, 83, 84, 85, 86, 87, 88, 223, 317, 326, 328, 330, 332, 333
King William's War.......... 142
King, Turi 50
Kronbeck, Elsa 264
Lake Calhoun 296
Lancastrians.......................83
Lansing, MI 243, 276, 291, 301, 302, 303, 304, 313
Laskin, Hugh....104, 105, 116, 118
Leach, Sarah..................... 141
Leicester...11, 12, 1, 3, 4, 5, 6, 7, 8, 9, 10, 11, 12, 13, 14, 18, 20, 21, 22, 23, 29, 30, 36, 39, 42, 45, 47, 50, 51, 53, 55, 57, 59, 60, 64, 65, 66, 67, 75, 76, 78, 79, 80, 81, 82, 83, 84, 85, 86, 87, 88, 89, 95, 97, 100, 109, 119, 120, 125, 217, 219, 223, 225, 317, 318, 320, 321, 322, 324, 325, 326, 327,

328, 329, 331, 333, 334, 335, 336
Leicestershire 7, 18, 20, 33, 37, 38, 39, 42, 44, 45, 46, 47, 48, 50, 51, 52, 53, 56, 61, 66, 67, 70, 89, 225, 318, 320, 321, 322, 324, 325, 326, 327, 328, 329, 333, 334, 335, 336
Lexington, MA ... 97, 177, 178, 179, 180, 324, 333
Litchfield, MN 264, 266, 267, 268, 303
London... ......5, 18, 36, 42, 48, 49, 51, 59, 63, 64, 70, 76, 80, 89, 91, 109, 124, 125, 129, 216, 218, 219, 225, 317, 320, 325, 326, 327, 330, 335, 337
Lupas, Hugh 67
Lyon's Whelp ..30, 31, 32, 45, 59, 82, 90, 99
Marlette, Mi 294
Massachusetts Bay Company 105
Mayflower . 30, 124, 125, 126, 127, 128, 129, 319, 326, 330
Mayflower Compact 125
Mercia 36, 37, 38, 39, 41, 42, 45, 317
Methuen, MA 170, 171, 173, 175, 176, 177, 183, 184, 193, 194
Michigan State University... 304, 309
Minutemen 177, 178, 180
Mobbes, Alice 22, 29, 59

Narragansett 107, 141
Naset 264, 266
Naumkaeg 99, 105
Nelson...11, 219, 264, 265, 266, 267, 270, 271, 328, 329, 333
Norman Invasion 47, 50
Normans 5, 14, 46
North Beverly Ancient Cemetery...97, 151, 154, 155
Nunda, NY 328
Oath of Freemen 105
Old Planters 99, 107, 116, 326, 335
Osborne, Sarah 144, 146
Peabody, Edward 59
Pequot War 107, 129
Perry, Thomas.................. 218
Pilgrims...31, 99, 116, 123, 125, 131, 139, 318
Plantagenets 325
Plymouth Colony 99, 123, 129, 141
Potato Famine 234, 261
Puritans 17, 18, 21, 22, 30, 31, 108, 123, 139, 142, 143, 144
Queen Elizabeth or Elizabeth I.... 4, 11, 17, 70, 75, 80, 336
Quist 264, 266, 267, 268, 269, 270, 328, 330
Repton 36, 37, 38, 42, 318
Revolutionary War ... 97, 136, 170, 175, 178, 180, 185, 191
Roddinge, Sweden 264
Rome-Arno Campaign.....296
Salem Witchcraft Trials... 141, 147, 157

Salem, MA 2, 117
Separatists 31, 123, 125
Simon de Montfort 67
South Side Cemetery ... 2, 164, 335
St. Giles church 3, 56
St. Martin's Church 13, 78
St. Mary de Castro 5, 12
St. Nicholas Church 12, 18, 23, 24, 25, 26
St. Peter's Church 10
Stutsmanville, MI ... 278, 285, 286
Tituba 144, 146, 147
Topsfield, MA 165, 170
Tudor, Henry 83, 84, 85
Vermontville, MI 97, 209, 230, 237, 243, 258, 273, 280, 335

Vikings.... 11, 5, 14, 35, 36, 37, 38, 39, 46, 50, 325, 326, 327, 329, 332
War of the Roses... 67, 71, 83, 84, 325
Washington, George 180, 182, 184, 193
White Boar Inn 10, 83, 86
Wigglesworth, Edward 184
Wigston Magna 52, 57, 324
William the Conqueror 3, 39, 46, 47, 48, 50
Woodhouse. 21, 219, 223, 225, 318, 336
World War II ... 218, 225, 227, 282, 295, 323
Wren, Christopher 80
Yorkist 10, 67, 83

www.ingramcontent.com/pod-product-compliance
Lightning Source LLC
Chambersburg PA
CBHW071147070526
44584CB00019B/2692